OTHER BOOKS BY CAROL OCHS

Jewish Spiritual Guidance: Finding Our Way to God
(with Kerry M. Olitzky)

Paths of Faithfulness: Personal Essays on Jewish Spirituality
(edited with Kerry M. Olitzky and Joshua Saltzman)

Song of the Self: Biblical Spirituality and Human Holiness

The Noah Paradox: Time as Burden, Time as Blessing

An Ascent to Joy: Transforming Deadness of Spirit

Women and Spirituality

*Behind the Sex of God: Toward a New Consciousness
—Transcending Matriarchy and Patriarchy*

Our Lives as Torah

OUR LIVES AS TORAH

Finding God in Our Own Stories

Carol Ochs

Foreword by
Rabbi Lawrence Kushner

JOSSEY-BASS
A Wiley Company
San Francisco

Copyright © 2001 by Jossey-Bass Inc., 350 Sansome Street, San Francisco, CA 94104.

Jossey-Bass is a registered trademark of Jossey-Bass Inc., A Wiley Company.

No part of this publication may be reproduced, stored in a retrieval system, or transmitted in any form or by any means, electronic, mechanical, photocopying, recording, scanning, or otherwise, except as permitted under Sections 107 or 108 of the 1976 United States Copyright Act, without either the prior written permission of the Publisher or authorization through payment of the appropriate per-copy fee to the Copyright Clearance Center, 222 Rosewood Drive, Danvers, MA 01923, (978) 750-8400, fax (978) 750-4744. Requests to the Publisher for permission should be addressed to the Permissions Department, John Wiley & Sons, Inc., 605 Third Avenue, New York, NY 10158-0012, (212) 850-6011, fax (212) 850-6008, e-mail: permreq@wiley.com.

Jossey-Bass books and products are available through most bookstores. To contact Jossey-Bass directly, call (888) 378-2537, fax to (800) 605-2665, or visit our Web site at www.josseybass.com.

Substantial discounts on bulk quantities of Jossey-Bass books are available to corporations, professional associations, and other organizations. For details and discount information, contact the special sales department at Jossey-Bass.

 Manufactured in the United States of America on Lyons Falls Turin Book. This paper is acid-free and 100 percent chlorine-free.

Credits are on p. 218.

Library of Congress Cataloging-in-Publication Data
Ochs, Carol.
    Our lives as Torah: finding God in our own stories / Carol Ochs; foreword by
    Lawrence Kushner.
      p. cm.
    Includes bibliographical references and index.
    ISBN 0-7879-4473-4 (alk. paper)
      1. Spiritual life—Judaism. 2. Jewish way of life.
    3. Jewish way of life—Anecdotes.
I. Title.
    BM723 .O36 2001
    296.7—dc21   00-11081
FIRST EDITION
HB Printing   10 9 8 7 6 5 4 3 2 1

CONTENTS

FOREWORD

ONE OF THE HAPPIER PARTS of my job as the rabbi of a congregation was making guest appearances in the preschool. Being a conscientious teacher, initially I prepared a short lesson plan until it dawned on me: I could tell them anything and they will never have heard it! I could say, "Abraham was the first Jew," and they'd say, "Wow! What's a Jew?" They were, in other words, a fairly easy group to teach.

A few years ago, as Rosh ha-Shanah and Yom Kippur approached, the preschool teacher asked me, instead of visiting their classroom, to give the children a tour of the prayer hall. I intended to talk about why their parents would all want to be in the same room at the same time. Then, for the *pièce de résistance,* I planned to open the floor-to-ceiling curtains at the front of the room that covered the ark—the chamber containing the handwritten Torah scrolls of the Five Books of Moses. Then I would remove one scroll, open it on the reader's desk, and invite the children up to the *bima,* where they could look inside and, if their hands were clean, they could pet the white part of the parchment. (It's what we educators call an affective lesson.) Initially, things went as planned, but before I realized it, the time must have got away from me. I saw the teacher at the back of the room discreetly signaling that school was almost over. Parents would soon be arriving. My time was up.

Not wanting to rush through removing the Torah scrolls from the ark, I decided to postpone that for a later lesson. "Next week, boys and girls, when we meet again, I'll open these curtains and show you something very special inside." They all said, "Shalom, Rabbi," and, like little ducklings, followed their teacher back to their classroom. The next morning, their teacher showed up in my office with the following story. Apparently, my hastily concluded lesson had generated a heated debate among the little people as to what exactly was behind the curtain. No one knew for sure! But the teacher swears they volunteered the following four answers. (I now suspect they may exhaust most, if not all, the available meanings of sacred text.)

One child, doubtless a budding nihilist, thought the ark would be empty. Another, of a more traditional bent, guessed that it held a Jewish holy book or something. A third, apparently already a devotee of American television consumer culture, opined that "behind that curtain was a brand new car!" But one child, the teacher recounted, explained to the rest of the class, "You're all wrong. Next week, when that rabbi man opens the curtain, there will be a giant mirror!"

Somehow that fourth little one intuited the great mystery of every sacred text: It is holy because in its words we meet ourselves. The idea is so elegant and yet so elusive that it must be rediscovered anew by each generation. Carol Ochs's extraordinary book is our guided tour back through the looking glass of sacred text and therefore into our own lives. She deftly guides us through the primary modes of life and demonstrates how the Bible can function not only as our own personal guide but indeed as our very own life story.

There is a fascinating passage near the end of Deuteronomy. It occurs as Moses presents the children of Israel with his swan song, his farewell speech, the Five Books of Moses: "And not until this day has God given you a heart to understand, eyes to see, or ears to hear. I led you through the wilderness forty years" (Deut. 29:3–4). In other words, for four decades the children of Israel had wandered clueless through the miracles of the wilderness.

Rabbi Aryeh Leib of Ger, one of the great Hasidic masters, recounts an interpretation he learned from his teacher, Rabbi Simcha Bunem of Przysucha. The passage means that the Israelites did not understand what God did during those forty years because everything that happened then was unique to that particular time. There had never been anything like it before, and there would never be anything like it again. The wandering Israelites never figured out what was going on because it never dawned on them that their lives were important enough to be part of a sacred story.

At the end of forty years, however, when Moses presented them with the Torah, the Jews suddenly realized that religious history was about to be clothed in their deeds, made from whatever they had done—and (this is what may distinguish the Hebrew Scriptures) not only just from the holy moments but from the mundane, the wayward, even the sinful moments as well. As Hanan Brichto, professor of Bible at Hebrew Union College, used to quip, there's no one in the Hebrew Bible you'd want your kid to grow up to be like. Imagine: ultimate truth, sacred text, clothed in the stories of your life. Now if you demur that the deeds of your life are simply too irreligious to be included in such a holy book, take comfort in the behavior of everyone from Adam through Joshua: murderers, lechers, liars, cheats, thieves. And the wilderness generation, that zany band of irreligious forty-year wanderers—who with their own eyes saw the Red Sea split and Moses ascend Mount Sinai, who ate manna for breakfast and quail for supper—these were the ones who built the golden calf, denied God at every opportunity, begged to go back to Egypt, and committed adultery with every tribe they met. These exemplary spiritual specimens were privileged to have the serial rights to their life story chosen for the script of the most holy document every recorded. (So there's hope for you and me yet.)

But for most of us, only at the end of a lifetime of forty years do we begin to understand that even our life stories are sacred and that God has been involved all along. We reread scripture not to learn about what happened to our ancestors but to learn about ourselves. The stories of the Torah are true not because they happened but because they happen. We reread the sacred text, and our hands tremble.

RABBI LAWRENCE KUSHNER

In grateful memory of my father,
Herman Blumenthal,
who by sharing his dreams shaped my own.

PREFACE

I HAVE LEARNED about essential theological questions by listening to people's stories. The more accounts I hear from other Jews, the more I appreciate how Torah is played out over and over again in the events of our lives. I feel privileged to be told how God is discovered in each life and how these narratives prove that our people's story is not just a historical event; it is also a very present reality.

Interpreting our own experiences and hearing the stories of others *as if they are Torah* opens us to countless creative possibilities. Of these, I have chosen to explore one of the many ways in which we are in the image of God: the act of creation. God creates by word alone (*And God said . . .*), and we too create by word—specifically, by *naming* our lives and the events they encompass. Calling our daily life *Torah* creates a life as revelatory as—if less dramatic than—the giving of the Law at Mount Sinai. Such an act of creation not only helps us understand why we live, it allows us to recognize how often we stand on holy ground.

Central to the story related by the Torah is the covenantal relationship between God and the Israelites. When we see our own lives as Torah, we name all our important relationships *covenants,* whether with our spouse, our children, or those people given to be in our lives. Regarding such relationships in all the complexity, richness, and eventual fruitfulness with which they are portrayed through the Book of Genesis, we recognize their creative potential. If we find ourselves seriously thwarted, we can apply Joseph's statement: "You meant it for evil, but God meant it for good . . ." (Gen. 50:20). Shifting our focus in this way, from our own agenda to God's, allows us to get beyond any setbacks.

Recognizing our lives as Torah transforms our sense of who we are, what we can know, and what we can hope for—the three major concerns any theological system must address. The process is not as difficult as it may seem. Each of us has a personal story, made up of the special and everyday events of our individual lives. Fitting our story to the Torah narrative feels appropriate because our people have identified with Torah for generations, and we all have at least a passing familiarity with the text.

So, armed with our personally shaped theology, we can face the adventure of living in the world with awareness and confidence.

o

This book would not have been possible without the generosity of the many people who have shared their stories with me. I am grateful to my students and colleagues at Hebrew Union College–Jewish Institute of Religion, whose interests and enthusiasm have nourished me. As always, my editor and life partner, Michael Ochs, has contributed to this book both professionally and personally, and my gratitude to him knows no bounds.

New York City   CAROL OCHS
Hanukah 5761 (2000)

Our Lives as Torah

INTRODUCTION

MY DAUGHTER'S GETTING MARRIED. I'm a nervous wreck!

Don't worry about it, I'm advised. There are books to help you, count-downs from the day of engagement to the wedding day, charts carefully listing each day's task, such as finding a location, choosing a caterer, hiring a band, selecting a florist, arranging for a photographer. Really, I'm told, it's no big deal.

Wrong—it's the biggest deal there is! I'm not worried about throwing a party or finding an outfit, but I'm awed by her entering into a covenant that will give shape and meaning to her whole life. As she takes her vows, she stands again at Sinai, promising to make her life sacred by imbuing the "ordinary" experiences of her future life with meaning and grandeur. She is pledging to see her life as Torah. This Torah, at its most expansive, includes not merely the Five Books of Moses, nor even the entire Hebrew Scriptures together with all the oral and written commentaries since the revelation at Sinai, but the entire story and culture of the Jewish people from the time of Abraham to today.

Seeing our lives as part of this capacious view of Torah both explains why we are awestruck at such life-cycle milestones and helps us get through them. Understanding our lives, and our children's lives, as Torah allows us to see our experiences as meaningful and opens us to recognizing God's power in and through all that happens to us. We can release our children, even though they are stepping into uncharted waters, because we can see the event partake in the unfolding story of God's engagement with Creation. When we see our children marry, we release them to form their own covenant. We may use the occasion to reflect on the way our own lives unfold as a story that begins with Creation and takes in all the narratives in the Tanakh, including Job, the Song of Songs, and the vision of Malachi: "Lo, I will send the prophet Elijah to you before the coming of the awesome, fearful day of the Lord. He shall reconcile parents with children and children with their parents" (Mal. 3:24).

Seeing our children get married is one of the great life-cycle events. But recognizing our lives as Torah is not reserved for special occasions—it is a viewpoint that transforms each day's experience and gives meaning and coherence to our day-to-day life. Our lives are not a collection of random events, they are part of the Jewish people's ongoing adventure, and we learn over and over that the adventure need never end. Our lives include countless incidents, some of which we barely notice, others we welcome, and still others we see as thwarting our dreams. Torah is a gift we receive to help us makes sense of all these occurrences. By providing examples of fundamental categories such as holy, trial, and covenant, the Torah helps us understand the text of our own lives, and, in turn, our lives help us understand the Torah. Our family experiences as children, siblings, lovers, spouses, and parents allow us to gain insight into the Torah stories. By dwelling within the text, we discover that regardless of what we currently experience, we find that others have gone through the same events, so we feel we are never alone.

An all-encompassing conversation has been taking place since our people stood at Sinai. As we recognize that our lives are Torah, we see that we have been invited to join this conversation not only to listen in respectful or awed silence, but to add our voice to the many that take part. The truths of our lives enflesh the Torah and make it relevant to the world of this historical period. The Torah stories didn't all happen once, a long, long time ago: they continue to happen, so now it is our turn to respond to the great challenges they offer. We, like the characters that populate Genesis, must learn how to reconcile with our siblings, venture forth to unknown places, find God's presence in and through our wanderings, and try to live a life of faithfulness worthy of the dignity we gained by being created in the image of God. Finding God's presence and living a life of faithfulness is an unending search for meaning, design, and purpose in life; it is, in effect, the search for a coherent, working theology. If we are to arrive at a theology that will draw out the full magnificence of our lives, we must first recognize that our lives are sacred texts and that our lives and the Torah, read together, elicit the deepest meaning of both.

○

We are meaning-seeking animals. We want to know who we are, what we can know, what we can hope for, why we were born. We seek meaning in the work we pursue, the relationships we forge, the homes we build, and the communities to which we belong. When we form congregations, participate in demonstrations, or volunteer in soup kitchens, we are really seeking meaning. This quest for meaning may be explicitly religious: an attempt to find meaning in life by looking to a traditional religion or by searching for a personal spirituality. But we may also look for meaning in a nonreligious setting, through wonders, scientific knowledge, and even political involvement.

Whenever and however we seek meaning in life, whether in the religious or secular world, the answers to the questions Who am I? and Why am I? define a theology—a special theology that is our very own.

Who Am I?

The term *theology* suggests that any answer to the question of who we are has to connect us somehow with God, a conclusion too serious to arrive at by definition alone. Who is God, and how do we relate to the holy? Could there be a Jewish theology that does not include God? How can it be that two books of the Bible, Esther and the Song of Songs, do not even mention God? Perhaps we can discover God in the silence of the text and in what the stories imply but don't say explicitly.

> SAM
>
> As Sam was reading the biography of a medieval rabbi, he felt a growing irritation. Though he thought that the book was worthwhile, the biographer kept invoking God in the text, and Sam felt these references were a major obstacle to his understanding the rabbi's life. He decided that since he didn't know what *God* meant, he would substitute *X* in his mind whenever he came across the term, thereby reminding himself that he didn't know how the author was using the word. Finally, when he had finished reading the book, he realized that only then did he know what *God* meant to the author and to the rabbi. *Maybe that's why it says, "You shall not take the name of Adonai your God in vain,"* he thought; *the word has such a history of misuse, coercion, and fanaticism that it takes an enormous effort to suspend judgment and discover what it could mean to me.*

Recognizing what we don't know and can't as yet define, we are still creatures trying to live in deepening intimacy with our Creator. All our stories, holidays, and practices are means to that end, and the end is our relationship with God. "All real being is meeting," writes philosopher Martin Buber. We aim to talk not *about* God but *to* God, not to analyze texts but to use them to shape our longing. Our holidays are mnemonic devices that remind us of this central relationship in our lives. Our practices set the stage for our encounters in prayer, in consecrated action, and in shaping our awareness.

Theology stands in the service of spirituality. We are trying to open our-selves to the reality of God's presence in our lives. Our deepest good is a growing intimacy with God. The answer to the enormous question Who am I? is not some chunk of our curriculum vitae, describing what we have done but not who we are. Who are we? We are beings searching in love and loneliness for our Creator. We find God in and through nature, through other people, and, on rare occasions, directly.

A useful exercise in spiritual guidance workshops begins with a reminder that we have been given the gift of story. The fact that Torah is in narrative form emphasizes the importance of the specific time, the loca-tion, and—above all—the individuals in the story. The workshop mem-bers then break up into *chevrutot* (pairs of partners). One of the pair relates a personal story to which the partner is asked to listen as though the story were sacred scripture. After the first person has spoken, the lis-tener may ask how God was present in the narrative. The listener "hears" the narrator into realizing the sacredness of the story. Finally, narrator and listener switch roles.

Next, we recall that when Moses asked to behold God's presence, God placed him in the cleft of a rock and shielded him until God had passed by. Only then could Moses see—not the face of God, but just the back. The rabbis commenting on this text understand it to mean that we can discover God in our lives in retrospect, but cannot see where God will be in the future, or even where God is in the immediate present.

Through the workshop exercise, participants can discover God's pres-ence in their lives in the past. After the initial round, they redo the exer-cise, recounting some event from the past twenty-four hours. Their earlier experience of being "heard" into recognizing the Torah in their own sto-ries helps them discover, in this second exercise, that God was present as recently as yesterday.

We can discover that each of our lives is a cosmic drama—that we are not bit players who must watch while all that is really significant happens to stars and celebrities. We begin to accept that our own lives are as important as any that have ever been lived on earth.

Finding God in our own stories is the beginning of our task. The next step is to grow in relatedness, in love. Because the ways of love are strange and unpredictable, and because they leave those touched by love unsta-ble, would-be lovers need structures of practice, of holidays, and of texts. The test of a theology is the love that doesn't merely move us but also shapes our lives. So truth in theology is whatever launches, sustains, and stabilizes us on the way of love.

We are seeking the transformation of our heart, soul, and spirit into expectant lovers of God awaiting God's presence. The formulation we want need not be ingenious or even elegant, but it doesn't come by itself: it comes to us only when we are ready to receive it. When we expect visitors, we clean the house, fix what is broken, and bring in needed supplies, all to make the house as welcoming as possible. When we expect God's presence, we clean up our act and repair whatever aspects of our larger home we can.

And Now the Task Is Ours

This book can help us find God in and through the stories of our lives and in and through our love, suffering, work, bodies, prayer, community, and experiences of death. If we follow the examples of Jennifer, Tamar, and Rose in this book, we begin with our story and then explore where love fits in, all too aware that loving deeply opens us to suffering. We recognize our relationship to a larger community and seek to make our contribution through work. We see that our work and suffering bring us face to face with our bodies and with the reality that we are mortal. Thus we raise questions that Mark and Ilana, whom we will meet shortly, had to answer in dealing with suffering and death.

We look at what meaning we can give to our practice of prayer, and we try, finally, to understand who we are and who God is for us. Each of these is a step, but the progression is not strictly linear—we recognize a need to return to some questions as we get further along in our thinking. So although we may begin with love, we are soon struggling with questions about our body and entangled in thoughts about death.

We need to keep all the balls in the air at once. That trick would be beyond us if the various topics didn't, independently, stick together: community connects us to love and to work and to all that we share with others, such as being embodied. Death, in which we support one another through community, leads us to the silence of prayer and to the question, God, who are you and where are you as we face this final mystery? All along the background drone is a story, and central to all of these issues are love and trust.

Philosopher Basil Mitchell (1961) has given us a parable, summarized here:

> One night in a time of war in an occupied country, a member
> of the resistance meets a stranger who deeply impresses him.
> The two spend the night together in conversation. The
> stranger tells the partisan that he himself is on the side of the
> resistance, indeed, that he is in command of it, and urges the

partisan to have faith in him no matter what happens.
The partisan is utterly convinced of the stranger's sincerity
and undertakes to trust him.

They never meet in conditions of intimacy again. But sometimes the stranger is seen helping members of the resistance,
and the partisan is grateful and says to his friends, "He is on
our side." Sometimes he is seen in the uniform of the police
handing over patriots to the occupying power. On these occasions, the partisan is berated by his friends, but he still main-
tains "He is on our side." He still believes that in spite of
appearances, the stranger did not deceive him.

Like the partisan, we recall those moments that formed the experiential basis of our trust in God. We have been experiencing God's presence
in and through our loves, our work, our participation in community.
Indeed, our relationship to God is the central theme of our story. We can
even find God through both the wonder and the vicissitudes of our body.
So in the face of suffering and death, our prior essential experience of
Presence gives rise to love, trust, and hope.

Forming a theology is intensely practical, shaping how we perceive the
world and choose to interact in it. We are born into a family, a tradition,
a culture, and as we are raised, we tend to absorb a world view unconsciously. But while the theology we received from our tradition may give
us the building blocks, the language, and even the questions to be
addressed, it cannot provide the answers. Just as no one can sense for us—
hear, taste, smell, or, in short, experience our life for us—no one can make
sense for us by creating our theology out of what we have experienced
and what our life has been about. Only we can do that, adding to what
we received and reshaping it as we live through the many seasons of our
lives.

Story

Step one in molding our informal theology is shaping our story. We do so
all the time, in bits and pieces. We may tell what has happened today since
we awoke, or we may focus on one aspect of our story—what, for example, is going on in our relationship with someone. But these fragments of
a story are merely episodes in the larger drama of our lives. Is our personal story a romance? a mystery? a comedy? a tragedy? As we think of
our life story, we reach back in our memory and also project ahead in our
imagination. Our culture offers us different story models: the journey of

the hero, or the rescue by Prince Charming. For millennia, Judaism has been offering its own model, with each individual's story an instance of the larger story of our people. The Hebrew Bible serves not only as the history of our people but also, as we saw in the exercise on hearing someone's story, as a tool we can use this very moment, to make sense of our own lives.

Over the course of the twentieth century, contemporary culture has employed the psychoanalytic story. First presented through the writings of Sigmund Freud, psychology has become an important model for understanding ourselves. Freud described three tasks of adult life: love, or expanding beyond the narrow boundaries of self to become part of a unit with another; work, or contributing to the world; and communal life, or relating to our fellow humans. Each of these tasks is an arena in which we use our theology and also develop it further, for our theology shapes our experience and in return our experiences shape our theology.

The Jewish story, as we will see, begins with certain fundamental assumptions, among them the reality of Creation, and of God, the unfolding of revelation over time, and our having been created in the image of God. It continues with our enslavement, our liberation, our covenant with God, our receiving Torah, and our wandering, and it ends with our entry into the Promised Land. Our story may emphasize some of these aspects over others, but to be the Jewish story it must affirm meaning and the reality of this world, and it cannot see us as essentially fallen and estranged from God.

Love

It has been said that at the end of life we will face an examination consisting of one question: What have we learned about love? The poet William Blake expressed the same sentiment:

> And we are put on earth a little space,
> That we may learn to bear the beams of love.

> —*Songs of Innocence*

A fundamental belief of Judaism holds that the intimacy, commitment, and trust we build with our human partner educates us for our relationship with God. The idea that human relationships mirror and help us forge our relationship with the divine is put forth by the prophets, especially Hosea and Jeremiah, and, if we accept the traditional interpretation, by the Song of Songs. Our experience of love and covenant is colored by Jewish folklore that extols the desirability and even divinity of marriage. (Question: What has God been doing since the Creation? Answer: Arranging marriages.) But along with familial love, the biblical text exhorts us to love our neighbor and to love even the stranger, "for you were strangers in the land of Egypt" (Deut. 10:19). Loving God enables us to love the stranger, because thanks to our love of God, we can feel nondefensive, safe, and generous. Loving God also leads us to love anyone God loves, however lowly (along the lines of "love me, love my dog"). Our love for God also allows us to discover God in and through our finite human loves.

Suffering

Love appears to open us to pain. Baruch Spinoza observed that "when a thing is not loved, no quarrels will arise concerning it, no sadness will be felt if it perishes, no envy if it is possessed by another, no fear, no hatred—in short, no disturbances of the mind" (1883/1949, p. 5). But we challenge sadness, envy, fear, and hatred by loving, knowing that the object of our love may perish or leave us, and we thereby open ourselves to suffering.

"Suffering is man's only biography," according to the philosopher E. M. Cioran (1955, p. 9). Judaism, by and large, sees little merit in suffering and has never approved of asceticism.

> One winter, a young man came to a great rabbi and asked to be ordained a rabbi himself. As the rabbi stood by the window looking out, the rabbinical candidate droned on with a glowing account of his piety and learning.
>
> "You see, Rabbi," he said, "I always go dressed in spotless white like the sages of old. I never drink any alcoholic beverages—only water ever passes my lips. I have sharp-edged nails inside my shoes to mortify me. Even in the coldest weather, I lie naked in the snow to torment my flesh. And daily, I have the *shammes* (sexton) give me forty lashes on my bare back to complete my perpetual penance."
>
> As the young man spoke, a white horse was led to a water trough outside the window. After drinking, it rolled in the snow, as horses sometimes do.
>
> "Just look!" cried the rabbi. "That animal, too, is dressed in white. It also drinks nothing but water, has nails in its shoes, and rolls naked in the snow. And rest assured, it gets its

daily ration of forty lashes on the rump from its master. Now, I ask you, is it a saint, or is it a horse?" [after Ausubel, 1948].

Even without seeking suffering, we have all too often experienced it and our theology must help us make sense of it. Nevertheless we reject the view that suffering is man's only biography. We are much more than what is done to us, though any theology has to give an account of our suffering and the sense we make of it.

Work

When we become aware that we are part of a community—our family at first, and later our people—we feel a need to contribute. This need is already expressed by toddlers, who want to help their parents set the table or sort the laundry. As we grow older, the desire to contribute is usually expressed in terms of our work. The Jewish view of work is also shaped by biblical and rabbinic texts. Paradise or no, Adam is directed to tend the garden, because work is an essential aspect of the human role in Eden. We read in Exodus that six days we must labor and the seventh is a day of rest. Clearly, applying ourselves to our work and keeping the Sabbath are *mitzvot*—religious obligations, or good deeds—that are equal in value.

From Abraham through the late prophets, some biblical personages feel *called* to a vocation (the English word *vocation* comes from the Latin for "call"). But despite its biblical origins, vocation is a concept Jews have largely ignored in theory, though not in practice. Many Jews *feel* called, and reminding ourselves of biblical precedents allows us to name our own experience in this way. But if we are indeed called, is our destiny predetermined? Is there a plan for each one of us? If so, does God shape it?

No matter how insignificant we may feel, the work we do leaves the world different for our having lived. Nomads and shepherds leave physical evidence of having passed through by contributing a pebble to a cairn or pillar of stones that they build in the wilderness. Our work may leave magnificent monuments, but even the grandest of these eventually crumbles, sometimes sooner than expected (think of Pennsylvania Station in New York City). The most enduring monuments are in the lives of the people we have touched in some significant way through the work of teaching, healing, and nurturing. Work is a two-way street: as we change the world through our work, the world changes and molds us. As the rabbis teach us, the work that Moses and David did as shepherds served to transform and train them to shepherd the Children of Israel: Once a kid escaped from the flock, and when Moses followed it, he saw that it stopped at all the streams, and he said to it, "Poor kid, I didn't know you were running after water. You must be weary," and he carried it back to the herd on his shoulder. Then God said, "Since you have compassion with a flock belonging to a man of flesh and blood, you shall pasture Israel, my flock" (after Ginzberg, 1968).

Body

A split between mind and body pervaded Western thought as far back as the second century, when it was central to Gnostic teaching. The split was reinforced in the writings of the French philosopher René Descartes. By and large, we still feel split off from our bodies, and social attitudes feed our ambivalence by insisting that our real selves are our minds. Also, because our bodies are always changing, we notice the deterioration of our physical selves long before memory loss raises the specter that our minds may be every bit as vulnerable. Sigmund Freud challenged the view that mind and body are independent; as a medical doctor, he knew that certain mental states had a physiological basis and believed that the future would reveal the neurological and biological bases of symptoms he treated by a talking cure alone.

JANICE

Shortly after the onset of adolescence, Janice suffered acute renal failure and received a new kidney. She survived, in part by deciding that she was not her body—which was in pain and was attached to various machines that kept her alive— but was instead her mind, her ideas, and her ability to dream. Her mind continued to function independently, she told herself, even if her body required machines to monitor her heart, regulate her breathing, and remove waste from her body.

After she was gradually weaned from all the equipment and restored to a normal existence, the "lesson" she learned—that she was not her body—remained with her. Though she took care of her physical needs, watched her diet, and exercised regularly, she felt as though her body belonged to someone other than herself, that it was not part of her own identity. She developed a provisional theology that was as dualistic, or split, as her own sense of self. Because she no longer trusted her body fully, she withdrew her engagement with the material world and became unable to recognize the holy in and through the world.

As she thought back on being hooked up to a respirator, she recalled the nurse attending to her during her return to consciousness—and her onset of terror. The nurse calmed her and spoke to her throughout the night, because Janice feared that going to sleep would mean dying. As she continued to recall the nurse, whom she readily termed an angel, she recognized that the nurse not only had her own body but used it to help Janice recover. She easily remembered the touch of the nurse's hand waking her from a lengthy slumber that blocked all positive physical memories so as not to deal with the acute pain she was suffering.

Just as Janice's reclaiming her body brought about a new wholeness in which her identity encompassed both her mind and her body, it also opened her to the larger reality that the world itself comprises not only ideas but also the physical reality of the earth.

Prayer

Many things bring us to prayer, but perhaps none so strongly as the sense of our own or another's vulnerability. In the horrors of a concentration camp, a group of inmates were passionately discussing the evil surrounding them, even putting God on trial for not preventing the unimaginable suffering they were undergoing. In the midst of the prosecutor's summing up, one man interrupted to remind them that it was time for *Minchah* (afternoon service), so the trial was put on hold to allow the participants to pray. Can we make sense of such a story?

What do we think happens when we pray? Why pray? Do we need to believe in God in order to pray? If we believe in God but don't believe in divine intervention, does it still make sense to pray?

HIRSCH
Hirsch went off to synagogue for High Holy Day services. His wife, Hannah, wanted to go too but decided to stay home with their sick daughter. All day long, Hirsch prayed fervently, and as evening approached and long shadows filled the *shul, Ne'ilah,* the last service of the day, began. Following the long blast of the *shofar* that marked the end of the service, Hirsch walked home with a sense that he had never prayed with greater focus or devotion. But God said to him, "You have prayed well, but not as well as your wife." When he came home, he asked his wife how she had prayed. "Pray?"

she asked. "I changed the cool compresses on Sarah's head, tried to get her to drink some broth, sang to her, held her. Who had time to pray?" And Hirsch had to admit that, indeed, she had prayed better than he.

Communal Life

There cannot be an "I" without a "we." Our communities not only bring us forth, they nurture and shape us. Raised in the wild, we cannot become human. Our communities reside around us, but they also live within our consciousness. We think in the language of our community and are shaped by its story and values. As Jews, we recognize that our community is based on the biblical stories and language, on the teachings of the rabbis, and on the tales, legends, and even humor that have coalesced to form a tradition. This heritage is constantly passed on and added to. When we consider the fundamental issues that our theology addresses—story, love, suffering, communal life, work, body, death, prayer, and God, we start with the language, examples, and stories of our people. So, we will see, not just any story will do.

As we gradually develop our perspectives on these and related issues, we may wonder how our own views relate to those formulated by others who claim the same background. Can there be religious community? Doesn't religious community require that we accept a theology forged and refined over many generations, rather than think these things through for ourselves? In a word, no. We are back to one of Judaism's great strengths (well captured in the expression "two Jews, three opinions"). Judaism has no credo that serves as the litmus test for who is or is not a Jew; rather, it emphasizes a way of life.

Death

To hang full-weight on the material world and on our own physical being is to confront death, life's universal mystery. Our natural if defensive response is to make a joke of it and thereby deflect our attention:

> An oft-repeated story tells of three patients—a Catholic, a Protestant, and a Jew—in an acute ward of a hospital. They are visited by a social worker, who informs each in turn that the doctor has determined that death is imminent and inquires if there is anyone the patient wants to see at this crit-

ical time. The Catholic replies, "I'd like to see my priest." The Protestant answers, "I'd like to see my family." The Jew says, "I'd like to see another doctor."

To paraphrase that old Jewish saying: "Two Jews, three opinions about death." Even though Judaism emphasizes life and generally refrains from speculating about what happens to us after death, fear of death informs all our views of life's end, as another story colorfully illustrates:

> When Rabbi Nahman was at the point of death, Raba entered into a compact with him to reveal the great secret of life and death after he passed away. Rabbi Nahman kept his word and appeared before Raba in a dream.
> "Did you suffer any anguish?" asked Raba.
> The spirit of the dead man answered, "The Angel of Death drew my soul away with as light a hand as one draws a hair out of a jug of milk. Nevertheless, I wish to assure you that even if the Almighty were to order me back upon earth to live life all over again, I would refuse because of my fear of death" [Ausubel, 1948, pp. 513–514].

The Jewish emphasis that life is good should not be taken to mean that death is evil. Judaism encourages medical care to the extent that all religious obligations are lifted to save the life of another, but it also teaches that a person on the verge of death should not be interfered with. Even more significantly, Judaism teaches us to appreciate and celebrate the material world and our own physical self, even when we might be tempted to flee to some incorporeal and thus less vulnerable world.

God

Just as Sam had to wait until he finished reading about the medieval rabbi before he could know who God was to that rabbi, we must think through all our views about our own relationship to the world before we can begin to understand who God is to us. There are essential differences between an idea of God received from the authority of a teacher or tradition, the idea of God we arrive at from inference and speculation, and the *experience* of God. Our theology may not keep pace with our experience, but it should be based on the reality of God's presence in our lives. Although God is much more than we can ever hope to experience entirely, the experience we do have of God is the foundation of our beliefs.

"And God Saw That It Was Good"

Existentialists see life as absurd or as a series of meaningless tasks. In *The Myth of Sisyphus,* the French philosopher and writer Albert Camus presents a protagonist whom the gods have condemned to push a boulder to the top of a mountain repeatedly, only to see it roll right back down. His punishment, in effect, is futile, hopeless labor, which Camus sees as the human condition.

Most Jews, by contrast, do not share the existentialist belief that life is a meaningless burden. We read in Genesis that God looked at Creation and saw that it was good, and our belief in that judgment helps shape our daily actions in the world. But how can people who have survived exile, pogroms, and even the Holocaust still claim that the world is good? Did this belief help them survive? Jews display an enormous will to live, perhaps because we experience life as a profound, meaningful gift to be celebrated joyously.

The fundamental Jewish toast is *l'chayim*—to life! So accustomed are we to that sentiment that we don't recognize the essential theological commitment it expresses. Many of the world's religions hold that life is not real, that it is an illusion from which we try to free ourselves. We may agree that "things are seldom what they seem," as Buttercup tells us in *H.M.S. Pinafore,* but that does not keep us from valuing life and finding what is real in and through what is merely apparent. Jews do not believe that life is a test and people should accept finite suffering in exchange for infinite reward in some afterlife. For Jews, life is neither an illusion nor a test: it is a gift.

The first thing we can say about a gift is that we don't earn it. If we did, it would not be a gift; it would be salary. We also recognize that the more we know about our gift, the more we can benefit from it.

> For her ninety-fourth birthday, a woman received an e-mail station as a gift from her grandchildren. All her life, she had been a fine correspondent in the world of pens and ink and stamps, but her grandchildren hoped to make it "easier" for her to keep in touch with them and vice versa. They simply showed her how to reply to a message by hitting the "reply" button, but they neglected to show her how to initiate a message. The gift became welcome only after she learned, a week later, the finer points of using it. Now she could e-mail one of her grandchildren who had not sent her a message in the first place.

Gifts can reveal and create challenges to the recipient, whether it is a grandmother being led into the information age or ourselves examining the gift of a talent we have and wondering if it implies some obligation. The most important thing we know about a gift is that it fosters gratitude, which is a fundamental stance in Jewish life. It is modeled for us by God's response to the six days of Creation, pronouncing it to be good, very good. Gratitude fosters awareness of all the wonders around us. Recognizing how gratitude deepens our appreciation of life, we can better understand the laws given to us at Sinai.

The Torah is a gift that allows us to be whole and healthy. Its rules foster virtue, which is the healthy condition of the soul. We have been given the gifts and tools of a text that opens us to wonder and gratitude, which is not merely a feeling but a way of doing and expressing. Torah opens us to love. Again, though love is certainly a feeling, it is also the shape of our lives. By accepting our people's story, we experience our kinship with the rest of Creation and so avoid the deadening alienation that accompanies the philosophy of existentialism. We discover the grandeur of our own identity. God has created and named us, and so we reject any attempt to categorize or label us. We find strength and resources to be countercultural because we have the perspective of being created in God's image.

Beginning with the gift of story, we add our own perspective and watch it change as we grow in our relationship with God.

It has sometimes been fashionable to think that depressing nihilistic philosophies are profound, but most Jews believe that joy is deeper even than sorrow. Nor does Judaism say, as some Christians do, that life is a trial to get through with clean hands, in order to achieve an eternal reward. Judaism does not rule out eternal life in a world to come, but its focus is on *this* life. Jewish folk images of an afterlife are simply amplifications of the joys found on earth: increased study of the Torah and eating at a heavenly banquet.

Circumstances may hinder our ability to accept this story and this way of understanding our lives. If we examine them carefully, we may well recognize how, instead, they can deepen our connectedness to God.

1

SEARCHING
FOR MEANING

WHAT INSPIRES US to begin our quest for meaning? We all have many experiences, positive and negative, that could motivate us: discovering love, suffering loss, feeling a sense of wonder, feeling empty. Or we may achieve a level of mastery over our lives that frees us to wonder if life concerns more than we have imagined. But such mastery alone may not be enough. We may be led to search out meaning when we hear our child raise a question we ourselves have asked but that we somehow bury. And sometimes it is none of these circumstances that inspire us to search, but rather something we might consider mysterious—a feeling that we have been "called."

JENNIFER
Jennifer was a social studies teacher in a private college prep school. She loved her students and found the work very rewarding. She felt that if she worked hard she would naturally progress in her career, and she was relatively unreflective about other people's experiences of unfairness and injustice.

In her sixth year at the school she was suddenly told that her contract would not be renewed for the following year. Because her reviews were excellent, she was totally unprepared for this turn of events. Her department chair made it clear that the decision was not his and that he felt terrible about it, but the principal was bringing in a long-time friend to take over her classes. The private school faculty was not unionized, so Jennifer had no choice but to use the remaining year looking for a different job.

As urgent as that task was, there was something even more pressing. She needed to figure out how she could have been an effective social studies teacher while avoiding any visceral connection to the injustices and abuses of power she saw around her. She was urged by friends to use her accumulated sick leave and simply stop coming to school. She felt anger toward the administration, but then she thought of her students. Sick leave was not the answer. But how would she be motivated to show up every day for classes when she knew that being an effective teacher had little to do with job security? Her students would, at some point in their lives, experience defeat as she just had, but they would still need to maintain their own standards. She realized that there could be no simple equation between what we do and what we receive; our doing and being must be grounded in something more significant than immediate reward.

Fairy tales and fables have morals that are tacked on too quickly, she thought. Life is more complex than that, and perhaps we will never see what it all means. But there was a more profound story that could give her perspective on this incident in her life. It was a long time since she had just read the Bible, and she wasn't sure she had ever read it with the deliberate purpose of making sense of her own life. But she felt called to the story, so she began reading the text that could help her discover who she was, why she was there, and what she should do with her life.

Jennifer intuitively recognized that theology is practical, not a hobby we can take up in some imagined future or "when we get less busy," because to live a meaningful life we need a working theology right now, provisional though it may be. Although its components stay relatively constant, some aspects of our worldview—which ones, we can't predict—change more and with greater frequency than others.

Why Create Our Own Theology?

Why does the meaning system we inherited from our ancestors no longer work for us? One factor is the increasing rate of change, visible from one generation to the next. Our grandparents' lives probably had much more in common with their own grandparents' lives than we have with our parents'!

In part, this rapid change results from scientific breakthroughs that have greatly lengthened life expectancy for most people. At the same time, inventions and developments in the twentieth century have influenced the way we look at the world. The youngest among us remember a world before cell phones, the oldest a world before electricity was ubiquitous. The time in between has seen distances shrink, first with the introduction of automobiles, then air travel, jetliners, and space travel. Communication by mail and telegraph gave way to the telephone and then, in short order, to radio, television, fax, e-mail, and the Internet. Still photographs moved, then started talking, then took on color. Handwritten documents and duplicates yielded to typewritten papers and carbon copies, photocopies yielded to computer printouts, scanners can make handwriting machine readable, and the machine can translate the content into hundreds of languages.

Meanwhile, psychological theory has us questioning our own actions and motives—even our accidents—while most recent research tells us that the fault lies not in our stars but in our genes (to misquote Shakespeare). Is it any wonder that given the dizzying rate of change, we find it increasingly difficult to discern meaning in our own lives by unquestioningly embracing an inherited theology?

Early in Genesis, we read that Adonai said, "My breath shall not abide in man forever, since he too is flesh; let the days allowed him be one hundred and twenty years" (Gen. 6:3). Knowing that our life span is limited, we are constantly aware of death. We have internal clocks reminding us that we won't live forever, or even indefinitely, so we determine how long we can spend on schooling, what age we must reach to see our children into adulthood and independence (not the same question as how long we might still be fertile), whether we should retire and if so, when. All such issues and questions are raised for us anew because our concept of time differs vastly from that of our parents and ancestors.

Our concept of space has changed along with our concept of time. We are now familiar with every part of our planet, and we are exploring our solar system and galaxy. The picture of Earth as seen from space has altered our ideas about our home. At the same time that we recognize the beauty and infinite worth of our planet, we human beings now have the power to destroy it. God made a covenant not to destroy the world:

So long as the earth endures,
Seedtime and harvest,
Cold and heat,
Summer and winter,

Day and night
Shall not cease.

—Genesis 8:22

But today we are under no such constraints. We can abolish the summer
by plunging us all into a nuclear winter, and we can bring on unending
night. So even though the psalmist could say

God established the earth on its foundations,
    so that it shall never totter.
You made the deep cover it as a garment;
    the waters stood above the mountains.
They fled at Your blast,
    rushed away at the sound of Your thunder,
    —mountains rising, valleys sinking—
to the place You established for them.
You set bounds they must not pass
    so that they never again cover the earth.

—Psalms 104:5–9

we have the capacity to make the earth totter and, undoubtedly someday,
to make the waters cover the earth once again. As we see boundaries so
strongly affirmed by the psalmist broken through, we are still trying to
address the human capacity for destruction. No one story in the Hebrew
Scriptures matches in moral horror what we witnessed in the twentieth
century, and no theology from the second half of the century can fail to
take the wars and Holocaust of the first half into account.

But even though our overall worldview is called into question, the
human condition is sufficiently constant that we can still be moved today
by the biblical narrative that dates back millennia. The story of the Flood,
described in Genesis, gives us one way to think about the breakdown of
the meaning systems we inherited from our ancestors. Until Noah's time,
everything is shut up behind its proper boundaries, but then the fountains
of the great deep burst apart and the floodgates of the sky break open. As
all the limits disappear, the ark and its inhabitants float above the crash-
ing flood, carrying the seeds for a new construction of the world. Reading the description of the biblical Flood gives us a hint of what the
breakdown of an old worldview might be like.

Every generation feels some need to question, reappropriate, and
reshape the meaning system of its ancestors. The theology that preceded

the destruction of the Temple, for example, was life-givingly transformed so that Judaism could survive the end of Temple worship and the entry into exile. Our urge to rethink the fundamental worldview we inherit—a challenging, even frightening prospect—is actually suggested repeatedly in our texts, which encourage us to "sing unto Adonai a new song" (Pss. 33, 40, 96, 98, and 144), to add our own voices to the songs we address to God. Some of these are songs of praise; others express our dismay, weariness, fears, and doubts. We can use the musical image to understand that we need many voices to achieve harmony. Indeed, music can affect us deeply, changing how we feel about the world and allowing us to reexamine our theology.

Developing a Personal Theology

The task of this book is to help us as we flounder while the old paradigms break apart; it is to help us find our own ark, floating above the chaos, that holds the bits and pieces of personal experience out of which we will piece together a coherent whole; it is to help us realize that we cannot neatly fence off our daily lives from this "construction zone." The book helps us make our quest for meaning explicit, suggests ways of approaching it, and offers some questions and techniques we can bring to the process.

Theologizing may satisfy our curiosity or help us build up our critical intellect, but its purpose is the practical one of defining and maintaining our relationship to God. Theology cannot substitute for this relationship, but theology can encourage it by helping us fight fears, sharpen our focus, and make conscious our experience of God's presence in our daily lives. In this effort, theology is eminently practical, shaping our expectations and teaching us how to be open to perceive the world in a new way.

Our personal theology is not subject to debate with others, though not because it is "perfect." On the contrary, it is always provisional and constantly being corrected as it is shaped by our experience and reshaped as we live longer and undergo change. We arrive at it and modify it through our life experiences, not through our speculative abilities. At the same time that our theology helps us form our beliefs about reality, these beliefs influence how we experience the world and how we interact with it.

As important as our theology may be for ourselves individually, it also has import for all of us. Together we are trying to figure out what it is to be human, who God may be, and where God can be found. Such a task lies beyond the individual, so each one of us must contribute our personal insight, perception, memories, and reflection to the larger whole of humanity's self-understanding. Similarly, we are nourished and strengthened by those who came before us and increased the repertoire of ways to understand reality that we can try on, modify, adopt, or discard. Our urge to make sense of our lives grows out of our feelings of loss, pain, and despair, and out of our need to know what we can hope for. People may also raise theological questions in the face of joy and gratitude: "What must reality be like, that I am so blessed?" For many, happiness feels natural—an occasion for joy but not for intense reflection—while for others, discovering love, wonder, or a sense of purpose leads them to reexamine their theology.

TAMAR

Tamar had been telling the same story about herself since her twenties, but now that she was well into middle age, it was time for a re-vision. The story of a twenty-six-year-old can no longer be the story of a woman who has married, raised her own children, and is now rethinking her life. But how do you change your story? Her first inkling that she was in for a radical shift came when her grandson, Shawn, asked her if she remembered her own first day of school. What began as a story for Shawn continued on in her own mind long after the child was in bed. Shawn was her link to the future; how, Tamar wondered, did she want the future to know her? What lessons could her life offer this vulnerable child? From the vantage point of the future, her life seemed very different from how she had always looked at it.

She found her thoughts over the next few days so fascinating that she decided to write them down. *Who am I?* she asked herself in wonder; *What has my life been about?* As these questions accompanied her on her daily walk, she realized that her life centered on loving relationships. What has all that loving taught her? How has it shaped her? What does it mean?

It began, as it does for almost all of us, with her love as a child for her parents and siblings. There was nothing simple about that love, she now realized, because she spent all of her adult life learning how to love the family she was born into. What effect did birth order have? her parents' relationship to each other? the stock market, even?

In her twenties, with her birth-family relations still decades from resolution, she married and began her own family. She read somewhere that she would never have as long a relationship with anyone as she would with her parents and siblings, and that struck her as inherently unfair. The years she spent building her own family while trying to forget the intensity of her growing-up time were no match for birth-family relationships, with their twenty-year head start. Marriage offered a magnificent challenge: three years of being a twosome followed by the birth of her daughter and son. But in and through the next thirty-two years of raising her children, and seeing them married and watching them become parents themselves, her relationship to her husband remained a major theme.

But where was God in all this? It was a question she learned to ask only recently, when a visiting lecturer suggested that it was the basic question to raise in all situations. She imagined Shawn as an adolescent (thankfully some years hence) asking her with scorn, "But what did you do?" She thought of her checkered work history, of reinventing herself while reentering the job market as a beginner. But she pushed the accusing question out of her mind in favor of the genuine questions, *What did I accomplish? What did all these jobs do for me and for others? What did I love doing?*

Two years earlier, when her doctor chided her for not exercising enough, she began her daily walks. *We take our bodies for granted when we're young,* she thought, *but aging brings us to an awareness of our physical selves with renewed appreciation.* But then she corrected herself: *we never take our bodies for granted.* As a short child, she was always made to sit in the front row of the classroom, when all the really interesting stuff was going on in the back of the room. Her body became a mystery and an embarrassment to her from early adolescence on. A few wonderful, less self-conscious years, and then her body carried life. Where was God in all of this? Easy, she thought—it was in the wonder of cocreating life, her daughter and son. It suddenly struck her with a start that her body transformed her theology before her intellect did. As the miracle of a new life was growing within her, she felt an almost indescribable sense of her connectedness with God in cocreating. Thirty-two years later, though, she still couldn't put the feeling into words.

But her body, and even the bodies of her friends, changed

her theology in other ways as well. Marci was an older friend she first met when their husbands worked together; Marci was the first friend (though not the last) to get cancer. Marci never asked Tamar "Why me?" So the answers Tamar formulated were her own desperate struggle with the trials and suffering of illness and, ultimately, with the idea of death. A long parade of friends, relatives, and colleagues departed this life following Marci's death; she recalled going through her address book, crossing out the names of the deceased.

It was different when she was a teenager and her grandmother died. That death was mediated by her parents, who prepared her and taught her how to act and answered questions she hadn't even asked. But Marci's death hit close to home; as an adult herself, Tamar was faced with somehow making sense of her mortality. But as she was asking herself *Why do we die?* she realized that she would first have to answer the question, *Why am I living?*

ROSE

Rose's husband, Lonnie, died of an aneurysm at forty-eight, without any warning. The shock and pain of it all left Rose immobilized. She knew she had to take care of the children, but her grief was overwhelming.

Two years after Lonnie's death, while she still had no energy or joy in life, her friends tried to persuade her to see a psychotherapist. She brushed the idea aside but did go to see her doctor, who did a routine physical, only to discover that she had a cancerous growth. The doctor suggested her tumor might be a response to her husband's death, maybe an unconscious wish to join him. Rose bristled: she knew she had two children to raise, and she was determined to live!

Faced with Lonnie's death and then her own illness, she stopped working. Eventually, after her health returned and her children were packed off to college, she allowed herself to explore the questions she had put aside during her mourning for Lonnie and her own illness and convalescence. (Who knew it would take years? She thought she would be done mourning when her eleven months of reciting *Kaddish,* the prayer for the dead, were up.) Even now, every twinge, sore throat, or muscle ache raised the specter of a more malignant danger. Never could she take her body for granted again.

Well, had she ever? She thought of friends, family, and synagogue members, all so loving and supportive during her deep
troubles, and she felt grateful for their presence, their caring.
But she could not accept their "answers," because they
weren't her own; she had to think things out for herself.

While the children were still at home, she didn't dare ask,
"Where is Lonnie now?" or "Where was God through all of
this?" Seeing her offspring happily involved at college, she
fought off the temptation to call daily so as to reassure herself
that they were safe. Instead of calling, she would write imagi-
nary conversations in her journal. By the time her daughter
was a senior and her son was a sophomore, she felt genuinely
liberated, ready to raise the questions that once seemed too
threatening. She could now ask herself, *What does my life
mean?*

To address the question, though, she realized she would
have to break it down into bite-sized pieces. Who am I? Is
there anything left of the hopeful girl who so loved nature
that she studied biology to help her form a deeper relationship to the natural world? She had been away from her field
too long to return to it. When she tried to read a scientific
journal, she felt like a novice in a field she barely recognized.
What to do?

The rituals at the time of Lonnie's death and the healing
services during her bout with cancer provided great comfort,
but where did Judaism fit in? Was it part of her personal
questioning? Could it help her make sense of what she had
lived through? Part of her felt it was self-indulgent to worry
about such personal matters. With an economic crisis loom-
ing and "police actions" sprouting all over the globe, who
was she to raise questions about the meaning of life based on
her loss and suffering?

Fortunately she recognized the charge of self-indulgence for
the temptation it was. If each life weren't so uniquely valuable, she wouldn't still be missing Lonnie. Also, neither the
vastness of the multitudes caught up in the horrors of war
nor, by comparison, the seeming unimportance of her personal concerns precluded meaning. Actually, she couldn't
envision anonymous masses and large numbers; what makes
us people is our lack of anonymity—our stories! God didn't
create nine billion people. God created Adam and Eve, and

later God chose one individual, Abraham, to guide a culture and a civilization.

Stories—that was how Rose would begin. In spite of the painful memories she would now be addressing, her excitement grew. She was undertaking a unique task. No one but she could make sense of her life.

MARK

In his boyhood, Mark believed in a God who allowed only good things, so he found himself forced to ask where God was when his father walked out on the family, his mother was institutionalized for bipolar disorder, and his stepfather used him for a punching bag. Later he could recognize that he erred in his premise. God can be present even in the midst of bad occurrences.

Neither he nor his wife, Ilana, a Holocaust survivor, professes to have any idea of why evil can happen, but both of them have concluded that God remains present, loving, and caring. As a result, Mark and Ilana no longer compound their suffering by believing that they have been abandoned by God. They find true comfort in the famous verse from the twenty-third psalm: "Though I walk through the valley of the shadow of death, I fear no harm, for You are with me." At the same time, they have come to recognize that the horrors and misfortunes they underwent were not punishments from God for any supposed wrongdoing of theirs.

These theological reflections led to immediate changes in how Mark and Ilana felt about themselves and about God. Instead of turning from God in guilt, anger, or even bitterness, they can turn to God for comfort, support, or refuge in times of trouble.

Does theology change what is happening? Yes, but not in the simple sense of making illness and evil go away. Instead, we come to realize that our lives are colored less by events than by our reaction to the events and that changing our theology transforms our reaction.

Two Holocaust victims who recorded their beliefs, Etty Hillesum and Viktor Frankl, forcefully exemplify this principle, but less-calamitous times have also yielded people asking and answering the fundamental working question: Where is God in what is happening? The awareness that God is present, and that we need to discover how that presence helps us, changes our entire quest. Rather than looking for a way out of our trying situation or yearning for revenge, we seek out what we can do with what has happened in our lives.

Move Toward the Light

A basic rule on the spiritual way, a rule much at odds with the practice of psychotherapy, is ignore the darkness and move toward the light—the light being God's presence in and through the dark times. If we move toward that presence, we can deepen our relationship with God and thereby transform how we interpret what has occurred.

Our most urgent job in the face of suffering is to ease it. For Joseph, in the Book of Genesis, that meant letting God's presence shape his actions (rejecting Potiphar's wife, dealing thoughtfully with his fellow prisoners). By contrast, he could not be relieved of his pain by divining the various motives behind his brothers' actions. Learning the motives (his favored treatment by their father, Jacob; his place in the birth order; his own pride; even the death of his mother) did nothing to ease his suffering. After his father's death, Joseph not only perceived God's presence but even figured out the larger purpose of his own being, long before he could understand the good of all he had undergone.

Of course, the effort to explore the dark can prevent its recurrence, but we should wait for the appropriate time, not try to do so while the patient is bleeding to death ("He died, but we couldn't stanch the wound while he was working out the reasons his brother hated him so"). In our own dark times, we are bled of hope, meaning, and self-worth. Locating God in such times restores our inner balance.

Theology Is Everyone's Task

All of us should be theologians. In a way, all of us are, but we do theology in a largely unexamined way, taking a bit from here and a dab from there, without asking if the two pieces really fit together. The writer Mary Oliver helps us recognize that we already have an unconscious theology: "Try to live through one day believing nothing is significant, nothing is governed by the unknowable, the divine. See how you feel by the end of such a day" (1999, p. 79).

Consciously recognizing our theology also helps foster our growing relationship with God, allowing us to view daily events in a positive light.

The following story is told by philosopher John Wisdom (1961):

> Two people return to their long-neglected garden. They find
> that amid the weeds, a few of the old plants show surprisingly
> vigorous growth. One concludes that a gardener has been
> coming and taking care of the plants, while the other, noting
> the weeds, believes no gardener has come. On looking further
> around the garden, the first person finds more and more evi-
> dence to confirm that a gardener has indeed been at work,
> while the second becomes convinced that not only has no gar-
> dener come, but a malicious visitor has been systematically
> destroying the garden. The first states, "A gardener comes
> unseen and unheard. He is manifested in his works, with
> which we are all familiar." The other counters, "There is no
> gardener." The difference in what they say reflects a differ-
> ence in how they feel toward the garden, even though neither
> of them expects anything different from the garden.

The difference in how the two feel about the garden affects how they
interact with it. When we know that a flower bed is someone's loved possession, we walk through it with care and appreciation. But if we believe
it to be abandoned, unclaimed land, we do not treat it with the same dili-
gence. We see that kind of difference in many aspects of our lives—for
example, in distinguishing between chronicle and history. In our day
books, we chronicle events without interpretation or hierarchy of importance. In our diaries, on the other hand, we weigh the events, discern patterns and meaning, and arrange them in the order of their significance to
us. A similar thought is expressed by theologian John Dunne: "Your story
could be told in many different ways, depending on the kind of future you
thought it was leading to" (1969, p. vii).

Judaism doesn't leave to chance what kind of future we anticipate. We
are educated about our past, made aware of God's faithfulness, and taught
our projected future; in other words, we are given a framework in which
our individual stories take their place. The psalmist shows how remembering God's past faithfulness becomes a warrant for future hopefulness.
Psalm 22 begins:

> My God, my God,
>> why have You abandoned me;
>> why so far from delivering me
>> and from my anguished roaring?

But in the fifth verse, the psalmist recalls God's beneficence to our ancestors:

In You our fathers trusted;
   they trusted and You rescued them.
To You they cried out
   and they escaped;
   in You they trusted
   and were not disappointed.

Yet still the psalmist worries, for there might be exceptions to God's concern:

But I am a worm, less than human;
   scorned by men, despised by people.

But finally, the psalmist is comforted in personally recalling the presence of God:

You drew me from the womb,
   made me secure at my mother's breast.
I became Your charge at birth;
   from my mother's womb You have been my God.

Locating God in our own story changes it and changes what we imagine the outcome of the story can be. The psalmist goes on to graphically portray a sea of troubles—

Many bulls surround me,
   mighty ones of Bashan encircle me.
They open their mouths at me
   like tearing, roaring lions.

—but then turns to the God familiar from earlier encounters—

But You, O Adonai, be not far off;
   my strength, hasten to my aid.
Save my life from the sword,
   my precious life from the clutches of a dog.

—pledges to spread God's name—

Then will I proclaim Your fame to my brethren,
   praise You in the congregation.

—and charges each one of us:

You who fear Adonai, praise God! . . .
   Adonai's fame shall be proclaimed to the generation to come;
   they shall tell of God's beneficence
   to people yet to be born,
   for God has acted.

We create our theology using many of the components of the biblical tradition, applying it freshly to our own experiences.

The Role of Memory

Each of us is charged to remember, to commemorate, to help others locate God in their personal history. "Forgetfulness is exile," Reb Nachman of Bratislava declared.

> ILANA
> Ilana found a powerful analogy to the exile brought about when we forget God's presence in our lives. Her father died when she was in her early teens. After the immediate intense grieving, she found herself trying to remember the exact nature of her relationship to her father. Twenty years after his death, Ilana found herself unconsciously calling her own daughter "my little ray of sunshine"; she suddenly remembered that her father had used this precise phrase to refer to herself. Those years of forgetting had cut her off from his love for her, and in now remembering, she reclaimed the gift of his love.

The *Haggadah* tells us that "we must remember what Adonai did for *me* when I went out from Egypt," in order to remind us of the love and intimacy we have personally experienced.

So now we set out on the adventure of theology. We recognize that our theology is something we urgently need to stanch a wound or to help us find our way. It is also something we contribute to our people's collective understanding of our relationship to God. With courage and a high sense of adventure, we set out.

2

FORMING OUR STORY

You, O Adonai my God, have done many things;
the wonders You have devised for us
cannot be set out before You;
I would rehearse the tale of them,
but they are more than can be told. . . .
"See, I will bring a scroll recounting what befell me."

—Psalms 40:6–8

WE TELL OUR STORIES in many ways. What makes our story Jewish is that the assumptions, language, and metaphors we employ are those we have absorbed from the story of our people. Adopting the story does not mean that we wind up with only one way of being human. The ways our humanity can be expressed, framed by the story of our people, are unlimited. I recall once seeing a whole class of girls wearing identical school uniforms. Yet no two of the girls looked alike. Several had hiked up their skirts to make them fashionably short. One had every button of her blouse buttoned while others had two—and one daring girl even three—undone. One managed to look military in her uniform while another was a rumpled mess, as if her uniform had been thrown together out of odd scraps of clothing. Individuality underlies every aspect of Creation, so that even in the simplest arrangement of a blouse, skirt, stockings, and shoes it manages to break through. How much more so in the ways we construct and construe the world in which we find ourselves.

If Judaism were merely a matter of rules, this richness would not be as apparent. But it is the story of our people—and we know how inventive the storyteller can be. Years ago, I was given a set of books containing a collection of ballads, stories in song gathered in the southern United States. The tomes document both the changes and the continuity in the oral transmission of ballads. For "Barbara Allen," a song familiar from my childhood, the book shows 167 versions.

Just as we have all enjoyed late-night song fests featuring variation upon variation of favorite ballads, I have also spent long evenings sharing the rich variety of ways in which each of us acquires and transmits the faith of our forebears. I feel a little like Francis James Child, who collected the ballads, as I listen with wonder and respect to the various stories and marvel at the magnificent ways people stretch the faith to accommodate the realities of their own experience.

Because the story we tell ourselves about who we are is our informal theology, it greatly influences how we perceive other people and situations. As we seriously examine this informal—and frequently unconscious—theology, we discover a new domain of freedom: our story can be modified.

> We can see two very different ways of viewing the same person. Two sisters, Jennie and Leah, have opposite and complementary reactions to their father. To Jennie, her father is stern and forbidding, and it has taken years to constructively view his actions as indicative that he loves her deeply. Leah had a very different childhood in the same household and so sees their father basically as someone who loves her; she dismisses his rages as his occasional need to act harshly.

What the Israelites received at Mount Sinai was not simply the law, in the narrow sense of rules and regulations, but the Law, in the full sense of the story of our people. The rules are embedded in the story, just as almost every story we know comes with implicit expectations and values.

A horde of people lived for hundreds of years with the story that they were chattel, mere slaves to the Egyptians. Then they were liberated not only physically but spiritually as well, in part by learning and internalizing the story that they were chosen by God and had a unique mission on this earth. Physical liberation is crucial, but without a new story it is difficult to sustain. With the gradual dying out of the slave generation, a new generation, raised and nurtured on the story of Sinai, emerged. Only then could the Israelites enter the Promised Land and have a vision strong enough that it could be transmitted and preserved—and could serve to preserve—the Jews for three millennia.

Our Informal Theology

Stories are the central component of our informal theology. We discover over time that they can be reformed and reframed, and how we choose to tell our story has practical implications shaping our perceptions and actions. We can emphasize different aspects of the Jewish story, so even though we have a common story the resulting theology is individual, customized to the life that bodied it forth. We keep returning to the larger story, both to foster a shared language with others (our quest for community) and to lift our day-to-day situations into a broader affirmative setting.

We begin with our own story, because we are the instrument through which any larger story is formed. Then we join our story with that of our people. But the story of our people is only one lens through which to look at a reality that is larger than our lives and efforts, larger even than our people's lives and efforts. Our story is essential, and our people's story is essential; but what we are approaching transcends both.

We begin in silence. This is the silence that comes before we even know that the things around us can be named. We learn language from our linguistic community. Wars fought over national language, disagreements about bilingual education, and the effort of many universal religions to have a special holy language all alert us to the power of a linguistic community. Perhaps through travel or study we become very comfortable in another language or even attain bilingual mastery.

We return to our first language, now able to contribute. We push the boundaries of language—and we end in silence. The silence in which we end is not the same as that from which we began, because our new silence has been arrived at through the whole process of loving, living, contributing, and recognizing all the contributions and gifts around us. Every language is a collection of a people's stories, as any careful examination of etymology will demonstrate.

Now, as we develop our theology—our way of dealing with the basic questions of who we are, what we can know, and what we can hope for—our starting point is our own story. We think of a story as a recital of events, a narrative account that has a beginning, a middle, a climax, a denouement, and an end. But we all know that the same set of events can be read in a thousand ways. The same movie, for example, can be judged by one critic to be hilarious and by another to be hopelessly sophomoric. Similarly, the same marriage might be equated by one partner with bliss, and the other with purgatory. It is not hard to conclude, then, that what counts is not the specific facts about our lives but how we interpret them, fit them together, and make sense of them. It is these procedures that we want to examine to help us identify our personal theology.

Personal story has also become the primary ingredient in psychotherapeutic relationships. Contemporary psychotherapy helps us develop a narration regarding our own history. This story, composed in the relationship between patient and therapist, mediates a common vision for both.

MARTIN
Martin, a twenty-three-year-old fraternal twin, ruefully told his therapist that his birth was the classic example of family planning gone wrong. His parents made it clear early on that they wanted two children, a son (his older brother) and a daughter (his twin sister). As the second son, he reasoned, he was unnecessary and had no place in his family of origin.

Rummaging through his memory, Martin recalled how close he and his sister had always been—still were—and the numerous times he had helped his sister. Once he came to realize that his twin sister benefited from his existence, he began considering some alternatives to his story. He also admitted the possibility that although his parents were necessary for his being, they were not the only force behind his existence. One day he independently announced to his therapist that "the stone that the builder rejected has become the chief cornerstone." He realized, both intellectually and viscerally, that whether or not his parents had wanted him, something or someone wanted his being very much.

Reshaping the story transforms how the patient can approach the future. The enhanced freedom that is supported by the new story fostered in the therapeutic relationship resembles the sense of autonomy and meaning we arrive at when we interpret our story theologically.

The Components of Our Story

Let's look at various elements of our story as if it were a play, a movie, or a television show. We certainly need a cast, sets, costumes, lighting, and either a script or an idea on which to improvise. But unlike a painting or a piece of sculpture, our drama also needs time in which to play out.

The Set

The set, at the very least, tells us where our story takes place. But the question is never this simple, because our stories occur in many venues, such as our place of birth, where we grew up, home, school, playground, synagogue, job. The geography includes internal as well as external space. Diarist Alice James, who was largely confined to her home because of chronic illness, nevertheless lived a full, rich inner life. Her caretaker thought James's day-to-day existence must have been unremittingly boring and could not imagine what she found to write in her diary. James was equally incredulous at how the caretaker could view her life as uninteresting. The caretaker, it is clear, saw only the external geography of James's story, while the diarist found delight and adventure in her mind's journeys.

Set also includes places and lands that feel like the intrinsic geography of our soul. In explaining why he was drawn to photographing the Sinai desert, photographer Neil Folberg wrote that the Passover *Haggadah* exhorts us to see ourselves as though we had been personally redeemed from Egypt. Carrying this suasion a step further, he believes that every generation should spend some actual time in Sinai. "Our sages teach that a man should make himself like a desert: humble and receptive to guidance from above. No wonder Moses and the Israelites didn't bother to raise monuments to their passage. Nothing merely physical is a monument to Divine revelation" (1987, p. 65). Set refers to where our body has been, where our mind has resided, and where our spirit has found a home.

Time

Time is the nonspatial realm in which the activities of life occur; it also measures the tempo of the activities. It can be experienced as fleeting, for example, or as burdensome. Careful attention to time is fundamental to Judaism; social psychologist Robert Levine (1997, p. 208) writes:

> Judaism is very much a religion of time. It gives more consideration to history and events—the Exodus from Egypt, the revelation of the Torah—than to things. The prophets teach, for example, that the day of the Lord is more sacred than the house of the Lord. Temporal settings, rather than spatial ones, frame the sacred Jewish texts. The Talmud opens with, "From when?" and the Torah with "In the Beginning."

Time, in which our story unfolds, stretches back to the distant past, and ahead to the imagined future. Because our story is ongoing, it partakes of the timeless. Awareness of past events that give resonance to our present undertakings, a vision for the future that shapes our current activities, and a sense of participating in an eternal drama all make time a central element in our story.

Lighting

Lighting tells us whether the actions in the story are clear and "well lit" or murky and mysterious. Much of what it means to become an adult is bound up in the ever-increasing light we experience. What originally was dimly understood and hardly controlled at all is later seen with clarity and often with some mastery. But when we turn in our story to look at God, the lighting shifts again:

> The Jewish understanding of God was rooted in the sense of mystery, of awe, and of the essential unknowability of the true God. The human person could not see God and live. . . . Paradoxically, the Sinai revelation was one in which God was said to have been encountered face to face. Here indeed is the central paradox of Jewish theology: that God is seen and yet not seen, known and yet unknowable, revealed but always in hiddenness and obscurity [Leech, 1985, p. 162].

What is true about our experience of God is also true about our encounter with ourselves, with others, and even with reality as a whole. As we age, we recognize that the lighting dims, our vision once more is obscured, and we have come to be aware of our ignorance.

Plot

In shaping our narrative, we encounter the large question of whether it has any meaning. Although story by its very form implies some purpose, the plot determines the meaning we assign to the whole. In hearing others' stories, we can often recognize what we may not see in our own story. We enjoy a special *frisson* of excitement when we see things clearly and wait to note when they themselves recognize that their stories have, all along, spelled out their own deepening relationship with God.

Since story is the fundamental component of our informal theology, we want to know how our story might be changed. Actually, we can find mutability in all its components. The setting can be expanded—that is, we can look beyond our narrow focus to everything that is going on around us—and our sense of space enlarged so that our set encompasses our whole world. Or time can be enlarged, taking us beyond our immediate past to include all the factors that might have influenced the actors in our story; we can even push the story back far beyond our birth to discover how our story fits into that of our people.

How we view the darkness and ambiguity in our story is also subject to change: we can learn how to see with greater clarity and learn to value mystery. The plot must be carefully examined. We thought the story was about one thing, but from a new perspective we may discover it is about something altogether different. As Tolstoy's character Ivan Ilyitch puts it, "It's as if all the time I were going down the mountain while thinking that I was climbing it" (1886/1964, p.110).

Cast

When we look back on our story, we realize that at first we focused narrowly and included in our story only those immediately around us. As we grow, and our interests and concerns expand, so does our interest in people outside our story. We find ourselves recognizing and reclaiming people in our lives whom we had previously forgotten. In thinking about the cast we want, we must decide whether the characters include the unseen: ancestors, fictional characters, those yet unborn, people we know about but haven't met. The unseen often embody aspects of ourselves viewed as separate entities: our passions, our aspirations, our memories. Also, we can change the cast of characters in our story, and additional characters should be considered. Has it occurred to us, for instance, that the major agent in our story might be God?

> REGINA
> Regina, a forty-five-year-old actor, director, and producer,
> took to the theater metaphor immediately. After hearing the
> components of story, she urged that we also consider all the
> so-called invisible people backstage who make the drama pos-
> sible: the hairdressers, makeup artists, and "techies" who pre-
> pare the props and find the telling details that make the
> audience identify the period of the play.

Like a play, our life is a production, and too often we overlook the people backstage who have made our own performance possible. In forming our story, we must be sure to examine the people and events that truly seemed of minor importance but that can now offer clues and turn out to be more significant than we ever thought.

Telling Our Story

If you are invited to tell your story, your first thought is probably, "Who asked?" Very likely, you then tailor what you say to how well you know the people who asked and what you know about them. But now you want an audience of one: yourself. There is no need to hide anything to shade meanings; this is the time to be completely honest. The raw ingredients of your story are not merely your actions and the events you have experienced; they also encompass what these actions and events have meant to you. You tell parts of your story all the time: when you meet other people, a piece of your story may serve as a good introduction, or when you hear the stories of others, you counter with your own. But this time, when you are telling the story to yourself, you are doing so in the service of theology. Put another way, you are trying to discover God's presence in and through your life.

Most Jews approach talking directly about God with discomfort or even a sense of horror. Merely to think that we are searching our story for God's presence may turn us off, except that we have probably not defined what we mean by *God* since we attended *talmud torah* (Jewish religion classes) after school at the age of eight. For now, let's say that we are seeking the aspect of the story that suggests we are part of something larger than our own life and effort. We are looking for the element that turns our daily life into something of infinite worth. We search our own memories to discover where there has been wonder.

We engage in reminiscence to help us discover God's presence in and through our lives. Our memories can be put in the service of theology: discovering who God is for us, where God can be found, and what we can know about reality. Memory is used to locate "the more"—the part of the story that cannot be accounted for by all the usual modes of explanation. Ultimately, we discover that every carefully recollected event, in addition to being whatever it purports to be about, is also a story of God.

The story we initially tell is narrower than it ultimately turns out to be. It is a first approximation of a personal theology that is, as yet, undeveloped. Making the theology explicit helps us shape the story and claim it. The formal theology that finally emerges is as unique and individual as the less formal story, though in comparing our stories we see family resemblances that result from certain shared assumptions, or commitments to beliefs.

Commitments Behind Storytelling

The first commitment is to the enterprise of storytelling itself, right down to the belief that stories can exist—or even further, that there is a before and an after. Some recent literature deliberately bypasses this belief, causing critics to decry the breakdown of the story. Thanks to scientists, many of our suppositions about time, space, causality, and meaning have been thrown into question, as a limerick suggests:

> There once was a woman named Bright
> Who tried to prove Einstein was right.
> She set out one day
> In a relative way
> And returned on the previous night.

If there is no general direction in which we're moving, how can we talk about before, during, and after—that is, all the components of linear time? How can we talk about whether or not we are nearing our goal? If our common notion of causality is questioned, how can we talk about responsibility?

Stories begin sometime and take place somewhere, but they also are about something. Every story—happy or sad, funny or tragic—affirms that there is meaning. Writers seem to agree. The novelist Isak Dinesen wrote, "All sorrows can be borne if you put them into a story or tell a story about them"; and Anatole Broyard wrote, "Stories are antibodies against illness and pain. . . ." Commitment to narrative form means we believe that revelation unfolds over time—that is, we know more at the end of a story than we knew at the beginning. Time itself becomes a medium of revelation. Stories also affirm the value of the particular, in that they concern specific settings and characters.

Although current literary theory may be challenging the age-old practice of storytelling, the psychotherapeutic community has understood therapy's function of getting to where the patient and therapist agree on a new story about the patient's life. The new story, reframing the events that the patient brings to the therapist, confirms the power of language and the word.

The power of story is evident in the political domain. People fight against repressive regimes by remembering better times, and by forming stories of liberation. Regardless of what Jews have undergone in the past two millennia, they recall that they were slaves and that, with a strong hand and an outstretched arm, God liberated them. This memory shows them the possibility of God's intervention on their behalf; it gives them a vision of possibilities and it keeps their hopes alive.

Many Ways to Tell Our Story

Stories are part of our nature, but there are many ways to tell them. The narrative form we choose reflects our authentic self. Poet Martha Collins suggests that our essential story concerns our mortality and vulnerability:

> The way to begin is always the same. Hello,
> Hello. Your hand, your name. So glad, Just fine
> and Good-bye at the end. That's every story we know
> and why pretend? But lunch tomorrow? No?
> Yes? An omelet, salad, chilled white wine?
> The way to begin is simple, sane, Hello,
> And then it's Sunday, coffee, the *Times,* a slow
> day by the fire, dinner at eight or nine
> and Goodbye. In the end, this is a story we know
> so well we don't turn the page, or look below
> the picture, or follow the words to the next line:
> The way to begin is always the same Hello.
> But one night, through the latticed window, snow
> begins to whiten the air, and the tall white pine.
> Goodbye is the end of every story we know
> that night, and when we close the curtains, oh,
> we hold each other against the cold white sign
> of the way we all begin and end. *Hello,*
> *Goodbye* is the only story. We know, we know.
>
> —"The Story We Know" (1985)

Collins's perspective sharpens our view of the many partings leading to the final one. Hello/goodbye is the central story of Buddhism, which focuses on the transience of life in all its aspects. But it is not the central story for Judaism.

Years ago a rabbi told me that if I wondered whether a particular concept was Jewish or not, I should try translating it into Hebrew. If it could not be easily translated, it was probably not a Jewish notion. I suggest a different type of translation, not into the Hebrew language, but into the Jewish story. If an idea or theme cannot be found within the Jewish collection of stories, it is probably not Jewish.

We live in a society that presents us with a wealth of stories, but because we are probably unaware of how powerful they are, we don't bring to them the careful critique they may require. At the same time, we may read and reread the Torah, and though we find many of the stories

disturbing, they create a world we can enter. Underlying the biblical stories is a belief in meaning, the reality of the presence and engagement of
God in and through all we see and experience. In other words, the invisible gives rise to the visible.

We can use the biblical stories to test other stories with which we are
raised and surrounded. For example, in Maurice Maeterlinck's story *The
Children's Blue Bird,* a brother and sister set out to look for the bluebird
of happiness. They are almost thwarted, and the lives of all the characters
in the story are endangered by a cat. At the end of *The Children's Blue
Bird,* the cat is comfortably ensconced in the kitchen. An illustration by
Herbert Pauls in the 1916 edition shows the cat still very much a menace,
but in a lovely scene that includes the children, their parents, and the bluebird.

The Children's Blue Bird thus gives us an example of encapsulated
evil—a picture in which evil is not destroyed but no longer dominates the
whole. What has changed is the story reframed within an enlarged perspective. Is the perspective that permits encapsulated evil a Jewish idea or
not?

We find that something analogous happens in the biblical story of
Joseph, the favored child of his father, Jacob, and the first-born of his
father's deceased wife, Rachel. He is estranged from all his half-brothers,
who plot to kill him but finally decide instead to sell him into slavery.

The earliest part of the Joseph narrative deals exclusively with Joseph
and his half brothers. When the brothers then journey to Egypt, the
perspective expands, and the story depicts their relationship to
Benjamin, Joseph's full brother, and to Jacob. A still larger perspective
shows Joseph's brothers to be more than simple villains. After Jacob's
death, the brothers come in fear to Joseph, but by that point Joseph has
entered into the largest possible perspective and can say to them, about
selling him into slavery, "You meant it for evil, but God meant it for
good." The capacity to reframe the story, and enter into this universal perspective is difficult, but we begin on the path by going beyond ourselves.

We live in a complex time, no longer nomads and shepherds. Yet we
find that the biblical stories resonate with our fundamental questions
about family, our essential goodness, suffering, our quest for meaning,
and our relationship with God. The Bible stories are difficult because the
characters are not simply heroes or villains. But the stories are instructive
for the same reason. The characters are flawed, and their flaws help us
examine, accept, and integrate our own flaws. According to a story at the
heart of the Jewish mystical tradition, the holy vessel was shattered at the
moment of Creation and sacred sparks flew out in all directions. Our task

(to extend the metaphor) is to gather these sparks, to draw out the good in the apparent evil, and to recognize the sacred in and through the profane.

Non-Jewish Stories

It would be wonderful if we could go about the task of formulating our story in a quiet, uncluttered atmosphere. But life is ongoing and new data comes in constantly. There is always busyness and noise, and we do not begin with a clean slate. From the moment we are born into a culture, we are born into multiple stories that compete for our allegiance. Some stories, such as the biblical story, are formally presented to us. Others are unconsciously absorbed, and these may have a deeper effect on us than we recognize. The fairy tales of childhood were not originally written for children; they were instead a folk culture's attempt at self-understanding. Their values, though frequently at odds with our own religious convictions, are rarely thought of as important influences to be challenged and debated.

Using the "translation" test, we are anxious to discover if our own story of wanting to explore, to be challenged, to grow, is one of restlessness (the late twentieth-century American story of midlife crisis) or one of more dignity (back to the biblical notion of call). How do the other stories of call handle the restlessness? Most of us are familiar with the 1939 film version of L. Frank Baum's fantasy *The Wizard of Oz*. Despite its great imaginative qualities, the movie is, finally, a putdown of restlessness. The character of Dorothy wishes nothing more fervently than to return home. When she finally responds to the question of what she has learned from her journey, she utters the immortal (and somewhat garbled) line at the very end of the movie: "If I ever go looking for my heart's desire again, I won't look any further than my own back yard because if it isn't there I never really lost it to begin with." The logical lapse aside, the point has been made: there's no place like home.

Cinderella and *Snow White*, two fairy tales by the Grimm brothers made into widely distributed Disney movies, are versions of the rescue story—the belief that "someday my prince will come" and save me from despair or death. When we try to apply the translation test to these stories, we find variations of the rescue story in foretelling the coming of the Messiah, although this is a very minor aspect of the Torah and is emphasized only by the few apocalyptic texts. As children hearing these stories, we come to believe that rescue comes from outside ourselves. But the major prophetic texts in the Bible call us to transform our way of life rather than merely await passively the coming of a rescuer.

Unlike *Cinderella* and *Snow White,* in which the protagonist waits for an external solution, *The Ugly Duckling* emphasizes an inherent value that is finally achieved and recognized. (The translation test recognizes that the biblical version of *The Ugly Duckling* may be Isaiah's vision that we are meant to be a light unto the nations.)

Heroes' journeys, such as that of Ulysses, are a frequent motif in folk and children's tales. The fundamental biblical story for Jews is, indeed, one of journeying, a story motif that lies at the heart of the Torah. We moved out of Egypt, wandered for forty years in the desert, and went on to reach the Promised Land. But the wandering of the Israelites differs from that of popular culture in that the biblical journey is undertaken with and to God. It is *not* a story of personal heroics but rather one of learning to follow the pillar of cloud and fire, and of being tempered and shaped by the desert sojourn. There is no direct one-to-one translation from our people's journeying to the popular myth of the hero's journey.

One Story, Many Points of View

Agreeing with the biblical story can *still* yield many theologies, which vary in the weight and emphasis they place on each component of the story. *Cinderella* offers a fine example of ways in which a story can be viewed. Here are five:

1. It is the story of what happens to a stepchild in a family with other children, in much the way the story of Joseph could be viewed as the story of what happens to a favored son in a blended family.

2. It could be viewed as the stepsisters' misprizing one whose beauty is more than skin-deep, in the same way that the psalmist can exclaim, "The stone that the builders rejected has become the chief cornerstone" (Ps. 118:22).

3. It is a story of special providence in the form of a fairy godmother, much as one can focus on the special providence evidenced in the ten plagues that led to the liberation of the Israelites.

4. It is a story about boundaries and limits (you must leave before the clock strikes midnight), not unlike the many rules that delineated the camp of the Israelites in the wilderness.

5. It is a story about the love of a prince for a beautiful creature (whom he is unable to recognize the next day when she isn't dressed for the ball) and the elevation of the despised maid of the cinders to be his bride.

Love and marriage are also components of the Jewish story, but unlike Cinderella, we are loved even as we struggle in slavery and our redeemer has no difficulty distinguishing appearance from reality. But over the centuries Jews have focused on family, virtue, moral beauty, chosenness, and *halakhah* (the laws that are unique to living out the role of Jews, as opposed to the seven laws of Noah, which apply to everyone). Judaism avoids giving prominence to the "happily ever after" of the *Cinderella* story. The few times that it has, political disaster followed, as during Bar Kochba's rebellion (132–135 C.E.) and the Messianic movement centered on Shabbatai Zvi (1626–1676). But if *Cinderella* can yield so many diverse emphases and theologies, how much more so can the rich, multi-valenced story of the Jewish people.

We have briefly considered the views in *Cinderella* and *The Ugly Duckling*. What is the essential Jewish story, and what does it say about our own basic theology—who we are, what we can know, and what we can hope for? Like all good stories, it starts "in the beginning"—in this case, God's creation of heaven and earth. After setting the background and preparing the way, God creates people and informs them that they are created in the image of God, unlike the rest of Creation.

The primordial history, which in the biblical narrative applies to everyone, ends with a destructive flood, after which the Torah's focus shifts to the calling of one person, Abraham. The spotlight stays on him and we then follow his descendants for the rest of the Torah. We find them moving to Egypt during a famine, becoming enslaved there, and serving their masters for four hundred years, until Moses is called by God to lead them out. Now liberated, they are led through the wilderness for fifty days, entering into covenant with God and receiving revelation—the Torah—at Sinai. They wander in the wilderness for forty years and reach (but do not yet enter) the Promised Land, all the while growing into the revelation they have received.

Within this basic structure, we find many particular stories about each of the patriarchs, about the brothers of Joseph who become the eponymous heads of the tribes of Israel, and about other characters. Those of us who identify with the larger story have already committed ourselves to the belief that life has meaning. We have also committed ourselves to a belief in God, whom we discover in and through Creation and history; and to a sense of our "amphibious" nature—that is, we are creatures like others in our environment, at the same time that we are creators in God's image. (Identifying with the larger story commits us to other beliefs as well—for example, that we are not yet who we are meant to be, that we have fallen into some form of slavery, that we have been liberated and led toward some Promised Land, that we have entered into covenant with God, that we have received revelation, and that we wander, trying to understand our full promise and striving to achieve it.)

Most of us have no trouble with the first point, that life has meaning, because we believe that God created the heavens and the earth, and Creation itself would not have occurred without any purpose. Anyhow, if we did not believe in meaning, we wouldn't be trying to discover our own theology. Simply forming a story, *any* story, already commits us to meaning.

The second point, the existence and presence of God, presents us with a problem: What do we do with the contradictory images of God found in the text of the *Tanakh* (Torah, Prophets, and Writings)? Here God is portrayed as compassionate, there as angry, here as patient and merciful, there as petty and even murderous. So we decide that since God is discovered in and through Creation and history, we focus on our own discoveries about God.

The third point concerns the nature of our own identity. That we are both creatures and potential creators is a piece of the story we can resonate with. If we were merely creatures, we would not be seeking to create a theology. It's no problem for a cat to be a cat, but it *is* a problem for a human to be a human.

The idea that enslavement is an aspect of our personal story looms as a major facet of the story. Can we recognize how we are less than free? Can we begin to name our metaphoric pharaohs?

What about covenant? Our first recognition is that love and commitment are essential to shaping a world. Later we realize that there can be no freedom without commitment.

Revelation may be the thorniest aspect of the story. What is it? What was revealed? How detailed and extensive was the revelation? We can avoid getting caught up in biblical criticism by focusing, always, on how the biblical story serves as a structure onto which we can map our own story. Can we, out of our own experience, give any meaning to the word revelation?

Applying the Basic Story to Our Own Narrative

Some of us find that our stories have gaps. We may believe, for example, that God was present in our childhood and is present now, but somehow absent between late adolescence and our early to mid-twenties.

ERIC

Eric enjoyed a loving childhood growing up in the suburbs.
He attended services with his family on the Sabbath and holidays. But when he went off to college, his synagogue atten-
dance went on hold. He was busy trying to figure out which
things really belonged to him and which actions he did only
to please his parents. He explored several political causes and
Eastern religions, and even joined a fraternity. Along with
wanting to find out if he was attractive to women, he was
also trying to do well in his prelaw courses (even though he
wasn't sure if he really wanted to become a lawyer—did he
choose prelaw because it was expected of him?).

Somehow, it never occurred to him to address all these
questions to the God he had known in his childhood, maybe
because he had to imagine that he was doing all this on his
own. In time, he graduated, completed law school, and married. Three months into his wife's first pregnancy, he suddenly
realized that he was standing on holy ground. There had been
such a long silence—could he now still address God? He
began by praying for his wife and his unborn child. After
expressing his fears, he began to express his thanks. As time
passed, his gratitude kept growing, and he found he could go
on and on appreciating all that had sustained him in his unreflective years.

Reflecting over the course of a few months allows us to see that the
God we now know couldn't have been absent. We reexamine those years
and find that the story has changed. God wasn't absent; *we* were! God
was patiently waiting for us to renew the conversation. When we recognize God's abiding presence and our own past indifference, we are struck
with gratitude and love. Then, when others tell us of the absence of God,
we are neither judgmental nor angry; we listen for the indications that the
other's story of indifference may also have a deeper dimension that sym-
pathetic listening can help elicit.

JONATHAN

Jonathan was a Jew by choice. He had studied for a long time
and, in part because of the intense effort that went into his
conversion, he tended to discount the sacred moments he had
experienced earlier. His engagement with religious questions
had led him to explore Judaism. To now be a joyous member
of the Jewish people did not negate his whole earlier life.

Judaism, it turned out, was an optimal way for him to live out and express his relationship with God, which began not in the *mikvah,* the ritual bath taken at conversion, but in the womb. Changing the way the story was framed had consequences not only for him but for his parents and the rest of his family, and even for the Sunday school and church of his childhood.

Sometimes stories are too tidy, too nice, too happily-ever-after to contain all the richness and ambiguity of life. The story never stops being written; the adventure is still unfolding. Also, we do not know what an event in the present may come to mean. The story of Moses in the cleft of the rock remains a significant warning for all who are trying to make sense of things. Moses requests that he be allowed to behold God's Presence (Exod. 33:18), and God reminds him that no one can see God's Presence and live, but God places Moses in the cleft of a rock and shields him until God has passed by: "Then I will take my hand away and you will see my back; but my face must not be seen" (33:23).

God is not discovered in the future and rarely in present. Only in looking back do we begin to recognize God's presence in and through the working of our days. We can prove it to ourselves by comparing actions we performed a moment ago, where we can see no trace of destiny in our choice, with actions we took a month ago, where we (now) begin to recognize that if our action had good and agreeable results, it also had a twinge of inevitability. When we reflect on something we did ten or more years ago, we see the consequences of that act even more plainly, and it is hard to imagine how things could ever have been different. The further back we go in our memory, the more we come to recognize meaningful patterns.

We are committed to meaningful patterns through our commitment to Creation—not as a past historical event, but as an ongoing process that is renewed daily. We wonder how this awareness of pattern fits in with our own free will and our sense of self, and how we change from an isolated individual to one participating in a great design that is larger than our single efforts can achieve but that brings forth our deepest fulfillment.

What a Theology Does

Although a theology is likely to cover many areas, the three questions it seeks to answer are Who am I? What can I know? and What can I hope for?

Who Am I?

Probably no one is more of a mystery to us than we are to ourselves. We look all around us for clues to our own identity. We judge how people respond to us and even resort to taking magazine quizzes that purport to tell us who we are. Yet, as Jews, we have been given a profound answer to the question of our identity. We are told "And God created Adam in God's image . . . male and female did God create them" (Gen. 1:27). We don't know—indeed can never know—who God is. But if we take seriously that we are created in the image of God, then the vast mystery that is God exemplifies the vast mystery that is the self. No amount of successes in the human genome project suffice to describe who we are because, like our progenitor, we are irreducible mysteries. In emphasizing that we are created in God's image, Rabbi Akiba stated that whoever sheds blood destroys the image.

> SAM
> Sam, whom we last encountered reading about a medieval
> rabbi, responded to this view by adding that the Jewish view
> is not untempered. The Torah has no unflawed hero, and the
> Jewish view of human nature as developed by the rabbis
> states that we should go through life with two pieces of paper
> in our pockets, one saying "The world was made for me" and
> the other saying "I am but dust and ashes."

What Can I Know?

Because we bring the unknown self to the knowing situation, Torah shows that how we are in the world is clearly illuminated, yet at the same time shrouded in darkness. The light is represented by the stories that focus on what was given to us in revelation: both the clear rules found in the Decalogue and our capacity to interpret them through reason. But at Mount Sinai, we received the Law and experienced the presence of a dark cloud surrounding the mountain at the time, suggesting that unknowing may be an approach to a deeper knowledge.

> JOHANNA
> Johanna is an older woman. Early in her career, she displayed
> the brilliance and flash of the young scholar. Now, by con-
> trast, she finds herself giving off the steady warmth of endur-
> ing light. At the same time, she is now self-effacing,
> expressing a gentle humility. She has learned what she doesn't

know and can serve as a model of what the knowledge of ignorance can mean and how it can be expressed.

What Can I Hope For?

The biblical stories focus on two questions: What can we hope for in our lifetime? and What can we hope for after death? The Jewish view that focuses on this life emphasizes social justice and a day when the lion can lie down with the lamb and neither will be afraid. The Jewish view that focuses on the afterlife tends to stress values central to our life in this world: a chance to continue study, to be reunited with our families, and to live with awareness of God.

Judaism reframes the question even more radically, stressing not "What specific outcome can we have?" but "What do we recognize as *being* our hope?" For Jews, hope is the deepening relationship we have with God. Theology helps us foster and deepen that relationship.

Other Questions

In addition to these questions, we want to ask, Why is there evil? Specifically, why do the innocent suffer? What is the nature of death? What can we know about God? Do I have a destiny? These questions are never merely theoretical—we are deeply caught up in real situations that we want to resolve.

Using the Biblical Story

Some of us knew already in childhood what we should become, while others have wandered from job to job or have been doing something financially rewarding but ultimately empty. If we don't know what we should be doing or what we are called to do, we feel a growing sense of discomfort. As we think about our own sense of call, we look for biblical models in the calling of Abraham, Moses, Isaiah, Amos, Jeremiah, Rebecca, and Miriam.

We are looking for stories to help us make sense of our own experiences in love and our commitment to covenant. The Song of Songs, apart from being exquisite love poetry, is a complex story that shows some of the difficulties en route to genuine intimacy. We also find stories of God's love for us embedded in the prayer book. Stories of love and pain are not overt in the Bible, but we can read between the lines in the story of Leah. The fundamental Jewish story is that we learn to love by being loved—

that is, God's love for us, consciously perceived and entered into, allows us to love. Simultaneously, our love for a special individual opens out to our love for God.

> SARAH
> Sarah's story, which is presented fully in Chapter Six, gives us some of the visceral experience behind the whole question of mind-body dualism: Are the mind and the body separate entities, or are they two aspects of the same being? Sarah is an attractive, vivacious young woman with more ideas and enthusiasm than any of her contemporaries. She also has neuropathy, which causes intense pain in the nerve endings of her hands. Her ongoing question has been, "How do I claim and accept a body that seems to limit me?"

We may value the body, work to make it attractive to other people, and take good care of it, but rarely do we think of the body as our actual identity. When we die, is it our mind/soul that dies, or our body, or both? Judaism splits on the subject; no afterlife is mentioned in the Torah, but it does appear in Rabbinic literature and prayers. As a result, there is talk of a "world to come" but little thought given to it. So Jews are left with a vague notion of an afterlife that doesn't clear up whether we are minds or bodies. There are little hints of the integration of mind and body, fragments of stories: King David's faith is at one with his physical strength and military prowess; the aging of Abraham and Jacob seems consonant with their spiritual maturing. But there is no single memorable story that helps us consider the relationship of our mind to our body.

Similarly, death has no one memorable story. There is hardly a view on death that hasn't been accepted by some Jews at some time: resurrection of the dead, immortality through descendants, immortality through a "good name," immortality of the soul, reincarnation. But it is less important to find a single story than to feel comfortable with the stories we already accept, and to trust that there is meaning even if we, in our present consciousness, cannot know it.

The Middle and End of the Story

We are all in the middle of a story. We look back to our origins for nourishment and support. We also look ahead with some sense of the future, but the vision changes as we change.

STEFFI

The wisdom of Steffi, a social worker, makes clear how important the sense of a heritage can be for her clients. She recognizes that we are "middle people"—that is, we find ourselves between the beginning and the end of a story—and that this status can nourish and support us. If her clients can see that they are part of something larger than their own lives and efforts, that generations of people before them contributed to what they are now, they will feel strengthened in facing whatever life has dealt them. Moreover, she urges her clients to look to the future and thereby think about passing something on to future generations.

The Israelites were promised freedom, at the time of the Exodus—not merely freedom *from* the oppression of the slave masters but freedom *to* relate to God.

We need to explore endings as well. Happily-ever-after may be an acceptable fairy tale ending, but it is not the Jewish ending. Hardening of the adventurous arteries occurs if we decide we are where we're supposed to be and thus settle; we are no longer in process. So we can agree with two seemingly contradictory statements: the first, we are where we're supposed to be and who we're supposed to be; and the second, we will never be where we're supposed to be or who we're supposed to be. The first statement affirms the present condition we find ourselves in and our present value. We are all supposed to be in the wilderness; we are already loved, hence lovable. The second statement tells us that the adventure does not end and there is still more life, growth, and transformation ahead. Journey is not a trial but a mixed good. Yes, the journey is transformative, but it is also the time and place for our ongoing encounter with God. We are in no rush to get to the Promised Land, because the journey *is* the goal, and each step is an invitation to deepening intimacy.

Claiming Our Story

How do we choose and recognize our story? We may already be committed to the biblical narrative, but whether we are or not, we still need our own story—our informal theology—to give meaning and shape to our lives. Accepting the biblical story does not mean accepting uncritically its portrayal of God. Just as we can use *Cinderella* to make certain assumptions explicit but then modify it or reject it entirely, we start with the fundamental Jewish story and then examine, critique, and modify it as we try to chart our own experiences on this primordial Jewish map. The story incorporates the essential points listed earlier: Creation, being in God's Image, finding ourselves in that constricted place (*Mitzrayim*) of enslavement, liberation, covenant, revelation, wandering in the wilderness, and entry into the Promised Land. How these aspects of the story are interpreted in our present lives can be seen in two current examples.

> BEN
>
> Ben, an artist, acknowledges revelation as ongoing and as the source of his creativity. His belief in continued revelation shapes his whole artistic practice—how he arranges the colors on his palette, the care with which he sets out his tools, the sense of dedication and awe with which he begins each canvas.

> JOHANNA
>
> At her golden wedding anniversary, Johanna said, "Now I see the Promised Land." Her daughter Steffi later speculated that the statement implies that her mother's fifty years of marriage had constituted her wilderness years.

Certain subtopics are not explicitly covered in the Jewish story, such as theodicy (justifying God's way) and eschatology (the doctrine of final things—basically, what happens after life); yet the story in just the aspects presented here provides lots of room for our own theologizing.

Turning once again to our personal story, we can see how entire systems of thought emerge from emphasis on a single facet.

Creation

Creation has led many Jews to appreciate science and even to engage in it. To argue for meaning is to share with the whole scientific endeavor a belief in intelligibility. Things happen for a reason, and the quest for the reason is a religious one. Even though many people see Sigmund Freud as an enemy of religion (because he chose a different emphasis from that chosen by his detractors), he nevertheless enlarged the arena of meaningfulness. Dreams and slips of the tongue that were once discarded as nonsense are now accepted as meaningful in the unconscious domain of our selfhood.

God

Jewish mystics center their concern on God. Unlike Moses, who was restricted to seeing God in retrospect, mystics want a direct, *present* experience of God. But even for nonmystics who place God at the center of their story, the emphasis rests more heavily on the mystery of religion: the rituals, the laws that are not reducible to universal ethics, and the like.

God's Image

If we emphasize the idea that God has traces in us, that we are in God's image, and that we are the locus of God's ongoing revelation, we arrive at a theology that is close to humanism.

Enslavement

Enslavement has led many to explore how we fail to be who we can become. Teaming this emphasis with one on liberation has led to an understanding of Judaism as a movement for social justice and political reform, that is, a prophetic movement.

> SAM
> Sam acquired the sobriquet "Social Activist Sam" because of his engagement with the soup kitchen, his numerous petitions, his participation in every demonstration, and his youth group work. In quieter moments, he explained that working on behalf of people who need help lies at the heart of his understanding of Judaism.

Covenant

Covenant can be understood in different ways: in terms of the love poetry in the Song of Songs, in terms of the reciprocal obligations growing out of the 613 *mitzvot* (the traditional count of Jewish obligations contained in the Torah), and in terms of staying faithful to the human side of our commitment to God.

Revelation

Revelation leads some to follow punctiliously all the details and implications of the law, while it makes others (some of whom emphasize revelation combined with the idea that we are in the image of God) capable of receiving the truth available to those who live in holy concourse with Creation. Revelation can inspire artists and scientists as well as ecstatics.

Wandering

Wandering as an emphasis may lead us to focus on the frailty of all human society and culture and our obligation to serve as social critics.

Theologies

These few examples are meant to suggest the innumerable theologies we can develop from the basic Jewish story, suggesting that in the deepest sense there isn't just Judaism, there are Judaisms. All the varied forms in which Judaism has expressed itself over the past centuries can find grounding and support in one or more aspects of the essential story. Which one—or which ones—are right? Even more, which one is right for each of us? We can't find out, because a theology is more than a speculative exercise; it helps us function in the real world. In trying to live the best life that we can, we use our theology as our guide. Ultimately, the test of a theology is the life it yields.

Although the theology we arrive at is unmistakably our own, we find that in some ways it agrees with others (just as faces can have shared features—two eyes, a nose, a mouth—and still manage to be unique). Of course, there is sufficient agreement that we can worship in a community of Jews without too uncomfortable a fit. We value the same sacred texts, and we talk with other Jews on matters of faith and custom knowing that we will understand and be understood.

3

COMMITTING TO LOVE

Love is stronger than Death.

—Song of Songs 8:6

WE ALL KNOW what it is to love, so why do we need a theology of love? Because love has everything to say about who we are, what we can know, and where we fit into the world. It helps us discover who we are by transforming the boundaries of the self. It is crucial to our concept of what we can know because it reveals aspects of reality that are not open to us in any other way. What it tells us about reality goes to the heart of our theology. We need to discern what all our loving and separating are about, and what they might be showing. To think clearly about love, we have to forget all the popular songs that fill the airwaves and examine our own experiences of loving and being loved.

Being loved forces us to see ourselves as lovable, a difficult turn-around that gives us a startling new perspective on the world. If we reflect on the popular endearments in song and poetry, we discover how often we use the language of infancy. We become "baby" and now have the chance to amend the inadequate parenting we may have experienced in our chronological childhood. Now the one who looks at us with appreciative eyes is not rushing off to take care of another screaming child, or hurrying to work, but is showing us over and over again that we are lovable.

How We Learn to Love

We learn to love by being loved—as a child, a sibling, a friend, a lover, a parent. We come to love God as we learn to love our God-given parents and siblings, our friends, partners, and children. Ultimately, in all our loving, we express our love for God.

Parents

Although the relationship of parent to child is a natural one, it is so fraught with conflicting interests and values that no one would call it easy. We see the tension between generations spelled out repeatedly in the Genesis stories, where the differentiated love that Isaac bears for his sons Esau and Jacob lies at the heart of their rivalry. Jacob himself shows such obvious favoritism for his son Joseph that he creates a lifelong enmity between Joseph and his brothers. A puzzling silence in Exodus concerns the relationship of Moses' brother Aaron to his sons Nadab and Abihu. The two are struck dead during the dedication of the Tabernacle, but no mention is made of Aaron ever mourning for them. And Moses, our teacher, fathers sons who are never again mentioned in the Torah and who do not carry on his spiritual mission.

But as troubling as all of these relationships may be, none can disturb us more than the *akedah,* the binding of Isaac. As often as we read this story—it is the Torah portion read during Rosh ha-Shanah, and observant Jews recite it daily in the morning service—we cannot fathom that Abraham, or any father, would be ready to sacrifice his son, however much our sages explain the story. There it lies, at the heart of Judaism's inception, defying easy interpretation. We are sure we cannot learn to love God by sacrificing our beloved child to God. The *akedah* strikes us as a dark and troubling basis for the Jewish faith. Do the lovers of God have no religion but the love of God, as Rumi, a Sufi poet and mystic, once declared?

In forming our own theology, we quickly discover that the Torah is not God; rather, it is a way to the love of God. Wrestling with the text is valuable, but the God we have come to know and love would not demand the sacrifice of a child. The text challenges us and stretches our awareness, but it cannot counter our experience of God as loving and caring of *all* creatures as individuals and not as their parents' possessions.

Siblings

One of the earliest love stories in the Bible tells of Jacob's reconciliation with his brother Esau. Jacob, having stolen both Esau's birthright and his blessing, fled to his uncle's home, where he lived for the next twenty years. Then, on his journey back, he is told that Esau is coming to meet him with four hundred men. Panicked, he divides his holdings into two camps, spends the night alone by the river Jaabok, and finally faces Esau. He offers his brother two hundred she-goats, twenty he-goats, two hundred ewes, and twenty rams, as well as cows, bulls, and donkeys. Esau replies, "I have enough, my brother; let what you have remain yours." But Jacob responds, "No, I pray you; if you would do me this favor, accept from me this gift; *for to see your face is like seeing the face of God*" (Gen. 33:9,10, italics added).

We don't always recognize the creativity entailed in Jacob's vision of Esau, or the creativity involved in all our loving. During Jacob's night alone, he wrestles with God, as some say; or with an angel, according to others; or with his unresolved relationship with his brother, as still others maintain. These three interpretations may well amount to the same thing, because wrestling with God is facing the truth, wrestling with an angel is fighting with a messenger of this truth, and wrestling with our unresolved relationships is looking within and taking responsibility for our actions. Jacob emerges from the night's wrestling with both a blessing and a wound, as if he needed the infirmity to at last approach his brother slowly enough to really see him. Without his transformation, Jacob would have seen nothing; but with the changes wrought in his own consciousness by the night's wrestling, he could see God in and through his brother's love for him and in his own love for Esau, which he could not acknowledge earlier.

We don't usually recognize the role that our own contribution plays in creating the lovability of the people we love. We may see it more easily in the case of an inanimate love. We know that much of the love we have for our home comes from the effort we have made to fix it up, to meet our needs, and to style it as an expression of what we value. The time we invest in shaping it is part of what brings forth our love. We notice the same investment of time and love with the puppy we have trained. But an inanimate house or apartment, or even a living pet, is a long way from a person to whom we make a lifelong commitment. In fact, we cannot create that love for someone else, but we can cocreate it just as we cocreate our world. Our beloved is a real person, but one we can see only from our own perspective. The effort we make to be open to another person's reality is part of what leads us to love.

When Jacob saw the face of God in his brother's face, he was seeing the love that irradiated his former enemy. Similarly, when we see love in the face of our spouse, or our child, or our neighbor, we are seeing a manifestation of our love of God.

Partners

Genesis also portrays the love we form for our life partner, although the image may trouble us. Love can't be earned, although we keep thinking it can. Leah, for example, recognizing that Jacob does not love her, keeps thinking that she could earn his love by bearing him sons, even though Jacob loves Rachel, who is barren. So when Reuben, their firstborn, arrives, she exclaims, "Now my husband will love me." Later, after the birth of Simeon, and with the birth of her third son, Levi, she declares, "This time my husband will become attached to me." It is not until Leah bears Judah that she can finally say, "This time, I will praise Adonai."

Love is a gift, one that we are often afraid to accept, because like all gifts it is not under our control. We cannot earn gifts—if we could, they would be salary. The only correct response to a gift is gratitude, and the only way we should respond to a gift of love is to move from fear to gratitude, which is mature prayer. Gifts played a central role for the Israelites in the wilderness, where everything they received was a gift. In our own day-to-day lives we often forget how much we have been given. We even forget all the care and feeding we needed just to survive and grow—nurturance we could not have given to ourselves.

We begin learning about love from the moment we enter the world, but much of this learning takes place before we have language to process it. Only years later, when we ourselves take on the parenting or caregiving role, can we fully understand the love we received in being parented. Now, so many of the things that puzzled us in childhood begin to make sense as we try to protect this precious life that has been entrusted to us. Now we find ourselves seeking a guide as we wander in this unknown territory of parenthood. A closer look at the Torah, though, actually teaches us a lot about parenting—not by showing us people who were model parents but by detailing the relationship of God to Creation.

The Wilderness Experience as a Parenting Manual

The biblical description of the Israelites' time in the wilderness can serve as a parenting guide writ large. Manna, the strange food that sustained the Israelites in the wilderness, was parceled out like breast milk, in that the amount supplied was determined by the amount needed:

> That is the bread which Adonai has given you to eat. . . . This is what Adonai has commanded: Gather as much of it as each of you requires to eat, an *omer* to a person for as many of you as there are; each of you shall fetch for those in his tent.
>
> The Israelites did so, some gathering much, some little. But when they measured it by the *omer,* whoever had gathered much had no excess, and whoever had gathered little had no deficiency: they had gathered as much as they needed to eat [Exod. 16:15–18].

In the wilderness, as in our childhood, rules were lovingly given. But in our infancy, we are as unconscious of the love that gives life and sustains it as the Israelites were after the Exodus. In order to grow into a mature, functioning human, we must be challenged to grow. Just as the Israelites were challenged to grow into a grounded people able to face adversity, we are given many occasions in our developmental years to face trials and difficult experiences that both test and strengthen us.

Our childhood resembles the desert in another way: many of life's essentials are a gift. As children, we simply take for granted the regular care that nourishes and sustains us. The same was true for the Israelites in the wilderness until God specifically reminded them of what they had experienced: "I led you through the wilderness forty years; the clothes on your back did not wear out, nor did the sandals on your feet; you had no bread to eat and no wine or other intoxicant to drink—that you might know that I am Adonai your God" (Deut. 29:4–5).

We care for our own young in much the way God cared for the newly created Israelites. In our role as parents, we find yet another way of thinking about God. We now have a more mature perspective from which to view all those annoying rules and regulations that were put in place for our protection. Just as being a parent requires us, at last, to "let go"— though without for a moment ceasing to care—to respect the freedom and individuality of our child, we realize that we have been given the Law and it is up to us how we apply it (though without doubting God's underlying and enduring love and concern). The concept of free will has often been invoked to explain God's lack of intervention in times of suffering. Yet we should know from our own experience of trying to foster freedom in our children that free will is not merely a psychological concept, or a convenient answer to a knotty theological problem. Free will is a gift of love, a gift we sometimes wish had not been bestowed. But we are called to grow into human beings and so must accept the ambiguity of being human, vulnerable, and loving. We accept Deuteronomy's injunction, "So therefore choose life," and recognize that choosing life is the same thing as choosing love.

The Wilderness Experience as Marriage Manual

The account of the Israelites' time in the wilderness can also serve as a marriage manual. The wilderness is a land we cannot control or domesticate. If it sustains us, it is because of its surprising richness, not because we've cultivated it. Marriage, in all these respects, resembles a wilderness. The other cannot be tamed, and if what we want is control, we will not have a marriage but a form of slavery.

What the Israelites learn in the wilderness is precisely what we each must learn in trying to grow into deepening intimacy with our partner. We must learn patience, for just as God's time is not our time, our partner's rhythms may not conform to our own. We must also learn gratitude. The Israelites gradually recognize the many ways they were supported and cared for in the wilderness—the manna, the water from the rock, the fact that their shoes did not wear out—and they experience a deeper sense of joy and appreciation for their time of closeness with God. Finally, as we become attentive to the many gifts in our relationship, we find that life with our partner is a great source of blessing.

The Israelites grew to trust their relationship with God even though they could neither control nor predict it; similarly, we must grow to trust in life with our partner. The Israelites repeatedly experienced God's forgiveness for their failures—from their worshiping the Golden Calf to their crying out for meat and their sustained criticism of Moses and Aaron. Forgiveness is an essential component of any sustained relationship.

The Jews in the wilderness enter into a marriage, or covenant, with God. They learn to follow the pillar of cloud and fire. In marriage, we also learn to follow these two pillars: the fire, which leads us in the direction of greater warmth and light; and the cloud, which represents the everlasting mystery, the other. Being in the image of God, we can never be fully known, even by the most loving partner. So we learn never to reduce the other to a role, a function, or any collection of attributes.

Love Affects Structures and Boundaries

In the wilderness, the Israelites experienced a need for structure. In response, they divided space (such as inside or outside the camp), time (sacred or nonsacred), objects (clean or unclean), peoples (we or they), and themselves (priestly or lay tribes). But over their forty-year sojourn, the boundaries that marked these strict divisions changed as the Israelites became more comfortable with their surroundings and their love for and relationship with God.

Something analogous happens in our own lives. As children we look for structure and familiarity. As we grow and become more comfortable in the world, our health, well-being, and happiness seem to be more under our control but in fact are inextricably connected to the well-being of those we love. Although we are less bound by structure, our happiness or unhappiness may be determined by this impetuous child we raised with love who dashes into the street without regard for traffic. Our boundaries may serve as barriers or they may constitute a growing edge, shifting as our love and trust expand.

Understanding the nature of boundaries and their relationship to love can help us explore the meaning of love. In the chapters that follow, we see that borders are central as well in suffering, where the breaching of boundaries is experienced as loss; in our work, which can show us a way to extend the boundaries of the self into the larger world; in our being embodied, which raises the essential question of how to grow in a healthy way (that is, how to expand the self without danger to its integrity); in prayer, which is a call to self-transcendence, another way to think about boundaries; in community, where we try to work out how Judaism defines its boundaries; and in death, which appears to be the boundary of all bodies, or the end to growth (but where we seek faith that the appearance is not the reality).

Finally, in the following chapters we consider God's promise to Abraham, "I shall make your seed as numerous as the sands of the seashore or the stars of the heavens," an expression of love and concern that expands the boundary of the self to include immediate offspring and even unimaginable future progeny that will embrace the whole world.

The Song of Songs and Boundaries

In portraying spousal love, the Song of Songs deals explicitly with borders. Early in the book, the female lover says: "My mother's sons quarreled with me, / They made me guard the vineyards; / My own vineyard I did not guard" (1:6). So while her brothers try to control her by setting up boundaries, she transforms her boundaries to serve as her growing edge, moving into a new sense of self because of another. Both exhilarated and terrified, she recognizes all the vulnerability of love that lies ahead: "Do not wake or rouse / Love until it please!" (2:7), a refrain that appears twice more in the Song.

The erotic descriptions of the body in the Song of Songs invite us to transform our boundaries into growing edges. In times of vulnerability and defensiveness, we turn in on ourselves and close up, as a turtle pulls all of its most vulnerable self into the protection of its shell. But love is about expanding the self, opening up in increasing engagement with the world. The first line, "Let him give me of the kisses of his mouth," already betrays a changed sense of self. Her lover's response later in the book is to describe her teeth, her lips, her brow, her breasts, leading up to his appeal, "Let me in, my own, / my darling, my faultless dove!" (5:2). Her response, in turn, describes a set of events:

> I opened the door for my beloved,
> But my beloved had turned and gone.
> I was faint because of what he had said.
> I sought, but found him not;
> I called, but he did not answer.
> I met the watchmen
> Who patrol the town;
> They struck me, they bruised me.
> The guards of the walls
> Stripped me of my mantle.
>
> —Song of Songs 5:6–7

Not responding to her lover's appeal would have left her constricted within her prior boundaries. Acting as she did left her alone to face those who control the limits of the self: the guards of the walls, who strip her of her mantle. But the boundaries have been irrevocably breached, and she can respond with confidence: "I am my beloved's / And my beloved is mine" (6:3).

What does it mean to change boundaries? We are finite—which explains, in part, why love is so scary—but we yearn for the infinite.

HANNAH
Hannah recalled the terror she felt the first year she was married to Hirsch:

"I was so aware of how committed and connected I was to him that if he came home even minutes late I feared for his safety. The strange 'solution' to my terror was not withdrawing love but loving more—I wanted to bear a child that would incarnate our love. Now, even if we faced death, the world would be forever changed by the fact of our having loved one another—a new being would enter the world. And, of course, I worried about the new being as well, but after the terror of the awesome responsibility I felt in taking care of a fragile new life, a kind of comfort developed.

"For years my mother may have worried about me, but I blithely took her completely for granted. And then, when I was in my forties and she was in her late sixties, a cyst was discovered on her ovaries. Suddenly the love—and the life— on which all my other loves were built was at risk. Benign! One of the most beautiful words in any language. But now my consciousness of love and fear went backward as well as forward. We leap into the unknown and into vulnerability, to loss and to life. We cannot set up safety nets."

Seeing her borders stretching back to include her mother, Hannah reaches across to embrace Hirsch and senses the forward pull to incorporate their children and their children's world.

The Great Biblical Love Story

The Song of Songs is a patent love song, but the story of the Exodus, with its desert sojourn and entry into the Promised Land, can serve as an important love story as well. The Book of Job, by comparison, suggests itself as anything but a love story, given that the protagonist is made to suffer the loss of his family and his possessions. We are accustomed to reading Job as the classic biblical text that confronts the problem of evil, that is, Why can good people suffer? But if we begin with the premise that we all suffer, that all the losses experienced by Job may confront each one of us as we age, we can ask the text to answer a different question: What persists throughout Job's losses that allows him to recover?

In the end, Job moves on—with new children who do not *cause* his recovery but merely signify it. Agreeing once again to bring forth children means that he was ready to open himself to the awesome vulnerability of love. In this interpretation, we must read the Theophany, God's speech from the whirlwind, as God's love song to Job:

Take now behemoth, whom I made as I did you;
He eats grass, like the cattle.
His strength is in his loins,
His might in the muscles of his belly.
He makes his tail stand up like a cedar;

The sinews of his thighs are knit together.
His bones are like tubes of bronze,
His limbs like iron rods.

—Job 40:15–18

The Theophany may seem like a puzzling declaration of love, in that it does not flatter Job. Rather, it corrects Job's image of God, which had been falsely portrayed by the so-called comforters whose visits are described in the text. Adjusting that image is an essential first step, but Job's faith can be restored only by some positive vision.

In the Theophany, God gives Job an imaginative vision of reality that enkindles trust and fosters hope. In facing his losses and pain, Job follows the tendency most of us have to turn inward and close ourselves off from the larger community that might comfort us. God's gift to Job is the openness he retains that allows the world to affect him. The gift is Job's ability to release all the defensive systems he has constructed to keep reality at bay. It is an opportunity to leave where he is and enter into something new. It also fosters the hope that he can integrate all that he has experienced with all that God now shows him.

The gift of the Theophany lies in opening a new worldview for Job from which he can rise above his personal despair and gain a fresh perspective on it. The Theophany is a transformation of Job's boundaries so that, through God's guidance, Job is led to recognize love and concern for all of Creation, even those aspects that are not directly useful to humans:

Who cut a channel for the torrents
And a path for the thunderstorms,
To rain down on uninhabited land,
On the wilderness where no man is,
To saturate the desolate wasteland,
And make the crop of grass sprout forth?

—Job 38:25–27

The Theophany is also God as beloved, showing Job a way of knowing God. The comforters may have been able to utter true statements about God: God is the Creator, God is just. They may even have been able to know God in a performative sense: "I worship and bow down, I bend the knee before You." But by means of the speech, God is inviting Job to truly know Divinity by being able to see as if from behind God's eyeballs—to see Creation from God's perspective.

Loving and Knowing

When Job is invited to see Creation from God's perspective, he sees with the eyes of love. The story of Job comprises three distinct phases in his life: before his loss, at the time of his loss, and after the Theophany. At which of these times did he have the truest picture of reality? Or to pose a similar question in modern times, When do we best see reality: when we are in love, when we are in neutral, or when we've just broken up with a lover? Our "scientific" worldview suggests that neutral is best, but our own experience tells us that only when we are in love can we even begin to see the richness of Creation. There are things we know about our off-spring only through loving them, because love is a profound form of knowing. The traditional dualism of head and heart, or reason and emotion, breaks down in light of our experience. Loving is a way of knowing, and being loved requires us to open ourselves up—a prospect that may frighten us.

Part of the Theophany's power is God's obvious delight in Creation, as we can see in the passage about behemoth. What we have there is not a generic appreciation of Creation; rather each detail of the animal is lovingly recounted just as the ostrich and the horse are lovingly described. God knows every aspect of Creation, and every creature is loved and celebrated. Hearing this speech, Job can only think that he is part of what God has created, so God must delight in him as well.

We fear being known as fully as God knows all creatures, yet there is nothing we long for as much: to be completely known but still loved and accepted. A central issue in building our practical theology is moving from fear to comfort, safety, and a sense of home. But we are presented in the Bible with powerful though contrasting images that seem to map such a journey. The psalmist writes "Under your wings we take shelter," while the Book of Proverbs warns "The beginning of wisdom is the fear of Adonai" (Prov. 1:7). But let us bear in mind that the *beginning* of wisdom is the fear of Adonai—the beginning, and not the end—because the end is a relationship that transcends fear.

The Theophany in Job complements the biblical love story in the Song of Songs, a text that at first conjures up sunshine, flowers, spices, and the song of birds in the air. But once we recognize the inextricable connection between love and suffering, we read both texts somewhat differently. The two have much in common. Neither book is historical, that is, neither relates particular events, people, battles. They are not basically Jewish: Job's religion is undefined and the Song of Songs omits any explicit mention of God. Both are problem texts that had a hard time being accepted into the biblical canon. And both challenge our notion of borders and boundaries, thereby allowing us to move to a deeper understanding of our faith. The books do not supply all the answers, and sages disagree about what they are actually saying. (For example, the Song of Songs can be taken literally, or it can be viewed as an allegorical portrayal of God and the Jewish people.) But both books get to the heart of the human condition: to be human is to love, and to be human is to suffer. The Song of Songs adds that "love is stronger than death," a hope we explore in Chapter Nine.

The Death of Love

What happens to the beloved when love dies? It is strange for the beloved to continue existing but with the lover absent. What has cooled or destroyed the love that was once a raging flame? Now the boundaries are shaky—and the support experienced by the bereaved is unavailable to those whose lovers have left them behind and moved on. Do we dare to love again, or should we grow hard shells and teeth and claws?

> NANCY
> Thinking of all the ways in which loving Dave had fostered her own growth, Nancy wondered if she could bear to listen to "their" music again, read the authors he had recommended. In pain but showing great courage, she determined to live fully in her newly enlarged boundaries. "I will not hate nature because he was a biologist. Yes, I see him everywhere, and each new phenomenon of nature I now understand reminds me of him—but someday these interests and likes will be my own, so I will not lessen myself because he no longer loves me."

Love and Change

Is there anything that persists through change, even through the great change of death? The psalmist raises this concern:

> Humans, their days are like those of grass;
> they bloom like flowers of the field;
> a wind passes by and they are no more,
> their own place no longer knows them.
> But Adonai's steadfast love is for all eternity
> toward those who fear God,
> and God's beneficence is for the children's children

of those who keep God's covenant
and remember to observe God's precepts.

—Psalms 103:15–18

In Chapter Nine, we will explore what may persist for one who goes through death, but we know that for those left behind, changes definitely persist in the lives that were touched, the works left behind, the children who have come into being, and the memories that give shape and meaning to everything else. Because of change, memory becomes important in love—and also in Judaism, because Judaism is the larger story of God's love for the Jewish people.

Although the function of memory may be personal, its implications create an entire people. Memory holds those we have loved in and through all the changes and even losses, thereby helping us shape our self and our world. Memory is the instrument through which we seek meaning, as Abraham Joshua Heschel put it so eloquently: "God's grace resounds in our lives like a staccato. Only by retaining the seemingly disconnected notes do we acquire the ability to grasp the theme" (1955, p. 142). Elsewhere, Heschel points out that "the essence of Jewish religious thinking does not lie in entertaining a concept of God but in the ability to articulate a memory of moments of illumination by His presences" (1955, p. 140). He echoes the dictum in Deuteronomy: "Take utmost care and watch yourselves scrupulously, so that you do not forget the things that you saw with your own eyes and so that they do not fade from your mind as long as you live. And make them known to your children and your children's children" (4:9).

We see that all things are transitory. If anything endures, it is love. Loving God enables us to love our neighbor because we now feel nondefensive, safe, secure, generous. Loving God leads us to love whom God loves (or to modify a phrase, "if you love me, you'll love my dog"), and it allows us to discover God in and through our finite human loves.

SHARON

Sharon recalled tucking in her child late at night and recognizing that those were the years for which she is forever nostalgic. "I was happy, and I knew it at the time. Yet the transitoriness of everything—but *no!* Even now I can conjure up those nights and all the sense of love and wonder flood over me. One of the psalms says, 'For in Your sight a thousand years are like yesterday that has passed, like a watch of the night'" (Ps. 90:4).

All our time can be taken up into the eternal perspective,
Sharon thought, *allowing us to see from a timeless perspec-tive while recognizing that nothing is ever lost. No time is ever wasted, and no love: every love gives us access to what is holy.*

JESSICA
Jessica recalled a quotation she read in a graveyard: "We are shaped and formed by those we love, and even when they are no longer here we remain their handiwork." She found her-self agreeing that we really are constituted by our loves. Then she saw a connection with the sin of idolatry, which results from having been misshapen. Jessica concluded that it is right to love people—as the Torah says, "Love your neighbor as yourself" (Lev. 19:18)—but it is wrong to love riches, honors, and pleasures of the senses. It is right to love people as peo-ple, but we must never confuse them with gods. The problem is not love but disordered love. If we begin with the love of God, all our other loves line up in a healthy order. Loving others in this way keeps us from possessiveness in love: because we recognize that people belong to themselves and to God, we don't try to control them or have agendas for them.

"Happiness or unhappiness is made wholly to depend on the quality of the object which we love. . . . Love toward a thing eternal and infinite feeds the mind wholly with joy, and is itself unmingled with any sadness, wherefore it is greatly to be desired and sought for with all our strength" (Spinoza, 1884/1949, p. 5)

Love and Pain

Love is not pleasure: it is what furthers our God-consciousness or helps us grow to God. Love can cause pain, as when our loved one is suffering, but it leads us to grow spiritually and it expands our sense of ego bound-aries, so that our happiness or unhappiness no longer depends merely on our own narrow interests but includes the being and well-being of all those we have grown to love.

Love and Work

Erich Fromm wrote that "love and labor are inseparable. One loves that for which one labors and one labors for that which one loves" (1963,

p. 23). Love logically implies work, because love brings forth a need to contribute, and it is through work that we make our contribution to the world. But work is not simply a response to loving a person—sometimes the work by itself (independent of those for whom we work) can become an object of love.

For those who love their work, there is usually a discipline involved in pursuing it. The work to which we give ourselves makes demands. We know about the dancer's many hairline fractures of the feet, the shooting pain in the violinist's back, the damaged knees of the basketball or football player, the fatigue felt by the writer after a day of writing. Work, love, and suffering go together. Love makes us want to contribute, and yet there is something exhausting about it: we spend ourselves—we use ourselves up. "There is no greater good for people than eating and drinking and giving themselves joy in their labor" (Eccl. 2:24). Our happiness is connected to our love, and our love includes our work: "I collect my tools: sight, smell, touch, taste, hearing, intellect. Night has fallen, the day's work is done. I return like a mole to my home, the ground. Not because I am tired and cannot work. I am not tired. But the sun has set" (Kazantzakis, 1965, p. 17).

Pain in Loving People

No one doubts that training for a career in dancing requires pain: the muscles must be stretched if the dancer is to become graceful. Similarly, preparing ourselves for loving, which is no less creative than dancing, requires that our psychic structure be reshaped if we are to become selfless lovers.

NINA
Nina was engaged to Jack when he became critically ill, needed a kidney transplant, suffered severe complications, and remained in the hospital for seven months. When he was finally released, he wanted to marry her, the angel who had "pulled him through" his terrible illness. Nina's experience was the reverse of his; unlike Jack, she had not been strengthened by love but been profoundly wounded by the near death of her beloved. She needed time; Jack felt rejected. Cognitively he could understand her need for time, but emotionally he felt betrayed.

Nina set a wedding date sufficiently far in the future that she could truly reconsider whether or not she wanted this marriage, but not so far ahead that he would think she was breaking their engagement. Her family urged her to find someone else: "You don't want to spend your life taking care of him." Nevertheless, their relationship slowly began to heal. Nina awoke one morning knowing that the date she had set would, in truth, be their actual wedding date.

They have been married now for fourteen years, and although he continues to suffer from major health problems, she accepts his illness as part of the terms of their marriage.

One of the outcomes of Jack's surgery is that he is now sterile, so a particular form of immortality for them has been ruled out. By the time Nina learned that she could not bear his child, she no longer had any doubts about her commitment to him. Her mother's comment on learning about what she regarded as their "problem" was, "So that will be the end of our family line." Nina and Jack have since adopted two children (adoption was complicated by his poor health history) and are now learning another dimension of love.

JEREMY

Jeremy is divorcing his wife, who is mentally ill. He is proceeding with the divorce even though he would have stood by her if she had been physically ill. Somehow he feels that her identity is now tied more to her mind than her body, and he doesn't know this "new" person he is supposed to love. His wife's family is furious with him and tries to shame him in terms of his vow, "in sickness and in health." His own family members support his divorce and urge him to save himself from "ruining his life." The doctors can give him no assurance that she will ever improve. He feels a need to reexamine his own theology to weigh the strength of his covenant with a woman who is not the same person he married.

CHARLOTTE

Charlotte's story is fairly common. She loves someone who is incapable of making a commitment. Her struggle now is to remain open to other loves even though she is in terrible pain.

NAOMI

Naomi is raising issues of space—all the old boundary questions that are brought out in the Song of Songs, except now it is not a theoretical issue of boundaries but an experience of deep pain. It is unclear if she can open her partner's boundaries soon enough for their relationship to survive.

ELEANORE

Eleanore is afraid to leave the security of an unchallenging friendship for love. She is tempted by the old trick of psychic numbing: if I'm not really alive, perhaps I won't die; if I don't really love, perhaps I won't suffer the pain of loss. But life and love are beckoning to her, and she is getting ready to experience both.

Love and Fear

Love contains moments of great fear: of rejection, of the possible end of the relationship, of the prospect that the self might be lost, and of all the changes that have to be made.

DEBORAH

Before her marriage to Simon, Deborah was afraid to commit to marriage. Now, four years later and in her second trimester of pregnancy, she fears becoming a mother. She can look back on her earlier fear of marrying Simon and find it unfounded, even silly. This revelation reassures her somewhat as she tries to envision the months ahead, when she will be a mother.

Deborah can see that the man she both loved and feared loves her and helps her see herself as loved and lovable. Later, as she is caring for her baby, Deborah recognizes that her infant son loves her and that his understanding of the word *mother* is shaped by his experience of her. That realization is both wonderful and terrifying, raising yet another fear: Can she be worthy of the totally trusting love of her baby?

She imagines the terror she once felt before Simon and the fear she anticipates in caring for a vulnerable infant; how much more does this terror apply to loving God? What would it mean to recognize fully that she loves God and that God loves her? What would be demanded of her? She imagines that such a realization would change the way she relates to the world. There is fear—some of it surely justified—but deeper than the fear are the love and the joy.

A traditional English folk song tells us about a young British soldier, General Wolfe, who won fame by conquering Quebec. Though called "Brave Wolfe," he experiences fear in the face of his visits to his beloved:

I went to see my love, not to affright her.
I went to see my love, 'twas to delight her.
When I began to speak, my tongue did quiver,
I dare not speak my mind when I am with her.
Love, here's a ring of gold, long times I've kept it;
Love, here's a ring of gold, will you accept it?
When you the posy read, think on the giver,
Remember me, or I'm undone forever.

The title "Brave Wolfe" is not ironic. The ensuing verses describe his courage while facing death in battle during the British conquest of Quebec. But the text of the ballad reminds us of the terror we felt when we first approached our beloved. Fear may even be a necessary stage on the path of love, but if it is not overcome, it can turn into a major obstacle. "I'm undone forever" describes the feeling we have when recognizing that we cannot return to our former ego boundaries. Once we are open to caring about another, we can no longer draw back into a guarded perimeter.

As necessary as fear may be at the beginning, the continuation of fear is the greatest enemy on the spiritual path, or the way of love. The *Tanakh* provides repeated warnings to "have no fear" (Pss: 55 and 112; Prov. 3), "be not afraid" (Joel 2), and "do not be terrified" (Deut. 1, 7, 20; Josh. 1, Jer. 1).

> JUDAH
> Judah is a serious, thoughtful man of thirty-eight whose indi-
> rect awareness of God convinced him to study for the rab-
> binate. Although he fears the prospect of having a personal
> experience of God, he recognizes an important experiential
> aspect of his commitment that he must address. He has no
> doubts about his vocation, but he is seeking spiritual guid-
> ance for help in dealing with his fears.

We read in the Song of Songs, "I was asleep but my heart was awake" (5:2). The Song is telling us about a choice between sleeping through life and never waking up at all or facing life's great challenge: finding love. (We find the same thought expressed in a traditional saying: "If you are in love, then why are you asleep?") When the beloved finally ventures out into the street to find her lover, the guards strip her of her protective mantle. Their action symbolizes love's stripping away of appearances and our own fear of being really known.

From Terror to Comfort

One of the great lessons of the Torah is how the terror we experience when seeing someone we love can be turned into profound comfort and delight. We see the transformation illustrated over a large portion of Exodus, beginning with "And Moses hid his face, for he was afraid to look at God" (Exod. 3:6), and concluding with "Adonai would speak to Moses face to face, as one person speaks to another" (Exod. 33:11). The fear and fascination turn into friendship and love in much the same way you experience the "sleeping" sense if your foot "falls asleep" and then begins to awaken. The initial motion in the foot feels like an electric shock to the system, but once the foot regains its normal state, you have a new and greater feeling of comfort and ease than before the whole incident.

Moses was, in a sense, asleep in his role of shepherd to Jethro. His gifts as a potential leader, his moral outrage, and his concern for his fellow Israelites in Egypt were all asleep: "I was asleep, but my heart was awake." His heart was sufficiently awake for him to experience curiosity about the Burning Bush: "There was a bush all aflame, yet the bush was not consumed. Moses said, 'I must turn aside to look at this marvelous sight; why is the bush not burnt?'" But when God called out to Moses, who had turned aside, Moses' curiosity turned to terror: "And Moses hid his face, for he was afraid to look at God" (Exod. 3:2–6).

Over the ensuing chapters of Exodus, we read about God's charges to Moses, Moses' carrying out these commands, the Ten Plagues, the panicked flight from the Egyptians, the terror at the Red Sea, the triumphant crossing of the Red Sea to liberation, the gift of water and food in the wilderness, the revelation at Sinai, and Moses' growth in his role as spokesman for the Israelites. Finally, after the sin of the Golden Calf and Moses' pleading on behalf of the people, the Torah reports that "Adonai would speak to Moses face to face, as one friend speaks to another."

As we think about our significant friendships and loves, we recognize how they grew through time spent together, activities undertaken jointly, promises made and kept (or broken), understandings and misunderstandings, and the whole process of getting to really know each other. At the moment of Moses' greatest closeness to God, he is focused not on himself but on the needs of his people. Perhaps only in that context could he be sufficiently preoccupied to come into God's presence comfortably and easily.

Love and Joy

We accept the risk and the pain of love because the joy is even deeper than the pain. Joy lies at the heart of love and draws us on. We all have images of the joy and elation of love: of our heart being lifted just by seeing the beloved; of a young mother's nonstop singing during her children's infancy because she is so delighted just to greet them each morning; of being reunited with an old friend; of sensing our parents' love and approval (though perhaps not without an element of judgment).

But joy occurs on a level deeper even than feeling, because joy entails expansion of the self. We have all experienced the opposite, when we are dejected or hurt and we want to turn in on ourselves. In joy we unfold, open up, and reach out.

Love, Creativity, and Struggle

Being a friend or someone's life companion is a creative process. Pursuing love is like following a dance partner: you have to be present, attentive to changes in mood, ready to alter rhythm. Since love is a relationship—whether with people in our lives, or with the work to which we give ourselves—it must constantly change as we grow, and it cannot leave a lasting mark. This continual changing makes us struggle to keep our loving relationships alive, and in the battle we are tempered and transformed. To quote William Blake's lines once again, "And we are put on earth a little space, / that we may learn to bear the beams of love" (from *Songs of Innocence*).

So we carry on a lifelong creative struggle with our family of origin; we engage in seemingly endless striving with our partner and with our children; and we even wrestle with ourselves—with our bodies and our memories.

> MARSHALL
> Marshall has had an ongoing battle with his body image. He recalled having been an unappealing child, but childhood photographs bewilder him because they show a very cute boy who looks nothing like the misshapen creature he remembers. His wife created a photo album that began with his boyhood photographs and continued into the years of their marriage. Seeing the photos in the album caused him to rethink his sense of himself, in light of her evident approval.

We also struggle with our work. Our work is a way of loving, and also an arena of grappling. If we don't expend the time, effort, attention, investment of self, fatigue, and pain needed to engage the world, then aspects of the self atrophy. Through struggle we can improve our self-discipline, focus, and self-giving. We must learn to work, during the week, but then also to rest on the Sabbath. Every creation, whether a work or a relationship, is the trace of a magnificent battle. We fight against inertia and must continue doing so if we are to keep choosing life. Our relationships must stay fresh; our interests must spread out in new directions. We recall the waterhole that dries up in late summer. We too dry up unless we are fed by many streams.

Love and Loneliness

Loneliness is a central fact of the human condition. We all face the fear that no one understands, no one abides, no one cares. We feel isolated. The greatest threat in the Torah is not death but being "cut off," separated from all that gives meaning. We examine our own experience of loneliness within the context of God's promise: "I will be with you." We are lonely because we are made to be in relationship to God. As a result, we may love and lose, but we still return to love again, because in and through all the loves, losses, and other vicissitudes of the human condition, we find our steadying point and our shelter in God's presence.

This discovery was clear to the Israelites, who experienced God directly and made God a communal point of reference. In today's society, we find it more difficult to talk about God, as we will see in Chapter Ten. We may feel more comfortable talking about holiness, eternal values, authenticity. Whatever we take as our highest value is always that with which we struggle to maintain our relationship in times of joy and times of bereavement. It is difficult to stay in relationship, to stay with our enlarged ego boundaries, as Nancy struggled to do after Dave left, but it becomes possible when we are grounded in some supreme value—what the Israelites called God's love.

What is the relationship of love to loneliness? According to Plato, love is not a god and does not have all powers and gifts; rather, it is the daughter of need and resource. In Plato's dialogue *The Symposium,* the character Aristophanes retells the myth of how human beings were once simultaneously male and female. The gods, being jealous of these powerful creatures, cut humans in half so that each one would be only half as strong. The bisection done, each half was left with a desperate yearning for the missing half. Love, from Aristophanes' perspective, means always trying to reintegrate our original nature, to make two into one, and to bridge the gulf between one human being and another.

What we love, then, is that which completes us. The major insight we gain from Aristophanes' position is that the object of our love tells us who we are. If what we love is a person of the opposite sex, then who we are is a creature needing that other sex for wholeness. But this drama may not give us the clearest understanding of who we are. If what we most essentially are is defined by our relationship to God, then our loneliness is a loneliness for God, and our love is a love for God.

When we experience love, we may at first focus solely on the beloved— with time out for gratitude to God for letting that person come into our life. It is at a later, more reflective stage that we begin to discover God's presence not simply in the role of matchmaker but in our capacity to love and trust sufficiently to allow someone else to really touch us and transform our ego boundaries. Eventually, we discover God's love shining in and through all other loves.

The first thing pronounced "not good" in the Torah is being alone: "It is not good for man to be alone; I will making a fitting helper for him" (Gen. 2:18). We spend most of our lives trying to overcome our separateness. It is clear that the creation of Eve is not the solution to the problem of loneliness, which occurs at a level so profound that the simple being of another person cannot eradicate it. Something has to open us to the awareness of the other—not simply as other but as being and belonging to a separate self and to God. Since the central problems of the human condition are learning to stretch our ego boundaries and genuinely coming to love another, we can expect to find clues to their solution in the Torah.

Sacrifice, the major form of worship in biblical times, was mercifully abandoned and replaced by words, as the psalmist already suggests: "Take my prayer as an offering of incense, my upraised hands as an evening sacrifice" (Ps. 141:2). The offerings brought to the Temple did not truly belong to the people who sacrificed them: the people did not create or own the animals, birds, oil, and grain—or, as we saw in the *Akedah,* Abraham's son Isaac. In attempting to sacrifice, we come to a visceral recognition of God's gifts of Creation, love, and presence. Likewise, in attempting to praise, we discover that the words may be ours, but the lifting of our heart in love and gratitude is God's gift as well. In the process of sacrificing and praising we experience joy:

> Love is not primarily a relationship to a specific person; it is
> an *attitude,* an *orientation* of *character* which determines the
> relatedness of a person to the world as a whole, not toward
> one "object" of love. If a person loves only one other person

and is indifferent to the rest of the his fellow men, his love is not love but a symbiotic attachment, or an enlarged egotism. . . . If I truly love one person I love all persons, I love the world, I love life. If I can say to somebody else, "I love you," I must be able to say "I love in you everybody, I love through you the world, I love in you also myself" [Fromm, 1963, p. 39].

When I was teaching undergraduates, I could always tell who was in love and who was simply fascinated by the idea of love. Students in love invariably did well in their classes because love is expansive—it allows the entire world to be perceived as more interesting than before. When students claim they are in love but do not have time for their friends or fall behind in their assignments, there is a strong suggestion that they are not really in love.

Love and God

How does all of this relate to a theology of love? Fromm defines what it means for us to love God: "To love God . . . [is] to long for the attainment of the full capacity to love" (1963, p, 38). The person we love is an aperture through which we perceive God. In all our loving, we are loving God. All our loving and separating are attempts for us to stop staring at the pointing finger and finally turn to look at what the finger is pointing to. This does not make the various apertures illusory. Love is *never* a generic "to whom it may concern": we love through knowing the uniqueness of the one we love. We are supposed to love the particular individuals (parents, siblings, lovers, children), but to love them as they are *in* God. We already know that love is expansive. Life is a process through which we can finally let our love truly grow so that it allows us to see the irradiation of the whole.

4

ENDURING SUFFERING

I came upon trouble and sorrow
and I invoked the name of Adonai.

—Psalms 116:3–4

Happiness or unhappiness is made wholly to depend on the qual-
ity of the object which we love. When a thing is not loved, no
quarrels will arise concerning it—no sadness will be felt if it per-
ishes—no envy if it is possessed by another—no fear, no hatred,
in short, no disturbances of the mind.

—Spinoza, 1884/1949, p. 5

ONCE WE OPEN OURSELVES to love, we are inevitably opened to pain
as well. A theology of love must be followed by a theology of suffering.
Any complete theology must deal with the reality of suffering. We cannot
make suffering disappear (it is not a riddle to be solved; it is part of the
human condition), but it must fit within our definition of meaning. In this
discussion of suffering I do not include death because we cannot know if
the dead suffer, or even if death is evil. We do know that our immediate
task is to be alive and to live fully, and that death is a natural condition
that comes eventually to all living beings. The meaning and status of death
are discussed in Chapter Nine.

The Role of Suffering in Judaism

Many faiths have suffering as the baseline for their whole theology because it poses the question of meaning in a way that nothing else ever does. We go through life pretty much on the assumption that "if it ain't broke, don't fix it." So ordinary life—which in reality is anything but ordinary; it is a daily miracle, an ongoing re-creation—does not pose the question of meaning with the urgency we feel when suffering pain or loss. The Buddhist faith is premised on the Four Noble Truths, the first of which is "All life is sorrowful." Christianity posits an original fall, or rift in our relationship to God, based on an interpretation of the Adam and Eve episode described in Genesis 3, a text from which Jews draw a decidedly different meaning.

For Jews, the starting point is the calling of Abraham to leave his home and his native land. Instead of suffering, sin, or guilt, we find at the core of our faith a sense of curiosity that leads to wonder and to further experiences rooted in the real world. And though suffering is indeed real, it is not the first, or only, or most important, fact about our lives.

"We suffer in so far as we are a *part* of Nature, a part that cannot be conceived of by itself, or without the other parts." This sentence from Spinoza's *Ethics* (1883/1949, IV.2) expresses a Jewish view of suffering in its emphasis on those other parts, as described in Genesis 1: the creation of the "holding" environment that includes space, time, foods that nourish us, and other creatures. Only within the security of this milieu can Abraham experience the curiosity that allows him to answer God's momentous call.

According to a Jewish legend, Abraham came to an early recognition of God:

> Abraham arose and walked about and went along the edge of
> the valley. When the sun sank, and the stars came forth, he
> said, "These are the gods!" But the dawn came, and the stars
> could be seen no longer, and then he said, "I will not pay
> worship to these, for they are no gods." Thereupon the sun
> came forth, and he spoke, "This is my god, him will I extol."
> But again the sun set, and he said, "He is no god," and
> beholding the moon, he called her his god to whom he would
> pay Divine homage. Then the moon was obscured, and he
> cried out: "This, too, is no god! There is One who sets them
> all in motion" [Ginzberg, 1968, vol. 1, p. 189].

Once Abraham identifies God, he is open to hearing and responding to God's call: "Go forth from your native land and from your father's house to the land that I will show you" (Gen. 12:1).

Since this call to Abraham, we have experienced suffering within the context of a larger creation. To draw an analogy, we might say that Abraham's curiosity and God's answering call correspond to an infant's spontaneous curiosity and the resulting organic interaction between parent and child, reassuring the infant that the parent is there to help and protect. God's meeting of Abraham's spontaneous curiosity and worship assures Abraham of a world that will fulfill his needs and even take a personal interest in him. So, from the start, any suffering would take place within the larger perspective of a universe that is responsive and caring.

In pursuing his relationship with God, Abraham is, according to legend, the first to feel pain and show signs of old age—the first to experience suffering. Tradition also tells us that he faced ten temptations; he is even compared by some commentators to Job, but his suffering occurs only after he has experienced the supportive context that gives it meaning.

The folk tradition that grew up around Abraham's ten trials helps us understand the suffering of those who wrote down the legends. The commentators chose Abraham's departure from his native land as the first trial. To the Israelites' descendants, who suffered exile, expulsion, and countless experiences of emigration, this was a trial they could both identify with and discuss with great elaboration and insight. Scarcely has Abraham settled in Canaan, his new land, when a devastating famine causes him to sojourn for a time in Egypt. To leave his native land and begin the slow process of acclimatizing to his new home, only to have to leave it to avoid famine, is a major test of Abraham's faith in the God whose call he answered.

Abraham's third trial, his separation from his nephew Lot, makes it increasingly clear that his allegiance is neither to a specific land nor to any particular individual, but to God. As a direct result of his leaving Lot, he is drawn into yet another trial, a war with four kings to rescue his nephew.

Abraham's failure to have a son proves an ongoing trial that is resolved only with the birth of Isaac, which leads to his greatest trial, God's call for him to sacrifice Isaac. Casting out Ishmael, his older son by the handmaid Hagar, prefigured the call to sacrifice Isaac and constitutes another major trial. A final trial is the death and burial of his wife, Sarah.

Although the *midrashim* (expansions of the biblical text, often in the form of stories) that have grown around Abraham provide a context in which to study different types of suffering, we can gain a better understanding of suffering by exploring it directly as we have personally experienced it.

Pain and Suffering

Aristotle saw pain as an emotion, like joy; Descartes saw it as a sensation, like heat or cold. Spinoza defined it as one of the fundamental emotions: pain is the movement from a greater to a lesser perfection. Each of these philosophers recognized pain as an event that demands interpretation. However we define pain, we are not satisfied with simply suffering it; we have a need to make sense of it.

Pain and suffering are not identical. Pain is a physical sensation, while suffering is the way we interpret that sensation. When the sensation is cut off from interpretation, no suffering is experienced (which is what occurs when we are anesthetized). We can also experience a minor twinge but turn it into a significant pain because we fear that it signifies a serious illness. "Pain, after all, exists only as we perceive it. Shut down the mind and pain too stops. Change the mind (powerfully enough) and it may well be that pain too changes" (Morris, 1991, p. 4). So we can also mitigate a severe pain by the way we interpret it.

> JOY
> Joy, a dancer, had a bad fall and was carried to a hospital emergency room. How bad was the accident? After X rays and other tests, the doctor tested her leg and she let out a yell. He smiled. "Do you know what that means?" "It means you're hurting me," she grumbled. "No," he replied, "it means there's no apparent nerve damage." Suddenly, the sensation of pain became a signal for happiness.

"The experience of pain is decisively shaped or modified by individual human minds and by specific human cultures" (Morris, 1991, pp. 1–2). The culture of the love of God can transform the experience of pain. In the *musaf* service on Yom Kippur, we recall a group of ten Jews martyred during the Roman period. The death of each is described, but one story suffices to show how the love of God can transform the experience of pain.

> Rabbi Hananya ben Teradyon, the fourth victim, was wrapped in the Torah from which he had been teaching and placed on a pyre of green brushwood; his chest was drenched with water to prolong the agony. His disciples, watching the flames dancing over their beloved teacher, asked him what he saw. He replied: "I see parchment burning, while the letters of the Torah soar upward" [after Birnbaum, 1951, p. 844].

At a time of overwhelming agony, Rabbi Hananya could visualize the invincibility of the Torah. Pain is always more than a physical matter. "The culture we live in and our deepest personal beliefs subtly or massively recast our experience of pain" (Morris, 1991, p. 2).

The problem of suffering for humans is less its reality than it is our difficulty in understanding it. Our very capacity to understand renders a given experience "suffering" and not merely pain.

HANNAH

Hannah talked of how she controlled her pain when she went into labor but couldn't leave for the hospital:

"I was in labor with my second child and could not go to the hospital until my mother-in-law had come to the house to care for our older child. My husband was en route home, but I had to wait, and my mother-in-law would not come until she had finished cooking a pot of soup to bring along. I took out a book of *New York Times* Sunday crossword puzzles. I had never before attempted to do a Sunday puzzle by myself. I was so focused on the puzzle, I was able to banish all my concerns: anger with my mother-in-law for not rushing over, annoyance at my husband's late arrival, and the strong sensations that came with the regular contractions. My effort was successful on all counts—the contractions didn't bother me, I made it to the hospital in plenty of time, I delivered a wonderful baby, and I even finished the crossword puzzle. Later, I tore the puzzle out of the book and pasted it in the baby album along with my daughter's identification bracelet. It was very much a part of the experience."

Pain can be reinforced, and even created, by psychological and emotional states such as guilt, fear, anger, grief, and depression. To mitigate such states, Jews have developed rituals for the times they feel most vulnerable—for example, requiring mourners to pray in a *minyan* (a community of ten worshipers) for eleven months after the death of a parent, sibling, spouse, or child. Just when we feel most estranged and isolated, and most anxious to turn in on ourselves, we are thrust into our community and thereby forced to recognize that there is no house without death. In our loss, we pray in solidarity with others who have experienced loss because language puts us into community. If there is a word for it, then someone before us has experienced it. That explains why it is comforting to read the psalms and recognize that others before us have felt angry with

God, cut off from their fellow human beings, and abandoned to suffer this pain and loss alone:

> How long, O Adonai; will You ignore me forever?
> How long will You hide Your face from me?
> How long will I have cares on my mind,
>   grief in my heart all day?
> How long will my enemy have the upper hand?
> Look at me, answer me, O Adonai, my God!

—Psalms 13:2–4

> Turn to me, have mercy on me,
>   for I am alone and afflicted.

—Psalms 25:16

> I am like a great owl in the wilderness,
>   an owl among the ruins.
> I lie awake; I am like
>   a lone bird upon a roof. . . .

—Psalms 102:7–8

As we experience the many ways emotions can exacerbate (or mitigate) suffering, we recognize the urgency for developing our theology. In doing so, we should remember that meaning can transform suffering. Certain emotions are, by themselves, forms of suffering: they constrict us, pain us, and hinder our openness to perceive the magnificence of Creation. Chief among the culprits are sorrow, hatred, fear, despair, envy, and anger. Sorrow lessens our power to act, while joy increases it. We have all experienced how willing we are to accept pain that accompanies growth or achievement. We consciously ignore pain when straining to beat our personal best time in jogging, when leaping against the forces of gravity as we perform in a ballet, when sitting still while nurses stick needles into our arms, and when taking to heart the exercise mogul's article of faith ("no pain, no gain"). In each case, we accept the transient pain for what we consider a higher good.

The no-pain-no-gain view is one of many interpretations theologians have developed to understand pain. They have viewed pain as, for example, a test of faith, an expiation of sin, or a means of redemption. The *Tanakh* draws no distinction between emotional and physical pain because the *Tanakh* sees people in their totality, with no hard division between somatic and psychic pain. Consider being told about Bob, who cannot walk and must be pushed from place to place, who has no control of either his bladder or his bowels, cannot feed himself, cannot even form words. Our first thought is that Bob is a great tragedic figure. But if we are told that Bob is three months old, we regard his condition as perfectly natural and expected.

Our interpretation of suffering is directly connected to our expectation of what is natural and what is anomalous. There are real obstacles in this world that thwart our plans, rob us of the love we crave, and destroy our health. Many people have chosen to alleviate suffering by focusing on these very real obstacles. But others, who have chosen to focus on interpreting the obstacles, feel that suffering can best be alleviated by changing our way of understanding reality. We find both approaches to suffering in Judaism. The voice of the prophet rings down through the ages:

> No, this is the fast I desire:
> To unlock the fetters of wickedness,
> And untie the cords of lawlessness,
> To let the oppressed go free;
> To break off every yoke.
> It is to share your bread with the hungry,
> And to take the wretched poor into your home;
> When you see the naked, to clothe them,
> And not to ignore your own kin.
>
> —Isaiah 58:6–8

Suffering and Meaning

"He who has a *why* to live for can bear with almost any *how*," wrote Viktor Frankl (1973, p.76). The belief that there is a why—a meaning behind all the vicissitudes that were suffered over millennia of persecution and exile—allowed Jews to survive. If our own quest for meaning is to be effective, we must critically examine earlier interpretations of suffering.

One biblical view of suffering (a mainstream, popular view) holds that suffering is always punishment for evil. Eve's suffering in childbirth as punishment for transgressing against the Divine Will; Adam's suffering by having to work the soil for obeying Eve instead of God; Cain's wandering as punishment for murder; the Flood to counter the evil that had arisen in the land; the destruction of Sodom and Gomorrah for the sins committed by its people; the affliction of Miriam with leprosy for maligning Moses—sickness, wandering, and death are often presented in the biblical text as retributive justice, or punishment, in the form of suffering.

But two other biblical stories challenge this view. First, manna in the wilderness is provided in equal amounts to those who labored long and those who hardly labored at all. Second, the suffering of Job appears to have no relationship to his righteousness. Both of these stories suggest that equating suffering with having sinned is simplistic and that we need to probe more deeply in trying to understand suffering.

Let us begin with a mysterious omission that may be instructive for us, living as we do in the post-Holocaust era. The *Mishnah,* which contains early rabbinic Torah commentary, though written 130 years after the destruction of the Temple, fails to mention either its destruction or the radical transformation in the condition of the Jews in Palestine (formerly Judaea) that followed. This silence about the Jews' most significant reality of that period corresponds to the silence of our own theologians in the 1950s. It was too soon; the horror could not yet be taken in. The halakhic *midrashim,* which refer specifically to matters of *halakha,* or Jewish law, and were written somewhat later than the mishnaic texts, admit the reality of suffering, but mainly to establish legally acceptable responses, never to question God or to complain. Only when we reach the era of the Babylonian Talmud is the full range of biblical reactions to suffering offered to Diaspora Jews.

It has been suggested that it takes at least two—some say three—generations to complete an important work. I suspect it is still too soon for us to absorb the enormity of the Holocaust and somehow make it part of our people's story.

The five stages of grief identified by Elisabeth Kübler-Ross can help us understand our response to the Holocaust (or, in earlier times, to the destruction of the second Temple and the subsequent exile and torture of the Jews). The first stage, denial, is what we see in the *Mishnah.* The second stage, anger, is evident in texts that put God on trial or deny God's existence or relevance. The third stage, bargaining, we find in the halakhic *midrashim.* The fourth stage, depression or mourning, is as far as we have come. Whether the fifth stage, acceptance, should or can ever be reached in relation to the horrors of World War II is very much open to question.

Suffering and Love

Suffering and love are inexorably intertwined, as Rabbi Akiba concluded. He connects his position on suffering with his advocacy for including the Song of Songs in the biblical canon. Indeed, he sees suffering as something to be valued, thereby severing it completely from any sense of retribution in this world or in the world to come and regarding it as a supreme good for the servant of God. Akiba is quoted as saying as he was being martyred that all his life, he had been troubled by the verse "with all your soul," meaning that God would take his soul. When, he wondered, would he be granted his chance to fulfill that verse?

Akiba did not think of his suffering as retribution; rather, he conceived of it as an overpowering love of his soul in its yearning for God (Urbach, 1973).

Akiba also believed that the Song of Songs, a love poem, was the holiest book in the Bible: "If the Torah had not been given to us," he is said to have proclaimed, "the Song of Songs would have sufficed to guide the world." To complement my argument that the Book of Job is a biblical love song, let us see how the Song of Songs can be viewed as a book on suffering.

The lovers' vulnerability reminds us of our first childish encounters with the world: when we are in love the world appears to us as newly created. Everything begins so hopefully, but we know all too well what transformed boundaries can mean. How does the Song of Songs actually end? The final chapter reiterates a theme that has already appeared twice: "I charge you, O daughters of Jerusalem, that you stir not up nor awaken love until it please." This warning immediately precedes desert imagery, which reminds us of the essential love story of the Jewish people, whose identity is shaped by a wilderness sojourn: "Who is this that comes up from the desert, leaning on her beloved?" The beloved constitutes both a wilderness himself and whatever makes the desert habitable. The next verse declares an answer to the unnamed fear behind all commitment: "Love is stronger than death."

Judaism in biblical times did not teach any persistence of life beyond death. When it later came to advocate some form of life after death, it did so for both negative and positive reasons. The negative was to reduce the dilemma of innocent suffering (the balance will be restored after death); the positive was that the strength of experiencing God here and now makes it seem incredible that death will bring an end to the relationship. The reasons for believing in an afterlife are for justice's sake and, as suggested by the Song of Songs, because of the power of love.

How to Love in the Face of Loss

How can we dare to love what we know death will touch? We can look for answers in how the ancient Greek world viewed all problems of change. The Greek philosophers, who found change as confusing and troubling as we do, described four basic responses to address the problem of how we can know and control that which will change. One position suggests, unconvincingly, that change is only illusory and therefore knowledge is possible. Another position is despairing, like Ecclesiastes' holding that change is ongoing and therefore knowledge is illusory. A third position concludes that change is real, however our knowledge is not of this changing world but only of the changeless. According to the fourth position, change itself can become the subject matter of knowledge.

Analogously, we can deny the reality of the changes, including death, that we find in the entities we love—which is what the *Mishnah* does with respect to the Temple. Or we can deny that this changing world is worth our love and commitment. This position is explicitly addressed and firmly rejected by Jeremiah at the time of the Babylonian exile:

> Thus said Adonai, the God of Israel, to the whole community
> which I exiled from Jerusalem to Babylon: Build houses and live
> in them, plant gardens and eat their fruit. Take wives and beget
> sons and daughters; and take wives for your sons, and give your
> daughters to husbands, that they may bear sons and daughters.
> Multiply there, do not decrease. And seek the welfare of the city
> to which I have exiled you and pray to Adonai in its behalf; for
> in its prosperity you shall prosper [Jer. 29:4–7].

In other words, do not turn from this world, but in the face of loss and suffering, become ever more deeply engaged with this world and its well-being.

A third position is to admit the reality of change but focus solely on the changeless. This is a position chosen by other faith traditions, but Judaism makes it clear that we are called upon to concentrate on this life, this world, and the transformations we can bring about to make this world closer to what it is meant to be. Because we are called upon to help complete Creation, we must be actively engaged with the world of change and its subsequent losses. Finally, we can decide that change itself should not be feared but embraced. That is a Jewish view that the quotation from Jeremiah supports as well.

Judaism has rightly been called a religion of time, emphasizing time over space. Jews can live out their entire lives without entering the Holy Land, but to be observant, they must enter holy time—Sabbaths and festivals. Judaism also sees time as the medium of revelation; in other words, history is the unfolding of God's meaning. But time itself is the measure of change—the measure of the before and after. So a religion centered on sacred time finds its way to God in and through the vulnerability of change.

Responses to Suffering

What wrong answers to suffering have been advanced, and what are their failings? Any response that allows us to be complacent in the face of another's suffering is wrong. All of our history argues against suffering as punishment, which we see in the Israelites' enforced slavery in Egypt for four hundred years. Later, we see it in the distribution of manna in the wilderness:

> "Gather as much of it as each of you requires to eat, an *omer* to a person for as many of you as there are; each of you shall fetch for those in his tent."
>
> The Israelites did so, some gathering much, some little. But when they measured it by the *omer*, he who had gathered much had no excess, and he who had gathered little had no deficiency: they had gathered as much as they needed to eat [Exod. 16:16].

We see the suffering-as-punishment argument rejected most decisively in the Book of Job, which begins with the statement, "There was a man in the land of Uz named Job. The man was blameless and upright; he feared God and shunned evil."

In the Theophany, God teaches Job to perceive the wonders of nature around him. Those of us who see these wonders are struck by them and marvel that others don't see and understand. The Song of Songs also inspires us to contemplate nature, which is described in verse after verse in all its beauty. But the same ability to notice beauty also opens us to perceive suffering.

JOHANNA
Johanna returned to her vacation house for the weekend.
After settling in she noticed that the door to the guest room,
which was closed when she left the previous weekend, bore
strange markings, as if something had gnawed at it. She

opened the door, and on the floor she saw the tiny body of a baby mouse. The mother must have been out of the room when Johanna shut the door as she left the previous week. She found herself stunned by the scenario that formed in her mind: "Every time I think of the mouse gnawing and clawing at the door of the guest room trying to get at her babies, I know that suffering doesn't happen just on the human level. Animals love and fear, and that incident made me extremely sad. Can we afford to know how much suffering there is on this planet?"

Whether it is the opening to love in the Song of Songs or the love song of the Theophany in Job, love makes us fully aware that we live in a miraculous world. At the same time, we become all too aware of suffering, but being open to it means that we are also open to the teeming life and consciousness around us.

The experience of love and pain testifies that we are alive and aware. Pain, like love, is caused by emotions, in this case fear (that something will happen to the beloved), envy, jealousy, anger, hatred, and similar feelings. Pain that comes about through love can be lessened not by withdrawing love but increasing it.

Job's losses touch every aspect of his being. Foremost, he loses his children, whom he deeply loves. Their deaths also rob him of his own future after death, his symbolic immortality. The loss of his possessions is not dwelt on in the biblical text. He loses his status and finally his physical well-being. But greater than his loss of status or even his physical well-being is his comforters' inability to empathize with his undeserved suffering. At the heart of Job's ordeal is his isolation. He is cut off from his future when his children die; he is cut off from his whole meaning system, including the status he had earned in his community; and he is cut off from other people altogether when even those who come to mourn with him fail to ease his grief.

Many Holocaust survivors felt themselves to be twentieth-century Jobs. They discovered that people around them were as unwilling to hear their complaints as Job's comforters were unable to hear his. Their stories are gradually being told, in the hope that keeping them alive may benefit the people who hear them and the survivors themselves.

TAMAR

Tamar reported: I still remember the man I met at synagogue who told me how he had survived the concentration camps. There was a thorn bush beyond the barbed wire fence, he told

me, and he made a deal with the bush that if it survived, he
would survive.

A lowly bush can suddenly become the Burning Bush: God can speak
to us—call us into fuller life—from any bush or shrub. What Moses did
was stop. "I must turn aside to look at this marvelous sight; why doesn't
the bush burn up?" To turn aside is to stop our own forward motion, put
our own plans and agendas on hold, and be fully present for what is happening now.

TAMAR

Tamar reflected further on the survivor's report and continued:
"What do I want to know about suffering? I've concluded that
justice plays no part and that bearing it is all I know: Can I
remain faithful? Can my death affirm what my life has been
about? Akiba's death remains an image for me of a life well
lived and consistent even in its final moments. The Holocaust
does not change my image of God because I've always known
that people are capable of unspeakable cruelty and evil. I've
also known that even in that darkness, if any one of us turns
to God, God will be present to console and guide. We are part
of a people, and that people has shaped us and given us the
language and symbols to approach God. But each one of us,
individually, must then apply that language and those symbols
to the life situations in which we find ourselves."

It is true that life contains suffering, but it also contains joy, and with
all this comes awareness. The joys in life have little to do with riches, status, or pleasure of the senses. Almost all joy has to do with love, caring,
connectedness, gratitude, and wonder. We make compromises with life;
we think if we are not fully alive we may fool death. So we numb ourselves and refuse to acknowledge all the wonder around us.

We have learned from our ancestors' responses to suffering since the
destruction of the second Temple that we don't have to wait hundreds of
years to acknowledge and accept the biblical responses to suffering. We
have learned that there is room within our faith for numerous ways of
understanding the losses and pains we confront. God is not threatened,
and neither is our faith.

Responses to Suffering Summarized

Let us review the basic interpretations of suffering and responses that have
been advanced from Biblical times to the present.

Suffering as Punishment

The earliest interpretation is that suffering is punishment. This notion of retributive suffering is the most common view found in the Bible and later in the *Mishnah,* but thoughtful readers will recognize that it is already refuted in the Book of Job and even by our own experience. As we study the lives and teachings of the great rabbis, we are all too aware that some of the greatest, such as Rabbi Akiba, suffered martyrdom. The view that suffering is punishment compounds the victim's anguish and harms those who promote this view because their compassion is diminished.

When a loved one falls ill, we often feel that we are somehow to blame. We then need someone else to tell us that the same thing happened to them. Only when we look at the incident in the case of the other person can we see clearly that we are not at fault.

Suffering to Temper Us

Those who believe suffering exists in order to test or improve us see it as a loving, parentlike rebuke. "Adonai your God disciplines you just as a man disciplines his son" (Deut. 8:5). In some cases, suffering does serve that kind of loving purpose, but not if it comes too early or is too intense. We may admire or even marvel at people who have transcended their suffering, but we rarely credit the suffering itself with their greatness. There is, though, another way of looking at this view of suffering. We examine our aspirations—as artist, athlete, caring parent, devoted partner, and one who truly loves God. Each of these goals demands that we transform ourselves by self-discipline so that whatever stands in the way of progress toward our goal—recalcitrant flesh, say, or quick temper, or insensitivity—is eliminated. The self-discipline undertaken serves a precise purpose of tempering ourselves to function better in whatever work we are called to do.

Suffering in the Service of Love

Suffering in the service of love is a difficult and complex position advocated by Rabbi Akiba. Surely all of us remember the intense passion of early love, when we wanted to be challenged, tested, even made to face suffering in order to prove our love. "Why is it," sex researcher Havelock Ellis is said to have wondered, "that love inflicts and even seeks to inflict pain? Why is it that love suffers pain and even seeks to suffer it?" We may know that the gift of love cannot be earned, but we still seek to merit it through intense exertion and dedication.

Suffering as Vicarious Atonement

Vicarious atonement is a position expressed in Isaiah's description of the suffering servant:

> He was despised, we held him of no account.
> Yet it was our sickness that he was bearing,
> Our suffering that he endured.
> We accounted him plagued,
> Smitten and afflicted by God;
> But he was wounded because of our sins,
> Crushed because of our iniquities.
> He bore the chastisement that made us whole,
> And by his bruises we were healed.
>
> —Isaiah 53:3–5

The view of suffering for the sins of others also finds expression in the autobiography of the twentieth-century philosopher Morris Raphael Cohen: "We must be prepared to suffer and be punished for the sins of others; otherwise we are not entitled to the benefits which we all do derive from the virtues of others" (1949, p. 213).

Suffering Now for Reward Later

Suffering seems to be distributed indiscriminately. One response to this apparent injustice is that the imbalance will be resolved in the world to come. We cannot, of course, verify this claim, but we can understand the longing that makes this view one of the chief arguments for an afterlife.

Suffering as the Price for Free Will

Viewing suffering as the price we must pay to have free will is a position designed to defend God's ways to humanity. God didn't do it, the argument goes; we did it to ourselves. There is truth to this position: if suffering strengthens our resolve to take responsibility for our actions in this world, then it serves a significant function.

Suffering as Nonexistent

If we believe that no real harm can come to the good person, then we might conclude that there is no real suffering, that it is illusory or transitory. This position is put forward in the biblical book of the prophet

Habakkuk and in many of the psalms. It is found in the famous story of Akiba's martyrdom referred to earlier.

The idea that suffering does not exist finds expression in Elie Wiesel's description of Hasidim en route to concentration camps: "What cannot but astound us is that Hasidim remained Hasidim inside ghetto walls, inside death camps. In the shadow of the executioner, they celebrated life. Startled Germans whispered to each other of Jews dancing in the cattle cars rolling toward Birkenau" (1972, p. 38).

We have all met people who embody that position. They assume that everything happens to them for some good and that ultimately they will understand why the apparent suffering is really a great blessing.

Suffering as a Mystery

That suffering is ultimately mysterious and only God can understand it is a position that many readers find in the Book of Job. In other words, suffering is meaningful, but we cannot understand the meaning.

> ESTHER
> Esther has composed a series of "cat poems" to convey her theology. In one poem, she tried to express the view that we have too limited a perspective to understand suffering:

I do not understand
why I have to go to the vet.
I do not understand
the pain.
You hold me close.
You pet me.
You clearly love me.
I trust you.
The pain must be necessary.

—"On Being Taken to the Vet"

Suffering as Meaningless

Finally, some people simply opt out of giving a meaning to suffering and maintain that suffering is meaningless. This view, expressed in Ecclesiastes—"vanity of vanities, all is vanity"—actually compounds the suffering of those who are in pain. We may here recall Viktor Frankl's observation that people can bear with any *how* as long as they know there is a *why*. Because the rejection of meaning itself causes suffering, we find ourselves developing our theology to overcome this position.

The Real Good

People have identified suffering in terms of losing good things, such as riches, power, fame, sensual pleasure, and health. But do these constitute the *real* good or one that is merely apparent? The real good is our relationship with God. Can our love of God overcome our suffering? It can for some, if their question is not, "Why is this happening to me?" but "What should I do in response to the suffering around me?"

As we ponder so-called natural disasters, we recognize that some occur because we have failed to heed earlier warnings. In the face of devastating earthquakes and floods, we prefer not to attribute evil to natural earth processes. Indeed, we find that most of the damage is wrought because people rebuild their houses in earthquake zones and flood plains, and greedy builders save money by erecting buildings and dams that fall short of safety specifications.

Buddhism, as we have learned, focuses on the transitoriness of all things and concludes that life is sorrowful. Judaism, with the same information, still encourages us to build houses and live in them, plant crops, and harvest them. We cannot spend our lives defending ourselves against future sorrow; rather, we choose to live in gratitude for what we know we have: our relationship with God. Because of it, we recognize ourselves to be *b'tselem elohim* (in the image of God) and focus on alleviating suffering. Our social activism includes not only designating, as prescribed in the Torah, the harvest from a corner of our field for the indigent but also conducting research on cancer prevention and cure, on earthquake forecasting, and on methods for building safer structures.

By participating in the larger life system, we can prevent much suffering through studying the system and learning how to live in harmony with it. Before the twentieth century, for example, most parents suffered the death of one or more children. Now the rate of infant and childhood death is dramatically lower, thanks to the research that led to vaccines and to more effective medicines. We will age and experience debility, but for more and more people, old age can be a prolonged time of independence and continued ability to contribute.

Our reaction to other people's suffering is to try to alleviate it and to show compassion rather than judgment or distancing. Tolstoy's novella *The Death of Ivan Ilyitch* details the protagonist's descent into illness and death and shows how the insensitivity of others intensifies his suffering. The one exception to the deceit and coldness of Ivan's household is that of the servant Gerasim:

> He was contented when Gerasim for whole nights at a time held his legs, and did not care to go to sleep, saying:—
> "Don't trouble yourself, Ivan Ilyitch; I shall get sleep enough."
> Or when suddenly, using *thou* instead of *you,* he would add:—
> "If thou wert not sick . . . but since thou art, why not serve thee?"
> Gerasim alone did not lie: in every way it was evident that he alone comprehended what the trouble was, and thought it unnecessary to hide it, and simply pitied his sick baron, who was wasting away. He even said directly when Ivan Ilyitch wanted to send him off to bed:—
> "We shall all die. Then, why should I not serve you?" he said, meaning by this that he was not troubled by his extra work, for precisely the reason that he was doing it for a dying man, and he hoped that, when his time came, some one would undertake the same service for him [Tolstoy, 1886/ 1964, p. 102].

Pain transforms our world, continually unmaking and remaking it. Yet pain could not unmake Akiba's world, or Etty Hillesum's, or that of the Hasidim en route to Birkenau. Martyrdom is not something we aspire to, but when it occurs, it tests our beliefs about reality. George Orwell wrote, in *Nineteen Eighty-Four,* about the power of a totalitarian state to transform the consciousness of the hero by threatening him with what he most feared (rats). But pain is not the whole story, as the closing line of *The Death of Ivan Ilyitch* suggests:

> And suddenly it became clear to him that what oppressed him, and was hidden from him, suddenly was lighted up for him all at once, and on two sides, on ten sides, on all sides.
> He felt sorry for them; he felt he must do something to make it less painful for them. To free them, to free himself, from these torments. "How good and how simple!" he thought.
> "But the pain," he asked himself, "where is it?—Here, now, where art thou, pain?"
> He began to listen.
> "Yes, here it is! Well, then, do your worst, pain!"
> "And death? where is it?"

He tried to find his former customary fear of death, and could not.

"Where is death? What is it?"

There was no fear, because there was no death.

In place of death was light!

"So that's what it is!" he suddenly said aloud. "What joy!" [Tolstoy, 1886/1964, p. 116].

The transformation in Ivan Ilyitch's consciousness and in his experience of dying comes about because of love. Most of the novella is about his suffering, his pain, and his distance from those around him, who lie to him about the gravity of his condition so they can continue their trivial pursuits. About his past, which he reviews without insight, Tolstoy comments: "Ivan Ilyitch's life had been most simple and most ordinary and therefore most terrible." In this statement, Tolstoy conveys how ordinary is the slide into alienation from all that we once valued and all that might give meaning to life's vicissitudes. As Ivan Ilyitch thrashes around on his bed after three days of unceasing torment, just two hours before he dies, his hand strikes his son's head, and the boy catches it, presses it to his lips, and begins to cry.

It was at this very same time that Ivan Ilyitch fell through, saw the light, and it was revealed to him that his life had not been as it ought, but that still it was possible to repair it. He was just asking himself, "What is right?" and stopped to listen. Then he felt that some one was kissing his hand. He opened his eyes, and looked at his son. He felt sorry for him. His wife came to him. He looked at her. With open mouth, and with her nose and cheeks wet with tears, with an expression of despair, she was looking at him. He felt sorry for her.

"Yes, I am a torment to them," he thought. "I am sorry for them, but they will be better off when I am dead." He wanted to express this, but he had not the strength to say it.

"However, why should I say it? I must do it."

He pointed out his son to his wife by a glance, and said:—

"Take him away. . . . I am sorry . . . and for thee."

He wanted to say also, "*Prosti*—Forgive," but he said, "*Propusti*—Let it pass"; and, not having the strength to correct himself, he waved his hand, knowing that he would comprehend who had the right [Tolstoy, 1886/1964, p. 116].

In the twentieth century, Viktor Frankl writes of speaking to his fellow prisoners in the concentration camp:

I told my comrades (who lay motionless, although occasionally a sigh could be heard) that human life, under any circumstances, never ceases to have a meaning, and that this infinite meaning of life includes suffering and dying, privation and death. I asked the poor creatures who listened to me attentively in the darkness of the hut to face up to the seriousness of our position. They must not lose hope but should keep their courage in the certainty that the hopelessness of our struggle did not detract from its dignity and meaning. I said that someone looks down on each of us in difficult hours—a friend, a wife, somebody alive or dead, or a God—and he would not expect us to disappoint him. He would hope to find us suffering proudly—not miserably—knowing how to die.

And finally I spoke of our sacrifice, which had meaning in every case. It was in the nature of this sacrifice that it would appear to be pointless in the normal world, the world of material success. But in reality our sacrifice did have a meaning. . . . I told them of a comrade who on his arrival in camp had tried to make a pact with Heaven that his suffering and death should save the human being he loved from a painful end. For this man, suffering and death were meaningful; his was a sacrifice of the deepest significance. He did not want to die for nothing. None of us wanted that [1973, p. 104].

Putting It All Together

How should we react to our own suffering? If we need to grow angry, we should do so, for anger too is a form of communication and relationship, and God does not need our lies. As we saw earlier, we long to be completely known and still loved, and satisfying this longing requires that God knows and accepts us as we authentically are, with all our anger, doubts, and confusion. Job's comforters, in their fear of his suffering, told pious fictions not to comfort Job but to reassure themselves. By maintaining his integrity, Job deepened his relationship with God. Do the rabbinic answers help? Sometimes, in some contexts. But we are all too aware of exceptions. We are awed before Akiba, Hillesum, and other spiritual giants. We pray not to be tested as they were because we doubt we can pass such tests. Fortunately, martyrdom is not a test we are likely to have to meet. Those who were martyred did not mitigate their distress because they hated God or denied God's existence; more likely, their denial intensified their suffering.

People do not *decide* to be angry at God; rather, they *experience* anger or deadness or doubt. It is the next step, what they do with these emotions, that is crucial. If they can honestly claim their emotions, their suffering can be addressed—not with someone else's answer but with the one that genuinely emerges out of a long relationship and a long struggle.

> I was angry with my friend:
> I told my wrath, my wrath did end.
> I was angry with my foe:
> I told it not, my wrath did grow.
>
> —William Blake, "A Poison Tree"

Each of us must personally choose how we respond to suffering. As we have seen, our models come from many centuries and take many forms. We do have one minimum criterion: whatever answer we finally arrive at, we must not look with complacency on anyone else's suffering. Our theology has practical implications, meaning that it can be tested by our way of being in the world. Not only can we not turn away from another's suffering, but we also cannot respond to suffering by disengaging from the world. As we read in Deuteronomy: "I kill and I bring life; I wound and I heal" (32:39). There is only one source for all that is, and the source we rail against for killing is also the creator and sustainer of all life. Finally, the source of our wounds is also the source of our healing. We know this is true because there is only one line of causality—from God—and we also see that it's true when we look at particular aspects of our own lives. Jewish folklore illustrates this insight with the story of the flawed diamond (after Ausubel, 1948, p. 66):

> A king owned a diamond of which he was very proud, but one day it became deeply scratched. He consulted with diamond cutters, and they told him that they would never be able to remove the imperfection. But a lapidary, who had recently arrived in the capital, said he could make the diamond even more beautiful than it was before it was scratched. With great delicacy, he engraved a rosebud around the deep scratch, using the scratch as the stem. Everyone who saw the diamond agreed it was even more beautiful now than it had been before.

Our greatest flaw, or woundedness, can become the source of our greatest virtue.

5

UNDERTAKING OUR WORK

Know before whom you toil, and who your Employer is
who will pay you the reward of your labor.

—*Pirke Avot* 2:19

JENNIFER
When she lost her job as a social studies teacher in a private
school, Jennifer thought she would have little trouble finding
a new position. Six months passed, and she did not make the
short list of any of the schools to which she applied; she
found herself anguished in a way she could not explain.

Financially she was not yet at any great risk. Her despair
took the form of wondering if there were a place for her in
this world. Her family did not cease to love her; her friends
(with a few notable exceptions) did not suddenly abandon
her. But her need to find a place where she could contribute
felt almost like a physical pain. She was tempted to take a job
in a supermarket, but her friends reminded her that she had
not earned a master's degree in education in order to become
a bagger at the local supermarket. If she accepted the wrong
job, she would have less time to look for the right one. An
older friend persuaded her to work on some curriculum
development while she waited. It turned out to be the most
exciting and useful suggestion she received. In the months
that followed, she developed creative syllabi for elective
courses in American history. But at night, she also spent time

trying to understand how her sense of place was associated
with work and with her developing theology.

While researching her curriculum, Jennifer met someone
who knew about a job opening at the school where he taught;
she also gained foreknowledge of a suitable opening that
would occur in a related agency. Both jobs sounded to her
like candidates for what she was supposed to find. She wrote
to the school but never even got a reply. At the agency, she
was dropped before the interview stage. Many months later,
looking back on the anguish of her unemployed state from
the excitement of a new position, Jennifer decided that
the false leads reflected a major change in the way she
approached her work and related to it. Instead of seeking status, wealth, and power, she was trying to discern God's will.

Freud wrote that the tasks of adult life are love, work, and communal
life. It may initially seem strange to think about a theology of work, but
as Jennifer's experience shows, our contribution to this world is a major
and personal decision. We need to reflect on our identity and how our
work fits into it, our connection with the rest of Creation, and our relationship to God.

Dignity of Work

Augustine of Hippo, a Roman bishop, deemed all work degrading
drudgery because of its association with bondage. Augustine's view has
its modern expression in the Marxist principle concerning the alienation
of labor and its philosophical counterpart in the twentieth-century writings of Simone Weil: "Death and labour are things of necessity and not of
choice. The world only gives itself to man in the form of food and warmth
if man gives himself in the form of labour. . . . He exhausts himself by
work in order that he may eat, and he eats in order that he may have the
strength to work, and after a year of toil, everything is as it was when he
began. Only if his labour is illumined by the light of eternity will the
monotony become bearable. . . . Manual labour is either a degrading
servitude or a sacrifice" (1982, p. 47).

Judaism challenges this view. Unlike the Greeks and the Romans, Jews
saw an essential dignity in work. After they settled in the Promised Land,
the Israelites could labor without associating the work with their earlier
servitude because work expressed their deepest natures. They were now
serving God, not Pharaoh. According to the fundamental Jewish story, we

were put on earth to be partners, or cocreators, with God, so the work of Creation is part of our essence. We praise God by taking part in the creative process and being engaged in the world. In rabbinic tradition, even those who find their primary identity in religious study are expected to contribute to the day-to-day duties of material existence, so that most rabbis, in addition to studying and teaching, are also expected to work as tailors, lens grinders, store owners—whatever suits their own needs and the needs of the community. They have their labor, which fulfills their obligation to the ongoingness of Creation, and they have their study of Torah, which is *lashamayim* (for the sake of Heaven). Today, with the many additional roles they must fill, rabbis hardly get done ministering to their flock, let alone find the time to take on any further occupation. But the earlier model reminds us of the dignity of work.

In direct opposition to Weil, Jews believe that the earth was created to nourish all its inhabitants, not to consume us as we try to find sustenance. The world portrayed in the first chapter of Genesis has fixed boundaries for all the creatures and definite ways in which they can interact to allow for mutual sustenance. Once the story moves out of Eden, the idea of work becomes more complex; but other than the servitude in Egypt, work is never thought to be onerous. On the contrary, it is seen as a place to make a contribution, bring us into community, and stretch us.

False Gods

It is easy to forget that through our work we seek to grow and transform, make a contribution, and sustain ourselves and the people we care for. Certainly our jobs are economically based, though status may also be a factor.

Unemployment, even when there is no immediate financial crisis, can be likened to the desert experience. The usual ways in which we define ourselves are gone: we feel left without a place or a meaningful task. Everything that structures our time when we are employed abandons us. As we deal with unemployment, we find ourselves thinking about the meaning that waiting and trust have for us. If unemployment persists, we may find ourselves frantically grabbing at all possible hints and connections. We feel a desperate need to do something; yet when opportunity finally strikes, it may seem unrelated to all that we have done. We try to make sense of the many wrong moves that we make. But once we make the right move, what finally emerges feels like a gift. Jennifer's insight allowed her to feel the benefits of moving away from the wrong goals—riches, power, pleasures of the senses—and of seeing work as an arena in which to make her contribution and express her deepest selfhood.

Not all work is joyous: we feel degraded if we fall prey to false gods, that is, if work is not connected to our authentic identity.

DAVID

David's experience of false gods came from a different source. As a writer, David regards his work as creative. But though he loves writing, lately it is losing zest for him.

The feeling, which began when one of his books was rejected for publication, was exacerbated by a negative review of an earlier work and then the news that someone he didn't respect won a prestigious writing award. As he explains his situation, he no longer believes in any sort of honors, seeing them as political and meaningless. Yet in some unacknowledged part of himself, he knows that it was the desire for honors that motivated him, and he wonders if he should bother to continue writing.

But the thought of not writing deeply depresses him. Although writing is hard, he reasons, it's what he does—not really for honors or status or job security and certainly not for money or pleasure of the senses. As he sees it, writing is God's gift to him. Even so, he realizes that he has sometimes lusted after the false god of honor and in doing so sullied the gift of writing: the joy went out of pursuing his craft, and he longs for it to return.

For David, writing is deeply personal, and he does not want to let other people into his consciousness. He yearns to regain the quiet, the adventure, the joy of writing books. He reasons that his depression came about through idolatry. How had the "demon" of status thrown him so completely? He realizes that working for the wrong reasons brought him suffering. He now concludes that all work, like prayer, should be an offering to God. His writing should be like someone else's game of tennis: an intrinsic pleasure for which other people's praise or criticism is irrelevant. Seeing work as an offering or a prayer brings him closer to God. The same principle holds for any work: cooking, cleaning, caring for children, working the soil, building, tearing down, teaching, healing.

PEARL

Pearl has the gift of making any occasion special. She lovingly prepares for every family birthday with favorite foods and carefully chosen presents. The Sabbath she welcomes with hand-baked *challah*, dessert, and a feast of soup and roasted chicken. When Pearl's children were younger, she made it a point to begin baking something about half an hour before they were due home from school. They would come home and follow their noses to the kitchen. With a warm snack and a glass of milk, they would begin to recount the events of the day. Their first stop home from school, before anything else could distract them, was the kitchen, to bask in the comfort and presence of their mother.

As the children got older, Pearl made it a habit to turn away as they began complaining about their teachers and classmates. She studiously cleaned the stove's burners so the kids would feel free to say anything without having to watch her reaction. One day, Rima, her daughter, said, "I bet no one's stove is as clean as ours." Pearl realized then that Rima had caught on, so she just poured herself a cup of tea and sat opposite her daughter as the day's narrative unfolded.

Pearl listened not only to her children's concerns but to her sister-in-law's many troubles, her neighbors' affairs, and the problems of the many friends she had made over the years.

Although Pearl could give comfort and assurance to so many, she had severe doubts about her own worth. What had she ever accomplished? Thinking about the loving home she created was no comfort to her. She even joked that only a few days after she cleaned her stove, the burners would be dirty again. What lasting things had she done?

What can we create that makes a difference? Rima outgrew after-school snacks, left for college and work, and then became engaged to be married. Pearl's question was answered when Rima visited one day and showed her mother what she had accomplished. Rima sat in the sacred space of Pearl's kitchen and recounted what being home meant to her. Pearl, she said, had created a magnificent model, which she planned to emulate—making home a place of safety, acceptance, and presence.

A theology of work—any theology, for that matter—should make us more receptive to God's guidance, presence, and love; that is, it should increase our spirituality. But the trick lies in holding to it. Doing so is both easy and difficult: easy because it makes perfect sense and fits in with everything we believe; difficult in that the demons are fierce, the false gods seductive and tenacious. To some extent, we can verify a personal theology. We test it out in the flesh of our lives: Does it engage us in the world, allow us to experience the gifts of Creation, and bring us closer to God? Even though we may agree that all people are created in the image of God, we can get careless, tired, or hurt and think that "people are no darn good."

But believing that we are in the image of God gives us a far better perspective than we get when carelessly dismissing other people. If we know that we are already loved and accepted, we won't use our work to prove ourselves or to compete with someone else. Writing, or painting, or building, or planting are all ways of coming to God, and any question of how many books or paintings or monuments or rows of corn is beside the point. Other people can view our work from their perspective, which allows them to judge whether or not it pleases them, is internally consistent, is done in a timely fashion, and meets other external factors. But only we ourselves know whether there were moments in the process of genuine insight, freshness, discovery, or encounter. To the artist, painting, like every other form of work, should be prayer.

Contribution

One of the earliest impulses we have as children is wanting to help, to make a contribution. We want to set the table, sort the laundry, push the baby carriage—anything that lets us feel we are giving as well as receiving. At the end of a lifetime of hard work, even those who are terminally ill are grateful to be able to make some difference in people's lives. They willingly take part in studies that might benefit others in an earlier stage of their illness, or they participate in oral histories and psychological studies about the stages in accepting death.

In the prime of life, we seek a place to leave our mark. We want the world to be different as a result of our having lived. We could leave a physical mark by, say, contributing a pebble to the cairn built by nomads and shepherds, to show that we've passed through. But even elaborate buildings crumble. Most of us have lived or will live to see something we achieved undone. If work were only about tasks accomplished, then the undoing of our life's work (or even of a lesser accomplishment) would lead us to a sense of futility. But if our understanding of work expands to include a place where we can grow, be transformed, and even encounter the Holy, then we can accept that at least some of our undertakings can never be undone.

The most satisfying realm in which we can make our mark is in the lives of the people we have touched in some significant way through the work of loving, nurturing, and teaching. Somehow, the energy and life we invest in working with others can start a transformative process and help create worlds of meaning and connectedness.

Distinction Between Job and Work

From the start, we need to distinguish between a job and work, that is, between what we do to earn the money that sustains us and the tasks we find intrinsically worthwhile. The distinction between job and work helps us overcome the temptation to reduce people to their occupations. People are what they do, and they are more. Knowing the name of their job does not tell us what their real task may be. Their specific work may be to create a family, but meanwhile they maintain their dignity in a soul-numbing job. When they "retire," it is from their job, not their work—which continues until death. We work at aging and at making some sense of our lives.

> REGINA
> Regina was explaining how difficult it was for her to do the creative work she felt called to do but that she needed the income from her high-powered job. When asked how much she needed to live on, she replied that it was very expensive to live in New York. She talked about the cost of dressing for her job with a large firm, the cost not only of owning a car and insuring it but also of parking it in the city. The question did, however, get her to thinking: *I rarely travel out of town; I could sell the car and save the ongoing expense. If I quit my job, I'll lose the income, but I won't need the fancy clothes.* The more she thought about it, the more she realized that she herself is her only obstacle to answering the call.

Partial Identity

Work helps defines us. Although being may have primacy over doing, we are called upon to complete or contribute to Creation, so our doing is basic to living. The twentieth-century philosopher Karl Jaspers wrote, "We are what we do to others," an idea that broadens the scope of work to include working at relationships. The Jewish contribution to this definition is to suggest that while we are what we do to some extent, we are also more, and that is why our doing gives us a partial identity. In *Pirke Avot (The Ethics of the Fathers)* we read: "You are not called upon to complete the work, yet you are not free to evade it" (2:21).

If we are more than what we do, what, then, is the "more"? It is our being, our essence. It is the sense in which we are most in God's image. Doing is always external, that is, it can be seen and measured; being cannot. We can understand this difference well in the case of two people who have the same job but are doing very different work.

HARRY AND BOB

Harry and Bob are both employed at a zoo, spending their time cleaning out the cages and other animal areas. Harry took the job just to see the last two of his children through college, and it is only his love for them that makes it bearable. Secretly, he yearns for the day he can retire (840 days away and counting).

Bob, on the other hand, found that the job actually coincides with his work. He loves animals and nature, even the smells many people find offensive. His work not only keeps him around animals and takes him out into nature, it also allows him to contribute to its cleaning and maintenance.

Although he is five years older than Harry, Bob has no plans to retire anytime soon.

The Sabbath

Refraining from work and resting on the Sabbath is a concept so fundamental to Jewish law that it forms an essential part of both the Creation story and the Ten Commandments. Even our animals and the stranger within our gates may not work for us. If we turn around the seven tasks forbidden to Jews on the Sabbath, we get a sense of what we should be doing on the other days of the week—a description of what constitutes work:

1. Growing and preparing food
2. Producing and preparing clothing
3. Working leather
4. Providing shelter
5. Making fire
6. Completing an action
7. Transporting or carrying

On the Sabbath in the wilderness, the Israelites refrained from performing these tasks. Looking at just how they were able to do so allows us to recognize that everything was readied before they were liberated.

They were wanted, expected, and prepared for—as we are, too.

- On growing and preparing food: God "gave you manna to eat, which neither you nor your fathers had ever known, in order to teach you that man does not live on bread alone, but that man may live on anything that the Lord decrees" (Deut. 8:3).
- On making clothing and working leather: "The clothes upon you did not wear out, nor did your feet swell these forty years" (Deut. 8:4).
- On providing shelter: "Under God's wings you shall find refuge; / God's faithfulness is an encircling shield" (Ps. 91:4).
- On making fire: "Adonai your God . . . goes before you on your journeys—to scout the place where you are to encamp—in fire by night . . . in order to guide you on the route you are to follow" (Deut. 1:33).
- On transporting or carrying: ". . . you saw how the Lord your God carried you, as a man carries his son, all the way that you traveled until you came to this place" (Deut. 1:31).
- On completing an action: According to a Jewish saying, only God can rest on the seventh day—people's work is never completed. "Six days a week we wrestle with the world, wringing profit from the earth; on the Sabbath we especially care for the seed of eternity planted in the soul. The world has our hands, but our soul belongs to Someone Else. Six days a week we seek to dominate the world, [but] on the seventh day we try to dominate the self" (Heschel, 1951, p. 13).

Reading in the Torah, "Six days you shall labor and do all your work, but the seventh day is a Sabbath of Adonai your God: you shall not do any work" (Exod. 20:9–10), we see that doing and being are both accounted for. Both are necessary if we are to understand our own identity, and both weekdays and Sabbath are central to our lives.

Work as a Place of Encounter

In the Hindu scripture, the *Bhagavad Gita,* it is written: "If I did not work these worlds would perish" (III:24). The corresponding Jewish view would be, "If I did not work, my worlds of meaning would perish." Things become ours because of the life and effort we put into them. Work is thus a place of meeting, engagement, encounter, a place where we can be in relationship and be transformed.

We relate to people by seeing them in person, writing letters, making phone calls, sending e-mail. We relate to them by holding them in our minds and hearts as we pray about their concerns. Our relationships include our connection and identification with our bodies and, by extension, with the body of our environment. For many people, especially for

Jews, books form an important part of the environment. We impose order on pieces of paper by writing, thereby creating meaning and value.

TAMAR

Tamar describes her sense of discovery and delight as she arranges her books on a newly acquired bookcase. Each volume stirs memories of the mental journey she traveled as she worked her way through it. Some of the books are associated with specific times in her life, while others serve as almost constant companions, friends in the deepest sense. Arranging her books on the shelves allows her to recognize that an important way she creates meaning and value in her own work as a writer is by establishing order.

Like Tamar, most people experience that when they are doing a specific task that feels appropriate for them, they also feel the presence of the holy.

Work, where we make our contribution, is also a place where we express our love for another. When someone we love has needs we are unable to meet, we long for a way to do something.

MORRIS

When Morris's wife was hospitalized, he became greatly concerned that there was nothing he could do for her. Of course, he visited her whenever he was allowed into the hospital, kept all her relatives and friends informed of her condition, and maintained the household, but he still felt powerless to help her more directly. He could not, for example, actively make a difference in the outcome of her treatment. When his spiritual director suggested that he pray for his wife, he almost dismissed the idea but then decided to try it. He soon realized that his feelings of powerlessness in the face of his wife's illness no longer plagued him. He had found a way to express all the love, fear, and pain that he had carried during the weeks of her illness, because praying helped him feel that he was no longer carrying the burden alone.

Work Shapes Our Soul

It has been said that we are what we think about, and we are what we dream; either way, whatever fills our mind finds expression in our being and doing. Our work, which takes up at least half our waking hours during the week, cannot easily be put out of mind during that time.

LEAH

Leah took a routine filing job in order to keep her mind free for her real work, which was fiction writing. She soon found that the stultifying atmosphere of the job actually deadened her ability to think. The creativity she hoped to preserve in this unchallenging job was being crowded out with thoughts about the slow progress of the hour hand on the clock and dreams of recovering from boredom on the weekend. She concluded that her mind wasn't working at all, and within two weeks she left the job for one that was far more demanding, but life-giving.

We may shape things in order to leave a mark, but our work shapes us. Perhaps in conscious reference to Moses, tradition credits David's skill as a king to his earlier experience as a shepherd. According to legend, God said, "David knows how to tend sheep, therefore he shall be the shepherd of my flock Israel" (Ginzberg, 1968, vol. 4, p. 83).

So what if both Moses and David were shepherds? we may ask today. An undeniable feature of shepherding in biblical times was the lack of any competition. Shepherds may encounter other shepherds, but they all shoulder the same task of caring for their flocks, not competing with one another. They need to make certain that their flocks are properly nourished and exercised. We too have been given flocks to tend: our talents, which are the gifts that God has put in our care. We must protect them, nourish them, and allow them to grow.

Work as Prayer

That *tefillah* (prayer) is sometimes called *avodah* (work) suggests that our own work might be a prayer offering. Prayer offerings cannot be done once for all time; they are an essential part of a regular and ongoing relationship. They are also opportunities to lift our hearts and minds to God and truly encounter God. Our work, at its best moments, should similarly function as an ongoing relationship and an occasion for encounter. Hannah, whose job as a legal secretary helps her meet the needs of her family, sees her work as being Sarah and Esther's mother and Hirsch's wife. Perhaps at a later time she will find a different sense of work, but for now her work is about nurturing and relationships.

HANNAH

Every morning, Hannah gets out of bed before the alarm rings. She washes up and brushes her teeth. Brushing is not something she can do once for all time (although not brushing may eventually obviate the need for it once her teeth are rotted away). In other words, she needs to perform this task despite the fact that no matter how often she does it, the task will never be completely done. Brushing her teeth is both an ongoing relationship she has with a part of her body and a form of thanksgiving for its health, so it is right that the task should be ongoing.

Hannah sets the table for her family's breakfast, remembers to feed the cat, and checks whether the plants need water. These too are jobs that cannot be completed; rather, they are ongoing expressions of her connectedness. If she were to count up preparing some fifteen thousand breakfasts over her lifetime and changing the cat's litter box more than a thousand times, she might think she were undergoing some cruel and unusual punishment. But if she is told that she will give birth to two wonderful children who will have breakfast at home for the next twenty years until the last one goes off to college, that the husband she adores will continue to eat breakfast with her "as long as they both shall live," and that her cat will live a long and healthy cat life, then the same tasks can feel like a blessing.

Hannah does a final sweeping away of crumbs before heading off to her job, where her daily task is trying to clear off her desk. She imagines a clean desk but then realizes that if there were nothing for her to do, there probably wouldn't be a job for her either.

Work entails relationship and process. Some work has apparent stopping points, Hannah thinks; teachers, for example, have theirs at the end of every school year. But even as the teachers are closing the classroom doors on the last day, they have to prepare their roll book for the fall term. Court attorneys (to take an example from her actual job) have specific cases that come to trial and that, even with appeals, finally end. Hannah knows intellectually that those whose work just continues on and on can keep from being worn down by focusing on the process.

Hannah's meditation on her unending work came at a particularly difficult time in her life: Sarah's diabetes, which had been under control for years, suddenly flared up as her body underwent the changes of adolescence. Hannah was amazed when her meditating opened her up to one of those inexplicably joyous experiences. While thinking about her tasks as ceaseless, she suddenly felt herself in tune with the pulse of the universe. Afterward, she tried to find words to describe her experience.

Our work can be a form of prayer, and prayer is a way of being in relationship with God. Faithfulness to our work therefore has the potential to be transformative.

Call

We first meet the concept of call in the biblical calling of Abraham, Moses, and the prophets. The idea of being called has evolved from a purely religious application to one that includes specific abilities in secular fields. Hence *vocation* came to be understood as any profession we arrive at through something less serendipitous than the want ads.

The Worldview Behind Call

The worldview behind the idea of call changes our posture toward our work from active searching to receptive listening for direction. Someone who is out looking for a job and someone else who is responding to a call may be equally busy, but their energy is expended in different ways. When seeking a job, we network, write an impressive curriculum vitae, attend seminars. When answering a call, much of our effort goes into discerning both the nature of the call and the most authentic way to meet it. We may well be called to something beyond what we have ever imagined doing, so answering requires us to trust and to overcome fear.

Because call is a process, we usually cannot see beyond the initial stages. We really don't have to understand all that we are called to—we just have to be open. Along the way, we get indications of peace (even if we are called to something frightening or dangerous), love, and desire. We don't leave essential gifts behind but instead come to the call in our wholeness. For the first time, we can understand how all our disparate interests and talents fit together.

> SAM
> The call for Sam came when he was eleven, although he didn't recognize it for another decade. The day before he died, his *zayde* (grandfather) gave him a book; it was certainly not one he would have chosen, but Sam found himself

carrying it with him, as *Zayde* had done, and turning to it—occasionally at first, and later with increasing frequency. The book was a pocket edition of the psalms in English. The translation was old-fashioned and the cover was worn from where his grandfather had held it.

His bar mitzvah class intrigued him; he couldn't explain what it was that held his interest, but he found himself eager to attend class and mind carefully what was happening. His call came through interests that he didn't understand but to which he remained open. It was fully eight years after his bar mitzvah that he finally recognized where his interests were taking him, and he announced to his family his call to become a rabbi.

MARTIN

Martin's call came largely through his love of music. Only while he listened to Bach, Mozart, and the like did his internal critic stop its sniping and allow him to just give himself to the music. His call was not actually *to* music—that is, to become a musician—but *through* music, which helped him contact his own deepest feelings. The Indian Nobel laureate Sir Rabindranath Tagore may have had a similar experience in writing: "God respects me when I work, but God loves me when I sing."

Martin knew he had to experience the same openness and wholeness in his work as he experienced in music. He found it in college in an introductory psychology course, changed his major, and became a psychotherapist, a decision he has remained happy with for more than twenty years.

Not a One-Time Event

We continue to be called into ever deeper engagement, such that people in their forties, sixties, and eighties may experience being called to address different issues in the same line of work, to continue their education, or to reclaim gifts they left behind years earlier when they first entered the job market.

JANICE

Janice, the rabbi we met in the Introduction, has to be where the pain is. There were the usual number of illnesses and deaths in her suburban congregation, so it was more than ten years before she recognized that she still wasn't where she needed to be. She returned to school in the hope of invigorating her work. The courses put her more in touch with her sense that she was called to serve God—so the rabbinate was, indeed, the right response—but her call was specific, not generic. It took another three years before she realized her need to be closer to the pain of others. She is now head chaplain in a metropolitan hospital.

MARCIA

Prior to entering seminary, Marcia majored jointly in Judaic studies and art; yet her oil paintings were not specifically Jewish. Her paintings did show great dramatic flair and equal intensity, and they won praise from her teachers. She loved painting, but she knew that artists could rarely support themselves. She became a fine rabbinic student but like most of the students found herself much too busy between the rigors of coursework and her student pulpit to pursue her artistic inclinations.

Shortly before ordination, Marcia recalled the intensity, aliveness, and joy she felt when she was painting, even though five years had passed since she last picked up a brush. She spoke with her spiritual guide about mourning for "the road not taken," but her artistry did not die.

Behind her sense of loss lay an unexamined view of what God demanded of her. One phrase that she could translate, critique, and debate in her Bible class still held the power to affect her: "For the Lord your God is a jealous God." Did that mean serving God as a rabbi ruled out her ever painting? When her spiritual guide asked her what she would tell a congregant whose job cut her off from work, the unexamined assumptions about God's nature suddenly came to the fore. Not surprisingly, she was more sensitive to her hypothetical congregant than she had been to herself—but at least she could hear what she was saying. The image of God she presented to the hypothetical congregant was of one who wanted each of us to be fully alive, to use all our gifts—to rejoice.

As soon as Marcia handed in her senior thesis, she bought new paints and a few brushes, and one week before placement, she began her first oil painting in five years. She felt rusty, unsure she could still get lost in the process, but she began.

JON

Jon took early retirement from a job in the business world that allowed him to support his family in a very comfortable style. His daughters had both graduated from college and were now working; the mortgage was paid. He was only in his early fifties, but he could no longer justify the business grind knowing that it prevented him from giving his wife the attention he felt she deserved. He knew he wanted to leave his job, but he didn't know what he wanted to do next. As he put it, "It's as if I've been invited to leave Egypt but they forgot to tell me there's a Promised Land." What had he put on the back burner during those demanding years of supporting his family?

Suddenly, deeply moved, Jon recalled his student days and his passion for writing fiction. But he'd been extremely successful in business and wondered if he could accept being a rank beginner as a writer. Slowly he began writing. He'd complain that he was wasting time, but when asked, he maintained that he was still writing. Friends asked him what he was doing with his free time. "Nothing," he replied. By that careless remark he was denigrating his own—at this point, very dedicated—effort. He wasn't doing "nothing." He was working very hard and joyously; he just didn't feel like talking about it. Where was God in his writing? "Why, God is everywhere—in the energy I bring to writing, in the ideas I have. God is my audience. God is the joy I feel."

As in many a sense of call, things were not quite that simple. One morning, Jon said to himself despondently, "I love to write, but I'm just too old—no one starts at my age. My writing will never amount to anything, so what good is it?" Then he seriously considered the question himself: what was the good of his writing? When he thought about the product, he was right—he had never submitted anything for publication. But when he thought about the process, he began talking to his spiritual guide about his relationship to his grown daughters. He felt freer, more able to let go. He felt closer to his wife, who was very supportive of his writing. He found himself eager to get up in the morning and get to his desk.

But Jon thought, "Isn't my writing selfish? Shouldn't I be doing volunteer work?" Much of the problem, he realized, came from his happiness. Jon was much better at giving than receiving. He had spent many years meeting the needs of his family, but he flunked at just taking in the wonder around him. He felt he found God in and through his writing, as the cause of his ideas, as the source of his energy, and as his audience. So along with the joy he derived from his writing came gratitude that he could return to his first calling newly energized.

He still has friends who ask him what he's doing in his retirement. Some of his answers, though true, reveal only as much as he wants them to: "I'm working on the rhythm of language. I'm interested in the relationship of sound to meaning." He has also found two people with whom he can discuss his excitement about writing. He still wonders, from time to time, about submitting a story or an essay for publication, and he may submit one that's based on his recollection of a camping trip, but only once he's satisfied with it.

Each of these callings can be described as joyous, but are the decisions to follow them responses to God's call? We are all called into being, called further into becoming all we can be and, ultimately, into meaningful work. We are called by love, desire, and delight. But we have unique natures and unique gifts, so we are called through our own giftedness. One person's way is not someone else's, and even though we can find encouragement in watching others answer their own call, we need to find our own work, which we can discover only by staying open to our own feelings. The greatest obstacle to our progress is usually fear, particularly the fear that we don't know how to receive. But in fact, we are receiving gifts constantly in the form of blessings. We need only make ourselves aware of them: "So long thy power hath blest me, sure it still / Will lead me on" (Newman, "The Pillar of the Cloud," 1905). Gratitude reduces fear and increases our confidence. Once we recognize and acknowledge our giftedness, we begin to realize how absolutely we can put our trust in God and can delight in surrendering control.

Joy in Work

One thread that runs through all these stories of people finding their work is a sense of joy. Joy is a deeper, more lasting feeling than the immediate pleasure of the senses. Our call stretches us, and we feel a bit uneasy, but we are called to greater life, to wholeness, and to joy. Joy is consistent with pain (Janice found her place close to the pain). It is also consistent with hard work and discipline (Jon's daily writing, Marcia's painting). Indeed, the more we explore call, the more we are led to joy.

Freedom

Frankl wrote about the men who walked through the concentration camps "comforting others, giving away their last piece of bread. They may have been few in number," he writes, but they offer proof that everything can be taken from us but one thing: "the last of the human freedoms—to choose one's attitude in any given circumstances, to choose one's own way" (1973, p. 86).

Answering our call means identifying with our own most authentic nature. The call is always our own growing out of our essence and desire. And yet we often ignore our own deepest good or do work that counters our nature. But willfulness is not freedom; it is instead shutting ourselves off from discovering our true work. We do that for a reason—every action we take has a cause—but we do it unaware of our real nature.

When we do act out of our own authentic being and not because of something external (that is, no one is forcing us), then we are expressing our freedom. An action triggered by peer pressure, advertising, or unresolved issues from our past may appear to be free, but in reality it is simply unexamined. Perhaps we think we're free because we're conscious of our wishes and appetites and unconscious of the causes that have led us to these desires. So our apparent freedom lies only in acting to satisfy our appetites—many of which may have been created by Madison Avenue or the media. But we find our real freedom when we are no longer enslaved by desires for riches, status, or pleasure of the senses, and our actions grow out of our own identity.

Destiny

Etty Hillesum, who has been described as an adult Anne Frank, was twenty-seven years old when the Nazis occupied Amsterdam during World War II. For the next two years, she kept notebooks, which were published in 1983 as *An Interrupted Life*. The notebooks show how Hillesum, in the midst of suffering and apparent chaos, could experience increased meaning and freedom. In a series of journal entries, she explores the relationship she sees between freedom and destiny:

> Everything is chance, or nothing is chance. If I believed the
> first, I would be unable to live on, but I am not yet fully con-
> vinced of the second.
>
> It is a slow and painful process, this striving after true
> inner freedom.

> Something has happened to me and I don't know if it's just
> a passing mood or something crucial. It is as if I had been
> pulled back, abruptly by my roots, and had become a little
> more self-reliant and independent. Last night, cycling through
> cold dark Lairesse Straat—if only I could repeat everything I
> babbled out then! "God, take me by Your hand, I shall follow
> You dutifully and not resist too much. . . . I shall follow
> wherever Your hand leads me and shall try not to be afraid"
> [pp. 29, 56, 64].

Hillesum found her freedom in her growing response to being called: "And I listen to myself, allow myself to be led, not by anything on the outside, but by what wells up from within" (p. 81).

Her discussions of God are based on her experiences; though they may seem contradictory—"God take me by Your hand," and "I . . . allow myself to be led . . . by what wells up from within"—both statements describe her experience of God. What we take to be God's will is the same as our deepest authenticity: "Before I created you in the womb, I selected you; Before you were born, I consecrated you; I appointed you a prophet concerning the nations" (Jer. 1:5).

> I have the feeling that I have a destiny, in which the events are
> strung significantly together.
>
> Yesterday Lippmann and Rosenthal. Robbed and hounded,
> and yet? So much joy, human joy, more than that pale-faced,
> jittery, plundering official could imagine. And the recurrent
> feeling that one is complete master of one's inner resources,
> which grow stronger by the day.
>
> Instead of living an accidental life, you feel, deep down,
> that you have grown mature enough to accept your "destiny."
> Mature enough to take your "destiny" upon yourself [Hille-
> sum, 1983, pp. 91, 114, 136].

Hillesum could radiate joy while undergoing unimaginable horrors because she felt she had understood, accepted, and fulfilled her destiny, which she credits both to God and to her own inner resources. We can glimpse the joy that comes with following our own destiny by noticing with gratitude the plain old, ordinary joys of living this life with attentiveness.

The most seductive phrase in the English language is, "I need you." We love to be needed, we yearn to make a contribution. Ultimately we don't seek the easy job; we want work that stretches us and calls forth our best efforts and our talent.

Our work expresses our destiny because we were created to be ourselves. When we stop trying to be someone else or to act according to an external standard rather than our deepest nature, we are doing God's will. Part of our daily morning prayer, "The soul which you have given me is a pure one," reminds us that we can discover God's will for us if we keep the soul plain and grow still. We were created to be rather than not to be, and we were created to be who we are and not other. The logical conclusion is that we have a destiny. The idea of destiny fits in beautifully with the idea of a nonrandom, meaningful Creation, and it is totally compatible with freedom. Our destiny is to live out our lives fittingly and appropriately; it is not something foreordained or automatic.

Meaning

Our lives are serious and urgent. Our choice of occupation should accord with our sense of work, or call. We are called by God into the fullness of life in the native language of our soul, that is, in our giftedness. Our call may discomfit or even endanger us, and yet we experience it as a great gift because it is always a call to meaning. Once we are committed to meaning, we no longer feel that we live in a world of randomness and chance. Each of us is unique and irreplaceable, with a specific role to play.

Opening ourselves up to being called and beginning to examine the theological implications of the call can lead us to transform our values. How insignificant this year's fashions and fads seem in the light of a growing realization that life is meaningful—that it is a great design in which we have a serious role to play.

A Theology of Work

But what is the theology that emerges from these experiences? What have the people whose stories we've just read learned about the nature of their own freedom and destiny, their sense of self, meaning, and God? They have come to believe that we are all created with a mission, and they need to identify what it is, what gives meaning to their lives, a calling, a way to respond to God's gifts.

Some callings—such as a unique gift for science, art, or music—may show up clearly, while others may appear more subtly, such as the gift to heal and comfort those in sickness and pain. No one is dispensable; there are no "extras" in this cast, since each of us has been called into being and into meaning. Sam and Jennifer, and Marcia, and Jon, and Janice, and Etty Hillesum were all able to change from actively searching to passively but attentively waiting to discern. At least one of them felt great despair because she didn't want to do what she had been trained for. It was not a question of being unable to work, but rather of failing to recognize where their unique talents could be employed.

ELAINE

Elaine was very happy with her husband and with being the mother of two bright girls. Yet she felt despair when the second course that she was to teach as an adjunct professor in her community college was canceled because of inadequate enrollment. Suddenly she realized how deeply she needed to teach, and the need spurred her on to continue work toward a Ph.D. She found a positive use for a negative event, and her despair served as a road marker in finding her way.

The Three Central Questions

In addition to meeting our needs for physical sustenance, work really addresses three central questions.

• *Is there a place for us?* We are always wondering whether we are wanted or intruding, whether we are on the inside or trespassing in the world. Judaism addresses the specific question in two contexts. "In the beginning," the scene is lovingly set with all that is needed to sustain our being before we are called into existence. Then, in the years following the Exodus from Egypt, we learn the seven tasks forbidden on the Sabbath. When we recognize that God has performed each of those tasks for us, we know that we were prepared for and nurtured in our being.

• *Are we needed?* We need to receive, but is there something we can contribute? We work both to prove ourselves (mainly to ourselves) and to help others. We know we can make a contribution.

• *Are we loved?* We want to be loved for being, not just for doing, so that is why what we do is only part of our identity and why the tasks forbidden to us on the Sabbath are so important.

Work is, of course, about doing. Through our work, we come to recognize all that has been done to allow us to be and to endure. We also learn that we can participate in the web of contribution. And work is a place where we can encounter God.

6

CLAIMING OUR BODIES

I praise you for I am awesomely,
wondrously made.

—Psalms 139:14

HOW DOES OUR PHYSICAL BEING fit into our theology? We Jews believe that the material world was readied for us before our creation, so every morning we celebrate and give thanks that our consciousness has been restored to this world. But how does gratefulness for the physical world relate to our bodily self.

To answer this question, we must first ask who we are: a mind in a body (that is, an enfleshed set of memories, ideas, and values) or a bodily self that is more than a vessel holding our "real" self?

Transposed Heads

Would you be a different person if you had a different body? Your body shapes your experience of the world. A small child tends to notice things on the ground simply because the child is closer to the ground. If we suffer from a disability in one of our senses, another sense becomes dominant; thus, if we become blind we are likely to perceive the world in terms of sound and touch to replace our missing sense of sight.

Thomas Mann addresses the head-body question in a novel, *The Transposed Heads.* The character Sita is married to Shridman, a gentle thinker, but is attracted to his best friend, Nanda, who possesses a strong body. When the two men sacrifice themselves to the goddess Kali, she agrees to restore their lives if Sita will reattach their heads to their bodies. Sita does, but in her haste she puts the kind head of her husband onto the muscular body of his friend.

Bewildered as to which of these men is really Sita's husband, the three go together to a holy man. The holy man declares the one who has the scholar's head and the friend's body to be the true husband. To Sita, this seems like the ideal solution: she now has the gentle husband with the strong physique of the friend. But in time, the head and its habits return the new body to the flabbiness of the old. Sita, married to the man with the husband's head and the friend's former body, finds herself also loving the man with the friend's head and the husband's former body, because the head transformed that body as well.

Mann's novel shows that love embraces the whole, not just its parts. But it also demonstrates that inexorably the mind belongs to its body and not someone else's. Your mind has the body it needs; put another way, you have the body appropriate for your identity.

The Voice of Jacob but the Hands of Esau

Following Mann's example, we could try a similar thought experiment using a line from the story of Jacob stealing the paternal blessing that was meant for his older twin brother, Esau: "The voice is the voice of Jacob, yet the hands are the hands of Esau" (Gen. 27:22). In the biblical account, Jacob tricks Isaac, now blind, into giving him the firstborn's blessing by disguising himself in Esau's clothes and covering his arms with goat hair.

Let's take this situation a bit further. Suppose that Esau and Jacob, fraternal twins, differed more profoundly than in their hairiness. Let's change Jacob for Jacqueline, a woman. Now it becomes a very different story. We can easily understand why Isaac, in the heavily male-dominated society, would favor his son, Esau. We can see as well why the daughter, Jacqueline, would hang around the tents of her mother. Rebecca, the twins' mother, believes (in our version) that as long as men determine the line of the covenant there will be sacrifices and grief. Also, she realizes that the presence of hair on Esau's arms differentiates him from his sister, just as this same physical characteristic typically separates man from woman. So through disguising Jacqueline she helps her daughter receive the blessing that Isaac would otherwise give to his son Esau.

Most people hearing this variation on the biblical story express some confusion, and some even get angry, but no one remains unmoved by the change of sex. Whatever response we may have suggests that our bodies do influence how we experience the world, and one very important factor is whether we are male or female. But we should not conclude that biology is destiny, because we can sort out—at least to some extent—what is cultural and what is biological. Surprisingly to some, much of what we used to ascribe to genes is now regarded as societal.

Gender Differences

Role differences between male and female play out to extremes in the story of Jacob's daughter, Dinah (Gen. 34). The male is supposed to journey and see the larger world. Since Jacob dwells around his mother's tent, she and Isaac follow custom by sending him off to the home of Rebecca's brother in Paddan-Aram. But, Dinah too, goes on a journey, to visit the daughters of the land. She fares less well than her father, the patriarch: she is raped by Shechem. Incredibly, the rape is her own fault, at least according to Rabbinic commentary, because by setting out on a trip she violates the custom that wandering is reserved for males and forms part of their coming into full selfhood. Wandering by females is impermissible in biblical society.

Alterations

You change your body, and your body undergoes changes by itself. You color your hair or try a whole new hairstyle. You gain weight, lose weight, grow a beard, pierce your ears. Such changes to the body are external, affecting the parts that make up your appearance. Other changes may be more internal ("I don't feel like myself—I think I'm coming down with the flu"). You may also recall the sense of estrangement you felt in adolescence, when your body was changing so rapidly that you didn't quite know who you were. As you get older, you recognize the disjunction between the face you see in the mirror and the young person you still feel yourself to be. All these changes feed into the question of locating which aspects of the body constitute the self.

In developing our interests and values, we deliberately train and discipline the physical self. We learn to carry ourselves as a dancer does or to hear and discriminate musical timbres. We teach ourselves to see as only a thoughtful artist can, and we strengthen specific muscles we need to jump higher or run faster. We learn to breathe properly for singing, running, and giving birth. In doing all this training, are we merely developing the tool we use, or are we developing the self?

The Body and Truth

One possible clue may lie in the relationship between the body and the truth of being. We learn how to lie, and even how to lie to ourselves. But viscerally, we know the truth. Being honest means being grounded in Absolute truth; it also means being grounded in our bodies. The tensing in the back of the neck, the sudden upset stomach, the inopportune headache are nuisances, but they are also gifts, warning us of something toxic in ourselves or our environment. That the body doesn't lie suggests that it possesses intimate knowledge of ourselves that only the self can have.

> SARAH
> Sarah's neuropathy, as we learned, was related to her dia-
> betes, but on any particular day her symptoms were better or
> worse depending on what she was doing and with whom.
> Eventually, she figured out that her illness was giving her an
> excuse to restrict her socializing. She realized her greatest
> relief when she was seeing people she cared about and doing
> things she loved to do. Gradually, she cut way back on the
> time she spent with people who ranked low on her fondness
> meter. She also tried to increase the number of gratifying
> activities in her life, while keeping "downers" to a minimum.
> Finally she came to believe that her neuropathy actually func-
> tioned as a gift, a special sense that told her when she was
> going in the right direction and that warned her against being
> led astray. She liked to think that she was developing a sort of
> theology of the body.

A Theology of the Body

A theology of the body, like all theologies, must deal with the fundamental questions of who we are, what we can know, and how we fit into reality as a whole. The question of who we are is especially complex in a theology of the body because, even though it was obvious to our Jewish ancestors that as human beings we are ensouled bodies, our long Diaspora has led us into prolonged contact with dualism and subsequent estrangement from our bodies. A theology of the body must directly address our personal identity. It must also examine how our bodies take part in the knowing process. How do we weigh the evidence of our senses? Are our bodies obstacles to our knowing or sensitive instruments to help us navigate through the world? How you view your body directly conditions how you feel about bodies in general, including the body of the physical world.

The Body and Story

Our personal story begins at a particular time, in a particular place; from the start it is concretized. The story is the tale of the self as an embodied individual being.

> REGINA
> Regina, so skilled in theater, had an earlier, less successful time as a fiction writer. It was painful for her to discover that although novels are about ideas, disembodied ideas such as the good, the true, and the beautiful hardly make for interesting fiction. Readers want a story with characters living out situations that demonstrate ideas. So Regina could have written how good this relationship is, how true that person's way of living, how beautiful someone else's simple way of life. But she had little interest in making up and describing characters, so stories about embodied people were just not her metier.

Through our story, which is the verbal or mental aspect of the self, we discover its physical counterpart in our actions, including some that we call rituals. We can think of rituals as the physical analog to stories, as ways we construct reality and make meaning. If the dichotomy between belief and action, or mind and body, is false, we need to discover the rituals that exhibit, express, or foster our beliefs. Through our rituals, we narrate our existence and create a vision of life.

The Body in Love

We are taught to love virtues, values, and ways of thinking, but we find ourselves drawn to a smile, a touch, a voice. Judaism has given us the Song of Songs to guide us in confronting society's separation between spirituality and sex. You can learn, through the Song of Songs, to delight in your body because your beloved delights in it despite its imperfections. But the eroticism of the Song of Songs has a meaning beyond simple sexuality. Eros is the core longing of the self for connecting with others. It has been said that the door to the invisible must be visible. Similarly, the door to the abstract must be tangible. Love begins with the visible, the tangible, the embodied; Freud characterized the force of Eros as that which seeks to combine organic substances into ever larger unities.

The Body at Work

If you are not physically engaged with this world, life cannot have meaning. Even if your work consists largely of reading, analyzing, thinking, and other activities that we classify as cerebral, "work" is not done until you've committed fingers to keyboard, pencil to paper, or voice to sound pickup—in other words, until you have incarnated those thoughts in some way that finds material expression in this world. Only through your body's actions in the world can your ideas be realized. We are here not only to experience how good this world is and to express gratitude but also to experience how broken the world is and to help mend it through the best uses of the self. In feeding the hungry, clothing the naked, or healing the sick, we are God's hands carrying out those tasks.

The Body and Our Encounter with God

Even though we may find traces of the holy in and through the wonders of nature, we ourselves are wonders of nature. This wonder has aspects of both beauty and terror. That we are intricate and cannot fully fathom ourselves arouses our fear because we feel outside of our own control. But what we cannot control is still controlled; we live, and for that we are grateful. In our daily prayer service, we affirm the unity of mind and body and see both as being renewed daily when we awake from sleep. This process of noticing, or stopping in the regular round of life to appreciate our return from sleep to waking, or in the well-ordered functioning of our bodies, becomes one of the places we can encounter God. In this very personal experience of a greater control, we find a sense of God's presence and concern.

> FLORENCE
> Facing a life-threatening illness in her teens, Florence has made it a regular practice to survey her body and recognize its strengths, its weaknesses, and her own sense of God's presence in and through the intricate workings of her being. At the time of her recovery, she wanted to forget her body and make up for the time lost to her hospital stay and convalescence. She was tired of regular blood tests and weary of the

concern she saw in her parents' eyes. She just wanted to get on with living. But without consciously intending to, she changed. Those long hours on the ward and later in bed at home made her less interested in the scores of the school team games or the position of a particular song on the music charts. Even though her strength returned, she found herself needing to withdraw for an hour or more each afternoon, just to have time alone. It was during this time that she began the practice of surveying her body.

What began with a sense of terror—checking for any recurring symptoms—became for Florence a ritual of gratitude and praise. If her restored health was a gift, then there must be a giver. Slowly she became aware that the time she spent alone with herself was actually time she spent with God.

The Body and Prayer

The content of many prayers reflects the reality of our having bodies. In the morning prayer, for example, we begin with the first wonder we perceive, our own bodily well-being. We thank God for our most prosaic daily needs: "Blessed are you, Adonai our God, sovereign of the universe, who has fashioned us in wisdom and created in us many orifices and vessels. It is revealed and known before the throne of your glory, that if one of these be opened, or one of these be closed, it would be impossible to exist and to stand before you. Blessed are you, Adonai, who heals all flesh and does wondrously."

This blessing, which is recited only after we discharge our bodily functions, helps bring every physical act within the orbit of religion. Without the physical act of excretion, we could not exist and stand before God's countenance.

> RUTH
> Ruth had special reason to meditate on this blessing because she suffered from colitis. She watched her diet, took medication, and tried to discover what her body might be telling her about the stresses in her life. She decided to add to the traditional blessing her own prayer to her sphincter muscle, giving thanks for the times it works as it is supposed to and encouragement when it doesn't. As a result of her blessing, she was able to stop warring with her body and start recognizing its marvels.

The Body and Suffering

"We suffer in so far as we are part of Nature," Spinoza wrote, a part "that cannot be conceived by itself nor without the other parts" (1883/1949, IV.2). It is because we are only a part of a larger system that we find ourselves constantly bumping up against other beings who compete for life-sustaining resources. The truth that we are "part of Nature" is first apprehended bodily.

The body is an aspect of the self that is subject to suffering (as well as pleasure), but as we saw in Chapter Four, suffering isn't only bodily. We often exacerbate physical suffering by anticipating it, by how we interpret it, and by the many unanswered questions it raises. For example, fear of pain can cause us to distance ourselves from our bodies and thereby lose the possibility for joy as well. We also lose whatever insight can be gained by attending to pain, weakness, and limitation. In drawing out our theology, it is useful to contemplate what we know when we are physically weak that we do not know when we are strong. From the biblical perspective, Jacob needed to be wounded before he could become Israel: "The sun rose upon him as he passed Penuel, limping on his hip" (Gen. 32:32). It also was necessary for the favored Joseph to be enslaved and tortured before he could save the lives of Egyptians and Israelites in a coming famine. And the four hundred years of servitude in Egypt followed by forty years of wandering in the wilderness were necessary to forge a faith that would preserve its followers for millennia to come. We often learn something through pain that we would not learn through joy.

The obvious question to ask is, What do we learn through suffering? Before we can answer, we must accept that what we learn cannot be transmitted verbally or vicariously and that the suffering is by, and for the benefit of, the sufferer. Our identity undergoes a transformation through which we learn who we are, how we live, and how we *are* lived. It may be our pain, yet we neither cause it nor control it. Logically I cannot feel your pain—even if by some bizarre experiment I could attach your wound to my nerve cells—because as soon as *I* feel it, it becomes *my* pain. In a profound sense, my pain is part of what it is to be me.

The Body and Death

All persons are mortal; Socrates is a person; therefore Socrates is mortal. This syllogism is the first one taught in logic classes, and it is the first syllogism of life. In other words, life is a terminal illness: you cannot get out of this world alive. How do you deal with this seemingly morbid idea?

One response, as you know, is to alienate yourself from your embodied self so that what eventually dies is not really "yourself." But how do we deal with the inevitability of death if we are more in touch with our bodies? We know that after death, the body breaks down, so apart from any religious teaching, we may believe in the immortality of the soul but not in the resurrection of the body.

Unlike the ancient Greeks, Jews have no concept of a soul that is separate from the body. In the Jewish view, our consciousness has been shaped for dealing with *this* world and *this* life, and we cannot relate to an immortal disembodied soul. Believing that all our ideas, memories, loves, and interests have been bodily shaped, we may hold on to the hope that our more rarified thoughts must surely be nonphysical. Albert Einstein, one of the greatest thinkers of the twentieth century, reported that he had the theory of relativity in his muscles for three months before he could find a symbol system through which to express it. Even our language for relating to God is physical: "O taste and see that Adonai is good"; "In your behalf my heart says, 'Seek my face!'"; "Pay heed, My people and I will speak"; "You will be covered with God's pinions, you will find refuge under God's wings." One might argue that the Bible speaks the language of the people and therefore must represent God in a way we can understand. One way is through the body.

The Body and Community

Our first community is physical, set in the environment that surrounds us—in the biblical formulation, a garden in which all needs were met; now it is wherever we find ourselves. Our environment includes our physical and mental health, which is the primary medium for our basic way of feeling and being in our surroundings. This environment includes our work—even Adam and Eve tended the Garden of Eden. There, all of Creation is said to have cooperated in the balance of the Garden, though beyond its borders, work included struggle and opposition.

When Adam and Eve left the Garden, God made for them their first set of clothes, garments of skin (Gen. 3:21). Clothing, though external and seemingly trivial, plays a significant role in community. It is the first public announcement of who we are and what we stand for. In a war, the uniform may be the only part of the enemy that we see, or choose to see.

Our environment of clothing and other possessions has grown quite complex since the nomadic lifestyle of the Israelites. Even two or three generations ago, our ancestors crossed the ocean carrying only those belongings they could fit into two suitcases or bundles. We can see such suitcases and some of their contents in the museum on Ellis Island in New York City, where many immigrants first set foot in the New World. One way to gain a sense of the self in its material environment is to pose the question our ancestors' suitcases raise for us: If we had to re-create our lives in a new place, which things would we take with us?

Having established some kind of setting, we can now look at the relationships that constitute the special part of our environment that we think of as community: beginning with ourselves (although it takes some time to distinguish the infant self from that of the primary nurturer), moving on to other beings, and then considering a special other person with whom we choose to live out our lives. We read in Genesis that "it is not good that Adam should be alone." The story then expands to cover the dysfunctional first family, opens out to include members of the tribe, broadens to take in other Jews, and finally encompasses everyone. Just as our notion of community expands, so the daily prayer service goes from our individual needs and concerns to those of the Jewish people and the rest of Creation.

Coming to Know the Body

The world as we first experience it is physical. As we grow to maturity, a world of ideas takes hold, often to the extent that we have to reclaim the physical reality of the world and of our own bodies. We get a chance to reclaim our bodies as we raise an infant. In our culture, we pay little attention to smell; it is not considered polite to notice or mention it. But the smell of the infant is sweet and appealing, drawing us in. We learn to offer only the slightest touch to the soft skin and to feel the small head of very fine hair. The sound of the baby's laughter rings out like a tiny, clear bell— no cynicism, no cruelty. A baby is all body: when it is sad, unhappiness reigns from the top of its head to the tips of its curled toes, and no aspect of the self lies outside the total picture of distress. And oh, when a baby is happy! How long has it been since we have partaken so fully of happiness?

> BEN
> All of Ben's family was involved in the first analysis of infancy: he has this one's chin, that one's nose, another one's coloring. In each aspect of his physical being—and as far as anyone knew, that was all he had in those early days—his relatives were seeking clues as to whom he resembled and who he would turn out to be.

Ben, meanwhile, was fixed on the signals that came from within his body: hunger, heat, cold, satisfaction. After some weeks, he also began to notice signals that came from his interactions with the world: wet, hard, sharp, bright, funny. With the passing months, there were songs he came to recognize. He reacted to the crunch of autumn leaves and their smell as he sat down hard on the leaf pile, he felt the wind on his face, and he experienced the sight, touch, and taste of snowflakes.

From taste ("Oh taste and see that Adonai is good"), he gingerly moved on to touch—the soft fur of the family cat. Crayons. It hadn't occurred to him to draw something that was outside himself. He created great swatches of color and—when no one was looking—he wanted to chew the crayons. Does blue taste better than yellow?

Somehow fear has entered in and distorted our theology. Even the wonder of our bodies arouses fear, so that we avoid thinking about the million separate acts and conditions needed for us to maintain life; after all, we have no control over them, and one of them might fail. But if we do take note of them, we find ourselves opening up to gratitude, love, and trust. Psychologist Ernest Becker (1973) has suggested that we can live decisively only by not noticing how miraculous the world is, because our world is incomprehensible, so full of beauty, majesty, and terror, that if we could fully perceive it all we would be too paralyzed to act.

The Body and Change

Our theology can never be complete—can never explain everything—but our trust can grow. Looking back to our own earlier years, we discover God and see meaning in events we could not understand at the time. Although confusion may linger in the face of changes ahead, we can remember the trust we once had that indeed turned out to have been warranted. If we do reach the point that we can trust now, can we trust that even our aging and decline are meaningful? Our maturing made sense, although at the time, we would have been happy to stop, as Christopher Robin wanted to:

> But now I am Six, I'm as clever as clever,
> So I think I'll be six now for ever and ever.
>
> —A. A. Milne, "Now We Are Six" (1955)

Change is hard—always has been, probably always will be, especially when it appears to bring no improvement. But as change itself grows more and more familiar, we begin to recognize and accept it. As children, we are fascinated by stories about giants, seeing them as stand-ins for grownups. We can't understand how we could ever turn into adults, who seem like members of an entirely different species. Then, when we are grown, we find it hard to believe that we will ever become old. But gradually, we recognize how our aging is connected to the lives we've led, the interests and activities we've stressed.

Nowhere does change touch us more intimately than what we experience in our own bodies. We look at the boundless energy of children and joke, "Too bad we can't bottle it and use it in old age," and "Youth is wasted on the young." The dictum in Ecclesiastes, "To everything there is a season, and a time for every purpose under Heaven," describes the situation without explaining it. So we are left to figure out for ourselves what function is served by our aging.

Aging

Philosopher Robert Grudin has observed that change "fools our sentinels and undermines our defenses"; we "search for it around us and find too late that it has occurred within us" (1982, p. 6). Even so, we expect certain changes to occur, and we even imagine how we might proceed with dignity and a kind of noble stoicism, only to encounter a loss that was not part of our dramatic agenda. Etty Hillesum wrote, "I shall have to learn this lesson too, and it will be the most difficult of all, Oh God, to bear the suffering you have imposed on me and not just the suffering I have chosen for myself" (1983, p. 231).

The gains of old age can include the ability to distinguish appearance from reality and the opportunity to encounter God. The fact that aging leads to death raises a question we push aside as we get on with life: Is death the meaningless end of a meaningful life? Or, put differently, can we find meaning in death?

The biblical portrait of King David begins by showing him as the young shepherd boy who slays the giant Goliath with a stone from his slingshot. He goes on to be the sweet singer for the troubled King Saul, and in battle, when Saul slays thousands, David slays tens of thousands. He becomes king, marries numerous wives, and fathers sons and daughters. But then we read:

> King David was now old, advanced in years; and though they
> covered him with bedclothes, he never felt warm. His
> courtiers said to him, "Let a young virgin be sought for my
> lord the king to wait upon your majesty and be his attendant;
> and let her lie in your bosom, and my lord the king will be

warm." So they looked for a beautiful girl throughout the territory of Israel. They found Abishag the Shunammite and brought her to the king. The girl was exceedingly beautiful. She became the king's attendant and waited upon him; but the king was not intimate with her [1 Kings 1:1–4].

King David has lost his sexual power, his political power, even the capacity to maintain his body heat. Here we are shown the biblical figure, until then young and virile, in the final days of his life. Can we make some sense out of this trajectory?

The story of King David should lead us to ask ourselves what our own aging is about. Years pass, we find ourselves middle-aged, and although time itself appears to keep speeding up, the rapid transformations that characterized our youth have slowed down—so much, in fact, that we may think that our bodies are not so transitory after all. But then, the physical changes of aging make us see our bodies in a radically new way. Where once we leaped from our beds in the morning, we now find that getting up takes longer and requires more effort. No longer are height or strength, speed or agility very important, as smaller motions that used to appear insignificant now claim our attention. We marvel at our body's wisdom; indeed, we can let it serve as our pillar of cloud if we can discern what it is trying to tell us. It tells us whom we like and whom we don't by its visceral responses; it tells us when we are really unhappy despite our friends' exclaiming how happy we must be; it speaks to us through little bursts of energy, periods of relaxation, and a sense of physical well-being, while also warning us of problems by means of aches, pains, and fatigue.

In our youth, we are proud of ignoring the pillar of cloud and we revel in our stoicism. We don't let little things get us down. In middle age, we stock up on an arsenal of Band-Aids, pain killers, antacids, lotions, and ointments that keep us moving past trouble spots. How might our lives look if we were to take the body's wisdom seriously twenty or thirty years earlier than we do? For one thing, we wouldn't need to regret all the times we blocked the body's wisdom from reaching and affecting us. But the call doesn't stop, the pillar of cloud continues to lead, and it's never too late to explore how aging can still be an adventure and a glorious fruition.

CONSTANCE

Constance, who is eighty-five years old and going strong, sees aging as the culmination of her life. The desert has weathered and tempered her, but she stands witness to a life lived in deepening relationship with God, shining with a new happiness that old age has brought. At last she has overcome guilt and self-hatred. Living fully in the present, she accepts whatever comes, including the knowledge of her own mortality. Pain and grief for her are as real as they are for everyone; she deeply feels genuine loss and sorrow as one by one her relatives, friends, and acquaintances take ill and die off. But although she doesn't deny pain, she faces each new day with renewed joy in life, because however great her pain, the joy is deeper still.

The Body and the Mind

Despite the best efforts of Judaism to accept body and mind as two manifestations of one and the same being, the dualism that sees them as two separate entities keeps cropping up in our thinking and writing.

REGINA
Regina discovered her own dualistic view. "Once," she told a spirituality group, "I fancied myself a writer and set out to write a novel. Not one to pick something up and then drop it after a few dry days, I lived the story and spent every moment for an entire year thinking about it. At the end of that time, I was unable to give a physical description of the main character. I then rationalized that I was writing from that character's perspective, so of course I wouldn't be looking at myself, but rather, using myself to look at everything else. And I had, in fact, described the village in which the character lived, the texture of her clothing, the smell of her kitchen. But that character told me more about myself than I wanted to admit: that I regularly think of myself as disembodied."

Her remark brought forth many affirming nods, and then, one by one, others in the group described their discomfort with their own bodies, sometimes to the extent of disowning their physical selves.

JENNIFER
Jennifer told the group of shopping for some computer software. She noticed someone who looked vaguely familiar. She turned to look more closely—something about the posture, the gestures—and then realized with a shock that she was looking at her own reflection in a mirror. She herself was that vaguely familiar woman! She reported having been so shaken that she ran out of the store. Later, she sat quietly over a cup

of coffee and tried to figure out how her own body could be
only vaguely familiar to herself.

TAMAR

In a session with her spiritual adviser, Tamar described her
first visit to a gym since leaving college. She approached the
building with trepidation—she had never liked gyms—and
with the attitude that exercise was a kind of purgatory where
small-boned women were sent to avoid osteoporosis. She
didn't hate her body, which was basically healthy and ener-
getic (indeed, it had served her well), but she was far from
accepting it fully. It felt strange beginning to love her body
now that she had entered her sixties.

Can we really appreciate what we have, she thought, only
when we fear losing it? She used to think of her body as other
people's first introduction to her. Now she saw it from within,
with renewed appreciation perhaps, but also with a new feeling of terror, because so many friends and acquaintances were
experiencing their bodies as a place of suffering and a gateway to death. She thought of Sandra with her biopsy, Linda's
husband's bypass surgery—finitude, mortality. But she knew
that disowning her body would not make her less vulnerable,
so she entered the gym and scanned the row of torture racks
known as exercise machines.

She studied the beautifully toned body of a blonde, twenty-
something woman with a perfect figure and almost ran
screaming out of the place. But at least, she consoled herself,
her children and grandchildren would not wait until their sixties to consciously inhabit their bodies. The younger generation thinks of running, stretching, and other exercise with
some degree of pleasure.

RON

Ron thought his spiritual life was completely separate from
his bodily life. Of course, he recognized the role his body
played on Yom Kippur, the holiest day of the Jewish calendar.
Knowing that it would be twenty-five hours before he'd have
any more to eat or drink, he always ate too much before sun-
down and took one last gulp of water, leaving him with a
bloated feeling.

He'd enter the dazzling synagogue, brilliant with its white
covering for the ark and *bima* (podium) and the white robes
of the rabbi and cantor. Everyone was dressed to the nines,

except that many of the congregants stood in sneakers, running shoes, or socks, following the rule to avoid leather footwear on Yom Kippur, as they did also on the Ninth of Av and when sitting *shiva*. The relationship between Yom Kippur and these two mourning occasions, the first for the destruction of the Temple and the second for the death of an immediate family member, was not lost on Ron. The absence of leather helps keep us grounded. How tempting it is to flee this material world in the midst of such sorrow, or in the case of Yom Kippur, such religious fervor. All physical pleasures are forbidden on Yom Kippur, not just eating and drinking but also bathing (no wake-up shower!) and sex. The body is treated as if it were dead—even to the extent of dressing it in a *kittel* (shroud)—to be reclaimed only after it has been cleansed.

Sated from his pre-fast excesses, Ron usually felt no hunger on Yom Kippur morning, although force of habit nagged him into craving his regular morning tea and buttered toast. Why, he wondered, on the most spiritual day of the whole year was he being forced to be so conscious of his own body? He wanted to lose himself in prayer, reciting the long confession of sins. But to his embarrassment, he listened to the rumbling of his stomach—or was it the stomach of the person standing next to him? In the afternoon, he longed to give his full attention to the chanting of the Book of Jonah, but a dull headache was forming behind his eyes.

In the end, Ron understood: "Afflicting my body gives me a perspective on its role in my normal life. On Yom Kippur, I am directed to treat my body as if it were dead, and as a result of this process, my whole life and value system are shaken up and transformed."

Physical Aspects of the Holidays

Ron's account stimulated a lively discussion in his study group about how each of the Jewish holidays had some physical component: building a *sukkah* (a booth in which the family eats during the feast of Tabernacles), taking in the smells and sights of Hanukah candles burning, cleaning and preparing the house for Passover, or staying awake all night to study on Shavuot (Pentecost), which commemorates the revelation of the Torah at Sinai. We're supposed to "taste and see that Adonai is good," so to really get at our theology we need to do more than just read the *siddur*, or prayer book. We also need to try out recipes from holiday cookbooks; taste *teiglach,* or honey cakes, on Rosh ha-Shanah and hear the blast of the *shofar* (ram's horn); use our tools and carpentry skills to build a *sukkah* and taste the pine needles that fall into our soup; smell the *latkes* (potato pancakes) on Hanukah, the *hamentaschen* (poppyseed cookies) on Purim, and the thousand and one smells of Passover—the list is endless.

As Hannah realized, Judaism is more physical than we usually give it credit for. Food is physical, smell is physical, as are sight, sound, shaking the *lulav* (palm frond), smelling the *etrog* (citrus fruit), eating the *maror* (bitter herb), so that the bitterness of slavery is given a physical rather than a theoretical analogy. We can find part of the meaning of a holiday in the intense physical preparation for it that we undertake.

We find similar physical acts described in the Torah. According to Leviticus, the consecration ritual for the high priest included physical acts, such as touching the ear lobe, the finger, and the toe with blood. When Moses passes on his leadership to Joshua, he performs the laying on of hands. The passing of Aaron's leadership to Eleazar is marked by Aaron's ceremonial garments being stripped from him and placed on his successor.

The Temple services repeatedly reminded the people that they should worship God in their wholeness, using all of their senses: smelling the incense, seeing the splendor of the Temple and the vestments of the Priest, hearing the Levites sing and the animals bleat, touching the fluttering bird to be sacrificed, and tasting the offering. The closest we come today to the fully realized Temple service is our Passover meal, where the seder table becomes the altar. The bone-weary preparations, the sparkling white table cloth, the shining silver *kiddush* cups, the cooking smells, the holiday songs, the new clothes, and the taste of *matzah, maror,* and *haroset* all bring the spiritual together with the corporeal, or, as the psalmist says, "O taste and see that Adonai is good" (Ps. 34:9). In this way, God is more than an idea; God is real, and the holy can be grasped with all of our being. We discover the holy in and through our own body and then expand our interest and concern to the body of Creation.

Encompassing the Physical

Judaism is not merely a philosophy—an explanation for why things are the way they are—but a way of life in the real world of things and people. It requires thought and feelings, but it also calls for actions and practices.

If we search for language and a way to express the relationship of mind to body, we find some clues in the writings of Spinoza. His examination of the mind in the *Ethics,* his major philosophical work, is presented in the same form as Euclid's *Elements,* using definitions, axioms, and propositions. His very first definition covers the body; in other words, in order to discuss the mind, he believes, we must first define the body. Immediately we are brought to the questions that lie at the heart of the matter: How does the body relate to the mind? and Where or who are we? Was Sita of *The Transposed Heads* right to privilege the head of her husband over the body of her friend? Should Jacob's goatskin-covered arms take precedence over his soft voice?

Spinoza answers the mind-body question by noting that the first thing to form the actual content of the human mind is merely the idea of our own body actually existing. Without a body, we wouldn't have a mind. We can think because we have a body, and what we think is shaped by the particular body we have. Our body takes in the perceptions that form the content of our thoughts. This is what Mann was illustrating in his novel, and it is something we have discovered in our own experience.

Belief and Action

Closely related to the mind-body problem is the tie between action and belief. Owning our body makes us hang full weight in this world: if we were bodiless, how could we recognize any beauty in the physical world, given that we can see or hear beauty only through our physical senses? We develop our theology to be more than just a way of *thinking about* the real world; we want it to be a way of *acting, doing, and being* in the world.

Recall the story in Chapter One in which two people return to their long-neglected garden and find some of the old plants growing vigorously, prompting opposite conclusions about whether a gardener has been there or not. Flowing from their opposing conclusions are two opposing sets of actions, and even lifestyles. The first of the two people might want to express gratitude by weeding an area that he thinks the gardener has over-looked. The second might tread carelessly over a set of plants, thinking that no one cares about his actions. Of course, no complex of actions exhausts the full meaning of any belief, and it is just this complexity that lies behind Rebecca's puzzling action in persuading her son Jacob to steal his brother's blessing. All we know about the incident are his words and actions.

When Jacob protests that he will be recognized by Isaac and be regarded as a trickster, thereby earning him a curse rather than a blessing, Rebecca answers, "Your curse, my son, be upon me! Just do as I say and go fetch [the kids] for me" (Gen. 27:13). Did she respond that way because, as the Torah reports, "Rebecca favored Jacob" (Gen. 25:28), or because she was dutifully following the words of Adonai, who told her,

"Two nations are in your womb, two separate peoples shall issue from your body; One people shall be mightier than the other, and the older shall serve the younger" (Gen. 25:23)? We cannot know, nor can we make a simple move from some particular belief to the specific action, but we *can* affirm that beliefs have behavioral aspects, in terms of both the physiology of our bodies and the actions we take in this world.

If we accept the idea that dualism (the complete separation of mind and body) fails to agree with our perception of reality, then true religious beliefs and actions must be thought of as two ways of observing the same commitment. Institutional Judaism has been faulted for emphasizing the actions and practices of the religion more than any creedal statement. But since actions are enacted beliefs, this emphasis in no way diminishes the inner dimension of the religion. Three times a day we recite the *Shema,* which tells us to love Adonai our God. But love, as we have seen, can be lived out in many ways, so the *Shema* commands no specific action that demonstrates our love. What we do get from Judaism is the insight that our theology must be enfleshed. Our theology, is then, what we think, believe, feel, and use to make sense of things, but it is also what we do, how we act, and how we live in the world.

Beliefs that imply no actions are empty beliefs, as are actions without supporting beliefs. Religion is a way toward wholeness (holiness) and so must involve both. Just as the beliefs of some people underlie their actions, actions sometimes shape beliefs, or as Hamlet says to his mother, Gertrude, "Assume a virtue if you have it not." In much the same way, rabbis have traditionally taught their congregants to perform *mitzvot* (good deeds) and the belief will follow. In terms familiar to the modern and worldly, we find behaviorist psychologists saying that people can be cured of fears by "acting cured" (assuming a virtue), while cognitive psychologists argue that cures are effected through the subjects' insight into the underlying causes of their fears. A true cure includes both change in feeling and change in action; we need not emphasize either behavior modification or cognitive insight, because individuals may find one way more amenable to them than the other.

Theology has traditionally been understood as a system of thought, but ultimately it is also way of life that includes both thought and action. Although considering the body means introducing suffering and death into our system, we need these issues in order to come in wholeness to an understanding of who we are, what we can know, and what we can hope for.

7

ENGAGING IN PRAYER

If you seek me, you shall find me
if you search with all your heart.

—Jeremiah 29:12

OUR STARTING POINT is as visceral a reaction as we can imagine: a sense of awe and wonder, of mystery and fear, of loneliness and confusion. We are caught short, and our first prayer may simply be silence. Gradually, we learn to form words around our experience and move from a purely subjective sense of religion to something ordered and shared with a religious community. Reflection on our fundamental experience of awe and wonder may develop to the level of a theology. Theology describes how we view the nature of reality and where we fit into the world as a whole. A theology of prayer makes sense only if we believe that the world is more than the surfaces we see—that something underlies it, supports it, and infuses it with life, energy, and meaning.

A Theology of Prayer

Prayer is entering into God's presence with openness and humility. Prayer helps us come to know ourselves and come to know more about God. Here, *knowing* means gradually getting to know a person with whom we spend time, not amassing lots of data. The path of prayer is twofold: inward, to our own essential center, which lies deeper than language; and outward, to include our congregation, our fellow worshipers across space and time and, eventually, all of Creation. What we think of as most personal turns out to be most universal. A passage we recite every Sabbath afternoon can be applied to the whole experience of prayer:

> If I am not for myself, who will be?
> If I am only for myself, who am I?
> And if not now, when?

> —*Pirke Avot* 1:14

If I Am Not for Myself, Who Will Be?

We begin to pray with an immediate concern: let this happen, or don't let that happen. Does prayer make a difference? Yes, but not the difference we hoped for as children. Prayer is not magic, although there is a great temptation to confuse the two. It has been said that prayer is a form of attention. When we pray for someone or for some specific outcome, what are actually doing is thinking about that person or situation in the context of a larger perspective, our relationship to God. The isolation of fear and doubt is lessened if we realize that the words we utter from our *siddur* really convey our own experience, attesting that others have had the same fears and doubts. The isolation is also lifted because we sense God's presence, telling us that we are not alone.

We come to prayer with one agenda, but as we pray, we find that prayer becomes a context within which we find our concerns and ourselves changing. We may come to prayer small and needy, but through the process we find comfort and a changed view of self.

If I Am Only for Myself, Who Am I?

It may seem strange to talk about losing ourselves in prayer, but what we really lose, and want to lose, is our focus on the self. To draw an analogy: when the body is working healthfully, we tend to be unaware of it. When we do find ourselves intensely aware of a particular part of the body, whether stomach or left foot, it is because that part is somehow not functioning properly. All too often we spend time focused on ourselves but don't realize that the focus is a symptom of malfunction in the self as a whole. The self should be able to look at the world and act unobstructed. Losing ourselves in prayer serves to heal our relationship with our self.

And If Not Now, When?

We use the healed self, the fully claimed self, to find the Other in prayer. It is always now, in the present, that we are invited into Presence. We do not look back with longing or regret, or look ahead in hope and anticipation. We need to enter into the time that is given to us, and it is here that we encounter the Other. Prayer is expansive, transforming us as we open ourselves to the Other.

The Role of Our Shared Story in Prayer

As we come to understand how identity is formed, we recognize why we pray in community from a shared text in addition to praying out of our individual needs. We make contact with one another through both our shared past and our actions in the present. Our common liturgy names us and explains our values, ideas, and culture. Our shared history, recited in the prayer services, affirms our common ground, helps us relive the awesome moments at the Red Sea and Mount Sinai, and unites us in what we must face together. Memory supports the present because God's actions in the past give us a warrant for hope now. Memory is constructed through social interaction, but it also becomes individual; similarly, our prayers are given communal expression but also develop their individual language and elements.

Prayer brings us into community by telling our shared story and using it as a way into a relationship with God. Our shared text serves the same function as a letter of introduction: "Remember the person you entered into covenant with? I'm his descendant." But now we've been introduced; here we are, and what are we going to do? The prospect is exciting, awesome, and scary.

Prayer and Silence

The three daily Jewish prayer services (four on the Sabbath and holidays, five on Yom Kippur) are structured to lead us to the consciousness of the *Amidah,* which is recited *silently.* The morning service moves from the thanksgiving and the blessings for Creation to remembering redemption and being open to revelation. Since prayer is a relationship between two parties, we reach a point where we must grow quiet and be receptive to whatever revelation may come. "To Thee silence is praise," a line from Psalm 65, was interpreted by Moses Maimonides (1963) to mean "silence with regard to you is praise. . . . For of whatever we say intending to magnify and exalt, on the one hand we find that it can have some application to Him . . . and on the other we perceive in it some deficiency" (pp. 139–140). Maimonides focuses on how words finally fail before the majesty of God, but we need to grow silent so that we can hear whatever may be said to us.

Anthony Bloom (1973) tells the story of a congregant, a woman in her seventies, who complained that after years of faithful praying, she had never experienced the presence of God. "How can God get a word in edgewise if you never get quiet?" was Bloom's first reaction. But he reframed his response more gently: "After you have finished saying your prayers, sit quietly, perhaps knit or crochet, and see what happens." She returned joyously a few days later, reporting that she had indeed felt the presence of God. She told Bloom that she had followed his advice, sat down, and looked around her quietly and peacefully. For the first times in years, she felt she had permission to just sit. Now she could notice how peaceful and quiet the room was. She felt that the peace and silence that surrounded her—that had been outside—now came within her. The silence opened to a richer silence that was not merely the absence of noise; it had a richness all its own. At its center, she found God's presence.

Prayer provides the time, the space, the reminders to us of our deepest love. Prayer helps us grow in love by reminding us of occasions for gratitude; it allows us to be open to being loved, and it helps us put things together and see how they fit. Because of our active participation, prayer engages us in the larger story of which we're a part. Our active engagement is part of what arouses our love. Love is not a spectator sport; it is a way of thinking, doing, and hoping.

Prayer and Love

Prayer requires a relationship between two parties, the self and God. We can learn a great deal about prayer through our human relationships. We learn about waiting, patience, disappointment, reunion after separation. We learn how to begin the conversation once again, how to be honest, and how to admit our failures. Over time, prayer helps us grow both in our relationship to God and in our sense of just who the self is.

God awakens in us aspects of the self we did not previously recognize. At one time or another, we all experience a similar awakening when we fall in love: part of what makes the other so beloved is the transformation you recognize in yourself when you are in the beloved's presence. The same awakening occurs when the one you love—and recognize as loving you—is God.

Along with everything that is exchanged in the meeting—presence, warmth, gratitude, love—comes a sense of what cannot be given: the object of your love is so intimate yet remains so mysterious. Then this force that you hardly know is changing you into someone you may not recognize at all, making real prayer dangerous but also making it a risk you must take. The description in Exodus of the Israelites' meeting with God at Sinai, "thunder and lightning, a thick cloud upon the mountain," gives us a figurative model for all our meetings with God in that it suggests expectancy, excitement, fear, and an inability to penetrate and understand. We come face to face with the limits of what we can know.

The most transforming influences in life are personal friendships; of these, the most transforming is friendship with the friends of God and with God: "What a great wonder that we should be able to draw so near to God in prayer. How many walls there are between man and God. . . . Yet a single word of prayer can topple all the walls and bring you close to God" (Green and Holtz, 1977, p. 20).

Work, Play, Challenge, Attention

Prayer can take many forms: it can be work, when we are fulfilling a *mitzvah;* it can be play, when we do something because we love and appreciate it; it can be a series of trials and challenges, when we accept them as part of life; and it can be explicit prayer, when our attention is engaged in learning to know about God and to know God.

DAVID
We met David in connection with work, where the loss of his zest for writing and his subsequent depression were addressed. He later realized that these negative experiences were due to his pursuit of false goals in prayer. "Two years ago, I prayed that my book would be published and my zest in writing would be restored. In the course of praying, I recognized that I had allowed myself to forget that writing is a gift and had let false gods color my consciousness. My joy in writing returned, not because my manuscript was accepted,

but because the relationship I established in prayer transformed my values."

Space and Time

All the concerns we bring to prayer can be formulated within two sets of coordinates: space (both the personal space of our bodies and minds and the larger space of Creation) and time.

The Body and the Prayer Shawl

When we think of the articles and objects that people use in prayer, we become very conscious of how they relate to our bodies. The *tallit* (prayer shawl) enfolds us. Actually, in the process of putting on the *tallit,* we experience many of the spaces symbolized by this one garment.

SHOSHANA
Shoshana had been given a *tallit* as a birthday present by her children. As she described her own use of the *tallit,* she began by recounting how her husband's grandmother in Israel sent him a *tallit* for a wedding present. "We used that *tallit* as our *chuppah* [marriage canopy]. Because a *chuppah* represents a tent open at all sides to let everything in, my first association with the *tallit* is of opening out to welcome the whole world. I hold it over my head and recite, 'You wrap yourself in light as in a garment, you spread out the Heavens like a curtain.' This blessing gives me a sense of God's majesty.

"Then I draw the *tallit* closer so that it covers my head and serves as a curtain, shutting out all distractions, while I recite the lines, 'Human children take refuge in the shadow of your wings, they have their fill of the choice food of your house, and you give them drink from your stream of delights. With you is the fountain of life and by your light we see light.' God, who is over all Creation, is suddenly close to me, covering me under these wings. I am nurtured and sheltered. Then I let the *tallit* fall to my shoulders, covering them. Each time I put it on, I feel as if my children were embracing me."

Noticing how the *tallit* functions in prayer, we realize that the body need not be a distraction but can be joined with the heart and mind to bring us in our wholeness to God.

Postures

Our bodies also bring to mind different prayer postures: turning inward as we do when we lower our heads and bow at the beginning of the *Amidah*, reaching for the transcendent as we stand on tiptoe while reciting *Kadosh, Kadosh, Kadosh* (Holy, Holy, Holy) and rocking back and forth as we live out the psalmist's saying, "All my bones shall praise you."

The Body as Subject Matter of Prayer

In addition to reflecting about what our bodies bring to our prayer, we can also think about what traditional prayers themselves have to say about our bodies. We have already seen the prayer for recovering awareness of the body on awakening. It is no accident that this prayer is immediately followed by the blessing for studying Torah: "Blessed are you, Adonai our God, Sovereign of the universe, who sanctifies us with your commandments and commands us to study the Torah."

After the very personal, individual reclaiming of our physical being, we recognize that the mind has its communal aspect. Learning Torah is a path into the shared story of our people and a way for us Jews to understand all that has befallen us. The morning service continues with the prayer: "My God, the soul you have placed within me is pure. You created it, formed it, and breathed it into me. You preserve it within me. You will take it from me and restore it to me in the hereafter. So long as the soul is within me, I offer thanks before you, Adonai my God, God of my ancestors, master of all creatures, and ruler of all souls. Blessed are you who restores the soul to the dead" (*Talmud Berakhot* 60b).

Personalized Space

Personalized space is the place we inhabit when we feel at home in our bodies. Archimedes said, in so many words, that if given a place to stand, he could move the world. We *are* given such a place: our own bodies. We can lift up the world through our groundedness and our prayers, using the sacred space of *tallit* as an extension of the body to help in restoring us to our bodies.

When you are in love, you see that there is a place for you. That love of place can be nourished through prayer, as we read in the Psalms: "O God, you have been our dwelling place in every generation" (Ps. 90:1). Place, in the Psalms, also reminds us how transitory everything we value is, how quickly it fades from memory:

Humans, their days are like those of grass;
   they bloom like flowers of the field;
   a wind passes by and they are no more,
   their own place no longer knows them.

                      —Psalms 103:15–16

And place also reminds us of the boundaries and limits that make life viable:

   . . . the waters stood above the mountains.
   They fled at Your blast,
      rushed away at the sound of Your thunder—
      —mountains rising, valleys sinking—
   to the place You established for them.

                      —Psalms 104:6–8

But our personal place is where we stand when coming into relationship with God.

Transcendence and Immanence

In the libretto for *Iolanthe* (1882), W. S. Gilbert mocks the English for invariably following their parents' politics:

   I often think it's comical . . .
   How Nature always does contrive . . .
   That every boy and every gal
   That's born into the world alive
   Is either a little Liberal
   Or else a little Conservative!
   Fal, lal, la!

Similarly, each one of us born into the world alive thinks of God as either immanent, that is, close, or indwelling; or transcendent, that is, above or outside the world. But both apprehensions of God are essential for a complete image of God. A God who is only immanent does not draw us beyond ourselves, while a God who is only transcendent is removed from our ongoing concerns. A passage in the *Zohar*, the major text of Jewish mysticism, represents the view of God's transcendence, the distant and unreachable heights:

   "In the beginning" (Gen. 1:1)—when the will of the King
   began to take effect he engraved signs into the heavenly

sphere (that surrounded him). Within the most hidden recess a dark flame issued from the mystery of the *eyn sof,* the Infinite, like a fog forming in the unformed—enclosed in the ring of that sphere, neither white nor black, neither red nor green, of no color whatever. Only after this flame began to assume size and dimension, did it produce radiant colors. From the innermost center of the flame sprang forth a well out of which colors issued and spread upon everything beneath, hidden in the mysterious hiddenness of *eyn sof.*

The well broke through and yet did not break through the ether (of the sphere). It could not be recognized at all until a hidden, supernal point shone forth under the impact of the final breaking through.

Beyond this point nothing can be known. Therefore it is called *reshit,* beginning—the first word (out of the ten) by means of which the universe has been created [*Zohar* I:15a; Scholem, 1949, p. 27].

A nearby passage in the *Zohar* describes God's immanence, or inward-turning depths:

When King Solomon "penetrated into the depths of the nut garden," as it is written, "I descended into the garden of nuts" (Cant. 6:11), he took up a nut shell and studying it, he saw an analogy in its layers with the spirits which motivate the sensual desires of humans. . . .

The Holy One, be blessed, saw that it was necessary to put into the world all of these things so as to make sure of permanence, and of having, so to speak, a brain surrounded by numerous membranes. The whole world, upper and lower, is organized on this principle, from the primary mystic center to the very outermost of all the layers. All are coverings, the one to the other, brain within brain, spirit inside of spirit, shell within shell [*Zohar* I:19b; Scholem, 1949, p. 28].

The view of God's transcendence is developed in the medieval collection of mystical writings known as the Kabbalah, which holds that the source, or the Great Countenance of the Godhead, can never be discerned by humans. Those who focus on transcendence find their own way to God through an ascent to union with the divine, a journey upward and outward through a series of intermediate states. The ladder earns special prominence as a symbol: "Happy are they who have a ladder in their own house," meaning happy are they who have the means to rise within themselves. Transcendence also gives us the Greek notion of *entheos,* or invaded by God (from which our word *enthusiasm* derives). So we have the image of ascent and descent: ascend the ladder and "From the Depths I've called thee" (Ps. 130:1), which could mean calling God out from *our* depths.

People serve as the meeting point of the above and below and raise Creation to its root through the performance of *mitzvot.* The Book of Job plays an important role in Jewish mysticism because the problems of suffering and of evil can sometimes be best addressed through the direct experience of God's presence and caring concern. Job's words "Out of my own body I behold God" are taken in the Kabbalah to be a veiled reference to the analogies of the human body and elements of the higher world. Every human faculty is deemed a mirror of divine powers. The body reflects the ten *sefirot*—the emanations from the *eyn sof* (the God above the *sefirot,* the infinite) that we can apprehend.

We tend to fear the infinite—both the infinitely large and the infinitesimally small—until we recognize that we are the meeting place of the above and below. What is out there, transcendent and unreachable, is also within. Both transcendence and immanence can stretch us (as Robert Browning put it, "Ah, but a man's reach should exceed his grasp, / Or what's a heaven for?"), but both come with potential traps that we should recognize and avoid. Transcendence can make us feel distant and overwhelmed, or cut off and isolated.

Immanence can shut us off to the greater world, making us into worshipers turned within while unable to see the holy around us. These are the pitfalls; how do we avoid them? For immanence, we must keep in mind the thought expressed in the opening verse of Psalm 121: "I lift my eyes unto the hills whence comes my help." For transcendence, we take our cue from Psalm 139:

> My frame was not concealed from You
>> when I was shaped in a hidden place
>> knit together in the recesses of the earth.
> Your eyes saw my unformed limbs . . .

Psalms 139:15–16

The rhythms of immanence and transcendence correspond to the rhythms of knowing and being known, taking in and giving out. Intimacy requires both:

> O God, our God,
>> how glorious is your name throughout the earth . . .

When I behold Your heavens, the work of Your fingers,
    the moon and stars that You created—
Who are we that You should be mindful of us,
    that You should care for us?
You have made us little less than divine
    and crowned us with glory and honor.

—Psalms 8:2–6

I praise You,
    for I am awesomely, wondrously made;
    Your work is wonderful;
    I know it very well.

—Psalms 139:14

So whether we look beyond or within, we see the wonders of God's Creation.

Just as the *tallit* embraces us but also opens out to welcome the rest of Creation, the content of the full morning service forces us to move beyond our personal concerns to a larger perspective by bringing to mind the rest of Creation and the rest of time. Our parochialism is alleviated by the content of our prayer.

Whether we pray alone or in a group, we do so as a people that span both space (to include all the people who are praying the same words around the globe) and time—those who are praying now, those who prayed before us (our ancestors), and those who will recite the same prayers in years to come (our descendants). That is why much of the prayer book is written in the plural. Without that guidance, we might be tempted to limit ourselves to personal thoughts and words. Praying in community with a shared text keeps us open to concerns of all the people—indeed, to all of Creation.

Time

The Talmud begins with a series of questions: "From what time [may people] recite the evening *Shema*? From the hour that the priests come in to eat of their heave-offering, until the end of the first watch; . . . From what time [may people] recite the morning *Shema*? From [the time one can] distinguish between blue and white" (*Talmud Berakhot* 1a).

Prayers relate to our consciousness differently according to the time of day. How we feel when we awaken in the morning, how we feel during *Shacharit* (the morning service), during *Minchah* (afternoon service), during *Ma'ariv* (evening service), and during the prayer we recite before retiring. Our bodily rhythms are part of what we bring to prayer because we are the meeting place of the holy and the secular, and our responses to the times of day cannot be separated from our prayer.

> These questions about the kind of concentration that praying is, for me, led on to the thought that perhaps effective ways of contacting this Answering Activity might vary according to the time of day. . . .
>
> If it is ideas I am stuck for then, usually, they have to be collected in the early morning, a beach-combing after the tides of sleep have retreated. . . . The rhythms of dark and light, daily, often hourly, dying and resurrecting. . . .
> "Ripeness is all." Able to wait and yet not lose faith something is coming [Milner, 1987, pp. 52–53].

Time refers not only to the transitions between dusk and night and between dawn and day but also to the turn of the seasons that give us our holidays: the New Year, Hanukah, Passover, Shavuot. Yet each week we celebrate the Sabbath, which is not inherent in any structure in the universe. Months are based on the moon, years on the earth's orbit around the sun, day and night on the earth's rotation, but the week is set by divine decree.

The Sabbath

Observing the Sabbath expands our notion of time so that at any moment we can relate the present to how things were at the beginning. It shapes our consciousness into letting us put every event within the perspective of the larger story of Creation, revelation, and redemption. We find the self to both be and not be contemporaneous with Creation. Just as a single frond of a fern carries the design of the entire plant, we carry within ourselves the entire human condition. But though we can know the darkness on the face of the deep and the spirit of God hovering over the waters, we wonder if more recent and visible aspects of the self can be known as well.

If we have trouble understanding the world of our grandparents, how can we hope to understand the world of biblical times? The stories from biblical times concern the essentials, not the contextually based details of modern stories. Our biblical knowledge about the troubles and rivalries in blended families, for example, helps us understand corresponding problems today. So the Sabbath and prayer allow us to enact a relationship to eternity without losing sight of the present. For a while, we stop the forward thrust of time and stand once again at Creation.

A Historical Religion

Judaism is called a historical religion not simply because the Torah purports to relate events that actually occurred, but because we believe that events in time tell us something about the nature of reality. The passing of time brings with it the possibility for increased insight, both for the Jewish people as a whole and for each of us in our own lives. Time is not merely the passing of this hour, day, or year; it is the locus for events that are fraught with meaning. We carry within us many times and ages. The Jewish emphasis on time and on what we can add to the community's prayer suggests that memoir itself can be a form of prayer, as the psalmist recognized:

> Deliver me from a lion's mouth;
>   from the horns of wild oxen rescue me.
> Then I will proclaim Your fame to my brethren,
>   praise You in the congregation.

> —Psalms 22:22–23

In other words, the psalmist declares that it is God who delivers us from danger and that recounting the dangerous event constitutes a prayer of thanksgiving. In our own lives, we scrutinize each moment of our day to find any event in which God was present and thus locate an occasion for gratitude. "Know before whom you stand."

Remembering and Diaries

Virginia Woolf asked the trenchant question, "Who am I addressing when I write my diary?" People have answered that question in a number of ways. Some think they are addressing their later selves. The later self will, it is hoped, bring the diary entries a different perspective.

> Marta was raised by a mentally ill mother and felt unable to keep a diary for fear her mother would find it. Instead, she wrote on slips of paper that she hid. After she moved away from home, her brother found the slips, saved them, and a few years ago returned them to her. She read them, and from her adult perspective she saw God's presence throughout all the entries. She is now glad she was raised as she was, believing that it made her more caring and compassionate.

Rose believes she is writing her diary with the hope that one day someone, perhaps a grandchild—*someone* will want to understand.

Ilana writes both in the depth of despair and in the height of anger, hoping that her more authentic self will eventually let her put her current situation into a balanced perspective.

Jennifer reports that her journal is consciously and deliberately addressed to God.

What does it mean to address our diary to God, or for that matter, to anyone? Marta's audience, her later self, can conclude that she was on a conscious search for God; Rose in her quest for understanding, seeks someone who will really know her; Ilana writes hoping to locate the best part of herself. All three are, in effect, sharing Jennifer's very conscious address to God. The difference is that Jennifer's is explicit and has given her the thrill of knowing that she is treading, reverently, on holy ground. Occasionally, she finds herself writing things she could not know; it is then she realizes that her own writing is eliciting some sort of response.

Time and Mortality

We live in time and long for eternity, yet we don't know what the word *eternity* means. Words take on meaning through experience; for example, we understand the meaning of *sour* from having tasted something sour. But do we have any experience of the eternal that can explain why we would yearn for it? We have been seeing how prayer can expand us if we accept our bodily self. We can expand our temporal self as well. We can look back in our lives to our birth and project ahead to our death.

But beyond these limits, we can connect with our ancestors and all others who came before us, all the way back to the creation of the world, and we can project ahead to the next generation and the next, forever. So although we are finite, we have within us the capacity to identify with the infinite. When we do so, life take on a different meaning; we see it as part of something larger than our own life and effort. We are amphibians of a sort: we live in the finite but have touches of the infinite, when we step outside the domain and dominion of time.

At its best, prayer should regularly take us outside of time. We may, for instance, be on a journey outside the confines of time by way of the content of prayers—those timeless words that our parents, grandparents, and earlier ancestors recited before we were even born. The content itself reminds us explicitly of God's creative power and, indirectly, of our own creative power since we are in the image of God. We may also go beyond our narrow sense of time when our whole selves—mind and body—enter into the timelessness of contemplation. The process is, as Heschel has suggested, like cultivating a bit of eternity in our being. The self that we are in contemplation is not the constricted, temporal self.

Finally, the Sabbath, when celebrated wholeheartedly, can also feel like time outside of time. Here we are not makers and doers, that is, people who tightly control their lives, but those who have let go and are still provided for, as the Israelites were with the manna in the desert. The Sabbath gives us the gift of experiencing that what we don't control is still controlled.

The Emphasis on Time in Judaism

In the days of the Temple, Jews celebrated three pilgrim festivals for which they traveled to Jerusalem to worship in the holy edifice. With the destruction of the Temple, Judaism moved away from this emphasis on sacred space and turned instead to view time as sacred. Unwittingly, the change led to a denigration of the physical, material world. Jews never fell to the level of calling the flesh evil or to the dualism found in gnosticism and Christianity, but all the physicality of the Temple services—the preparatory journey, the incense, the magnificence of the building's courtyard, the colorful priestly vestments, the singing of the Levites—was replaced with words depicting the Temple rites. We now *talk* about worshiping and bowing down, but we do not kneel (except on Yom Kippur). Our minds may know the words by heart, but our bodies play only a small role in our worship. Heschel has written convincingly about Judaism being a religion that emphasizes time over space. But why does it have to be one or the other? Just as we want both immanence and transcendence, we want space as well as time. Physical space matters. Thus we return to the first of our coordinates, the space of our own bodies.

We have traveled full circle, from space back to body, and have seen how each element implies the other. Prayer not only unites body and mind, and space and time, but it also allows us to bring our whole selves into the praying encounter. We discover that God, who encompasses all space and time, can be encountered through the broken stammering of whispered prayer. God knit together the brokenness of Marta, whose scribblings in her journal became a fully realized way; God gave Rose a vision of a future to which she could contribute; God was the constant through the heights and depths of Ilana's emotional swings; and God is the partner in Jennifer's dialogue.

8

LIVING IN COMMUNITY

I will make you fertile and numerous,
making of you a community of peoples.

—Genesis 48:4

THE TORAH SUGGESTS that we were created to be in community, that
only in community do we sense the presence of God, and that only in and
through community can we become holy: "And as Aaron spoke to the
whole Israelite community they turned toward the wilderness, and there, in
a cloud, appeared the Presence of Adonai" (Exod. 16:10). "Adonai spoke
to Moses, saying: 'Speak to the whole Israelite community, and say to them:
You shall be holy, for I, Adonai your God, am holy'" (Lev. 19:1–2).

The charge to join in community raises all the perennial questions about
who we are, what the self is, and whether religion fosters salvation for the
individual or holiness for some larger unity called community or people.

Can we be Jewish and not be in community? A prior question has to
be, Can we be *human* and not be in community? Actually, even before
that, we have to ask whether we can exist at all without being in community. Certainly we cannot come into being without community, which
is necessary for conception, nurturance, and development; an infant cannot survive without being in a nurturing environment.

The questions surrounding humanity's existence lie even deeper. At
birth, we are only potentially human—we need a cooperative environment
and a precipitating force to fulfill the potential. The eye, to take an example, is potentially seeing and the environment is potentially seen, but seeing needs a precipitating force, in this case light. Analogously, the self is
potentially human; the environment is one that allows for all the human
characteristics of knowing, feeling, willing, and doing; and the precipitating force turns out to be other humans.

Our earliest community comprises all those in our immediate vicinity, such as parents, siblings, and other caregivers. But most people, including our parents, are part of a larger community into which we are educated. Much of our learning takes place through a kind of osmosis. How much of who we are is shaped, for example, by the aesthetics in which we are raised? Do we like Mozart or rock because our community does? Does hearing more Mozart, or rock, mold our consciousness to want more of the same? What is true about types of music also holds for ethical concerns and awareness of God. Only after we have reached a certain level of independence can we begin to contemplate dropping out of our community, but by then we have already internalized many of its values and perceptions.

Jews in Community

People who ask whether we can be Jewish without being in community have a more limited and specific community in mind. They are really asking, Can we be Jewish cut off from *institutional* Judaism? As we formulate our theology, we try to find out what genuinely belongs to us and what we have simply picked up that can be modified or discarded in light of our own experiences and insights.

Defining Judaism

How do we define Judaism? This is part of our task in formulating our own theology. We have tried to understand different human experiences in terms of the language of the Bible and the prayer book. Judaism has shaped our world view, but so have other things. Judaism furnishes us with a home, but few of us fully inhabit it. We do Jewish things: we may pray using the *siddur,* read psalms, and celebrate the High Holy days and Passover, but we frequently lapse in other matters. Has Judaism created a community to which we belong?

A basic argument in favor of institutional Judaism is that religion is not—cannot be—a solo dance, that we need partners: "Environment is stronger than your will. You will not attain your goals until you surround yourself with people who are actually striving toward similar ones," writes Gail Sher in *One Continuous Mistake* (1999, p. 73). Many Jews find their community in institutional Judaism, while others, who feel themselves to be just as Jewish, find their communities elsewhere or—consciously or unconsciously—form their own.

Environment

We need an environment that supports the worldview we have gleaned from Judaism. Numbers picks up the story of the Israelites, who are creating an environment that helps them become an *am kadosh,* a holy people. Environment includes space, relationship, possessions, work, health, time, and thoughts. Most of these are discussed in one form or another in the Book of Numbers.

SPACE. Space is determined by the location of the *Mishkan*—the Tabernacle, or Tent of Meeting—and the tents around it. Three millennia later, the structure described in the second chapter of Numbers influenced the structure of the Puritan village in New England. The ideal pattern, as described in the mid-1630s, was centered on the meeting house, the community's house of worship. Surrounding it were the dwellings of the faithful, "orderly placed to enjoy comfortable communion." The widening circles held fields for grazing livestock and for growing crops. Beyond the occupied areas were "swamps and rubbish waste grounds" that provided "the surrounding disorder within which the town would find its identity" (Stilgoe, 1976, p. 4; see also Lane 1988, pp. 112–113). We will return to this outer sphere, or "wilderness," later in this chapter.

Space, in the form of change in place, alters the perception of Abraham, who is called to leave his native land; Jacob, when he leaves his parents' house to live with Laban; Moses, who flees to Midian after being raised in the palace in Egypt; and the Israelites, when they leave Egypt and enter the wilderness. The power in Jewish history of place and of change in place structured our people's experiences in the wilderness.

RELATIONSHIPS. In Numbers, people are defined and numbered in terms of their lineage. Their work, especially any service that was done for the maintenance of the *Mishkan,* was defined solely in terms of their tribe. We can easily recognize the tension between the individual and the communal because it continues to this day. Like the biblical character Korach, who rebelled against Moses, we struggle to define ourselves even while we are still members of a family. Although Korach was punished by death, some of the most beautiful psalms are attributed to his sons. Perhaps we and the community of our children can also add to the beauty in the world.

POSSESSIONS. In the wilderness, the Israelites' possessions are limited to what they can carry while wandering. The simplicity of the nomadic life allows us to perceive more easily how the objects we carry, need daily, and use to adorn our tents define and create community.

HEALTH. As described in Numbers, illness is defined only by visible anomalies and has less to do with treatment than with impurity—what makes someone unclean. Suffering from a running sore was reason enough to be put "outside the camp." The view from there, from outside the concentric circles of belonging, affects our sense of community.

We might like to reassure ourselves that thrusting someone outside the camp was a primitive reaction that would never happen in our mature society. But when Marla's husband developed a brain tumor (we'll turn to Marla's story shortly), her coworkers suddenly had a hard time talking to her. They were embarrassed to gossip in her presence about their weekends or a movie they had seen. Their discomfort was only exacerbated by his subsequent death.

When tragedy strikes us, we find ourselves in danger of being pushed out of the community. To counter people's tendency to shun someone who has lost a loved one, the community sets up rituals that bind us closer to it. But when we ourselves become ill, a different sensibility takes over: we might be contagious. The community, thinking of the good of the whole, throws us out, without considering what we may learn from being "outside the camp" and how the new perspective will have changed us once we return.

It often takes an anomalous event, such as almost dying and then recovering, to give us a new perception of boundaries and borders. The boundary we reach in almost dying stays with us and shapes all the rest of our perceptions. "How shall he desire wealth, O Death, who once has seen thy face?" we read in the Upanishads. Once we've seen that boundary, the ordinary goals of life seem trivial and irrelevant.

WORK. Leaving work, too, makes us feel "outside the camp." For the Israelites, life outside Egypt is no easier than it was inside Egypt before Moses' return. The daily routines of slavery offered structure and predictability. The Israelites were all housed together in Goshen, where they knew what food they would eat each day. They developed a sense of community, albeit a community of the enslaved, not yet one formed in freedom around the love of God. Following the initial euphoria experienced by the Israelites after crossing the Red Sea, the dailiness of life in the wilderness, with its unrelenting heat, the ever-present grit and sand, the unchanging food (manna), and the realization that the Promised Land lay far, far way combines to make it almost painful to remember the miracles they experience.

TIME. The unstructured space in the wilderness is tempered by time, which is highly regulated and structured. Distinctions are drawn between Sabbath and weekdays, between festive and ordinary time, and between hours for worship and hours for work.

All these structured areas—space, relationships, possessions, and time—helped determine the Israelites' understanding of their environment and, by extension, of their community.

THOUGHTS. More than anything else, what we think and how we interpret events controls our environment and creates our community. Thoughts are the natural by-product of a shared story—a shared environment of space, relationship, work, possessions, and time. But the Torah never addresses thoughts explicitly in describing how the Israelites were shaped into a people that retains its identity even through the destruction or transformation of all its support structures.

Despite two thousand years in exile, space continues to maintain a formative influence on the Jewish people. Relationships remain central, although many Jews cannot trace their ancestors back more than a few generations. Possessions continue to tend toward the portable as Jews never feel quite secure in their environment. Our work remains the place where we can make our prime contribution to the community. And time is still rooted in the Jewish calendar, with its seasons, holidays, and daily schedules, regardless of our surroundings. But the message conveyed by "outside the camp" survives in all of us, both as Jews and individuals, as we struggle to be true to our own experiences.

The World and Communities

In an important sense, we each live in our own world, because as cocreators we each experience the world as it appears to us individually. Community is formed when we find we have a shared standard of perception. Accepting Torah as our fundamental story de facto creates a community across time and space with all those who share our understanding of God, Creation, covenant, liberation, and revelation.

To be sure, we have all experienced other communities when we face major disasters, such as floods, fires, or plagues. In sharing the perception of danger, our sense of compassion helps create community. As the doctor portrayed in Camus's novel *The Plague* characterizes it, we are the human community united against death and suffering. We may also come together when there is no danger (for example, to work for a political candidate because some aspect of the candidate's platform or character becomes a shared vision). There is, of course, the natural community of family, which implies some shared history and developmental experience that allows our worlds to coincide, although these common factors may or may not result in shared values. So part of the power of theology is not only to discover meaning but to cocreate it, and to do so in a way that connects us to others.

Entire cultures perceive the world differently, making it clear that the word *Judaism* defines a *people* as well as a religion. All religions, and Judaism most emphatically, create community; they aim at the border situations of life where we face diminished control, feel conflicted, experience guilt, confront suffering, or try to come to terms with death. When we feel most alone, the structures we have built support us.

> MARLA
>
> After her husband died of a brain tumor, Marla felt isolated at work. She found that her synagogue community supported her in ways her coworkers could not. She rose early every day to attend morning prayers before work, in order to say *Kaddish*, the mourner's prayer. Each day she sat next to a particular woman with whom she was not acquainted. They never chatted, but they rose together for the *Kaddish* and felt like partners in grief.
>
> Marla felt that every day, at least one person understood her journey of mourning, even if she saw no sign of comprehension at her place of work. Now she realized why mourners are required to pray in a *minyan* (community of ten adults) for eleven months after the death of a close relative.

When we feel most estranged and isolated, and most anxious to turn in on ourselves, we are forced to pray with others and to recognize that there is no house that has not experienced death. In our loss we stand in solidarity with all who share the human condition.

Language puts us into community. If a word exists for an experience we have, then someone else has already had that same experience, so we gratefully inherit language but adopt it to express our own unique perceptions. Using the same words, we can construct infinite variations on reality.

Religion functions like language in that it is not in itself reality but is a way of expressing reality. With the same building blocks, we arrive at the variety of Jewish religious experience.

Troublesome Issues

Community almost always implies borders and boundaries, whether those that demarcate inside and outside the camp or those we use to determine who is part of our community at all and who is not. As we saw earlier in this chapter, boundaries mark the limits of any individual or community. A border, the edge of a body, can be immutable, or it can be the growing edge that reaches out for new insights. Every group needs boundaries, but how do we decide where we draw them and when we regard someone as different, or other?

Being born into a community, we do not have to carry all the trials and vicissitudes of life alone. Our suffering is eased by Jews fulfilling the *mitzvot* of *birkat cholim* (visiting the sick) and *levayat ha-met* (attending the dead). Even so, if we stray from the values of the community or undergo some other transformation through opening ourselves to new ideas, we may feel isolated, not because we are physically alone but because we now have a new perception of the world. The wilderness experience of the Israelites gave them a new perspective, not only on their status as slaves but on Egypt's entire worldview.

Although our border remains a growing edge and we grow right along with the young, change in age can also transform our view of community. In some ways, our world is not sufficiently flexible. The aging of Jacob is marked by his inability to adjust to further changes. Moses, at the end of his life, cannot lead the people; someone from the next generation must carry on in his place.

But beyond the essential categories of space (leaving a place to gain a critical perspective on it) and time (finding community through people of our own age group), we know there are categories of understanding that are shared by the community of Jews, and we continue trying to determine which ones make up a minimal Jewish theology.

> LOIS
>
> In her adolescence, Lois found herself in conflict with the values of most of her peers: "My values were those of a community, though it took me a long time to discover that. When I did, I felt I had experienced the force of revelation. All it took was reading for the first time a dialogue of Plato. I realized then that I was not bizarre but that there were other people who thought as I did—indeed, there was a whole discipline that is concerned with questions I had struggled with for years.

The experience of recognition that we do, in fact, belong to a community can come to any of us. Every time we read a story or see an art work or hear a piece of music that speaks to us, we recognize that we are part of an invisible community.

Music binds people together and reinforces central roles and values. Liking "different" music can quickly move us outside our community. One way children begin to separate from their parents is to claim their own music. This move signifies the new generation's entering a new community and claiming its authenticity ("Sing unto Adonai a new song"; Ps. 149:1). Meanwhile those friends and family who are left behind lament, with the psalmist, "How can I sing Adonai's song in a strange land?" (Ps. 137:4). The music our children like is not the music of no-community but rather the music of a different community—not mainstream, maybe, but still community.

> RUTH
> When Ruth moved from junior high school (where she listened to top forty popular songs) to New York's La Guardia High School for the Performing Arts (where she listened to classical music), she underwent a change in community. Later, when she moved from classical music in general to Renaissance music in particular, she underwent another change in community. People like Renaissance music for different reasons, such as its ethereal sound quality and its fluid rhythms. What moved Ruth especially was its emphasis on sacred music, which reinforced her interest in the essential questions she had been addressing for so long.

What Makes a Community Jewish?

A Jewish community has, first of all, a shared history, beginning with the Torah stories and continuing through the vicissitudes of our people in the many lands of the Diaspora, right down to today. Second, Jews have a basic view of Creation—not a quasi-scientific theory but a shared assumption that the world makes sense and that it is therefore worthwhile to ask questions about meaning and causality.

Third, Judaism entails a response to God, although as essential as that component may be to our story, our sense of meaning, and our sense of self, it is increasingly difficult to talk about. The word *God* is used today in many cultures, but it doesn't always mean the same thing. Out of confusion or embarrassment, some people who think of themselves very clearly as Jewish have been reluctant to talk about God and prefer to limit their thinking to holiness or value.

Finally, Judaism subscribes to a specific sense of human potential. In biblical terms, all people are created in the image of God; secular Jews would say that each person has an essential dignity.

The Body and Community

Our fundamental story was created in an agrarian culture. Those who first heard the stories of the Torah or recited the psalms could relate personally to the references to shepherding. They knew that sheep can literally graze a field to death and that their waste fails to fertilize the soil because most of the nitrogen they produce goes into their wool. Since we no longer live in close contact with shepherding, few of us are aware of these fundamental realities, which served early Jews as powerful analogies for their self-understanding.

The conflict between the nomadic shepherd and the farmer, which harks back to Cain and Abel, raises questions about how we relate to the communities around us (the nonnomadic peoples). Unlike sheep, most beings process what they eat into waste that nourishes plants, just as plants give off the oxygen we need to breathe—a happy condition that allows both biological kingdoms to thrive. Indeed, we are reminded on many levels of our connections to larger communities. Unlike the cell, which has its own life agenda and presumably lacks any awareness of its role in the world, we can get occasional glimpses of the larger story.

The scientist and writer Lewis Thomas, reflecting on the mitochondria in his intestines, which are essential for his staying alive, wrote that they can hardly be said to be him, but

> I had never bargained on descent from single cells without
> nuclei. I could even make my peace with that, if it were all,
> but there is the additional humiliation that I have not, in a
> real sense, descended at all. I have brought them all along
> with me, or perhaps they have brought me.
>
> It is no good standing on dignity in a situation like this, and
> better not to try. It is a mystery. There they are, moving about
> in my cytoplasm, breathing for my own flesh, but strangers.
> They are much less closely related to me than to each other
> and to the free-living bacteria out under the hill. They feel like
> strangers, but the thought comes that the same creatures, pre
> cisely the same, are out there in the cells of sea gulls, and

whales, and dune grass, and seaweed, and hermit crabs, and further inland in the leaves of the beech in my backyard, and in the skunks beneath the back fence, and even in that fly on the window. Through them, I am connected; I have close relatives, once removed, all over the place [1974, p. 73].

That we harbor mitochondria in our intestines suggests that we are not individuals but conglomerates. Taking this idea beyond our physical selves, we realize that in our minds, too, we are conglomerates. "I am a part of all that I've met," wrote Walt Whitman, but we can change that to "All I have met feeds, nourishes, shapes, and becomes part of me." Lurianic Kabbalah, a Jewish mystical movement in sixteenth-century Safed, held that the drama of the individual soul both transcends the borders of death (via reincarnation) and challenges our notion of the borders that constitute an individual: "Luria teaches that every soul is given unlimited opportunities to work through its own individual *tikkun* [program of improvement] to fulfill more and more of God's commands, until it reaches its state of perfection" (Gillman, 1997, p. 182).

Without appealing to reincarnation, we can focus just on this life and verify how we are constituted by so many people we have known.

DAVID

David, a thoughtful person, sat down to examine his habits: the books on his shelf, his speech pattern, his taste for incense left over from the 1960s. In his rumination, he felt himself to be in a vast assembly of friends and former acquaintances. Though Bob was dead, David not only read the book Bob recommended but in turn passed the title on to many others. Somehow in the busyness of his life, David lost touch with John, but he recalled that John introduced him to the writings of Borges. As the list grew, David settled in his seat and congratulated himself that at least the sweater he wore he had bought himself—only to remember that it was Margaret who introduced him to catalogue shopping and gave him his first catalogue.

Did anything come from him, or was he simply a funny patchwork of qualities gained from his friends? He had retained some things and rejected others. Even when he discussed the book with Bob, the book he came to love as well, they read it differently. With all the similarities and differences, no two of us are alike, but we are all in the image of God.

In *Pirke Avot (The Ethics of the Fathers)*, we find some deep insights on community. The text begins by recounting the chain of tradition by which Judaism has passed on the wisdom received from the earlier generations: "At Sinai, Moses received the Torah and handed it over to Joshua, who handed it over to the elders, who handed it over to the prophets, who in turn handed it over to the men of the Great Assembly. The latter said three things . . ." (1:1). Clearly, what they said was part of a community across time.

Pirke Avot offers a similar chain of tradition for each quotation. For example, "Joshua ben Perachyah and Nittai of Arbel received the oral tradition from them [the sages]. Joshua ben Perachyah said: 'Provide yourself with a teacher; get yourself a companion; and judge all men favorably'" (1:6). Thus built into the idea of community is an awareness that isolation can be dangerous. We need to interact with others who can challenge our interpretations and offer new insights. A teacher can serve this role, according to Joshua ben Perachyah, but a friend can also open us up to new ways of understanding a text. Judging all others favorably is essential if we are to build a religion on community.

Rabbi Hillel is quoted in *Pirke Avot* as saying, "If I am not for myself, who is for me? If I care only for myself, what am I? If not now, when?" (1:14). Once again, a tension is expressed between the needs of the individual and those of the community. We must be concerned with self-preservation and self-cultivation, but without becoming self-centered and selfish. Modern Reform rabbis have interpreted this statement to mean that our concerns for social justice should not be restricted to members of the Jewish community. "We are required to transcend particularism and help all in our community who require assistance" (Kravitz and Olitzky, 1993, p. 10).

Hillel also said, "Do not keep aloof from the community" (*Pirke Avot* 2:5). Although remaining in and with community in its time of distress clearly helps the community, doing so benefits us as well. Hillel focused on the Jewish community. Twentieth-century theologian Fontaine Belford (1996) focuses on a larger community of people with shared concerns across many denominations:

> We find our families, those with whom we can be as God
> called us to be, with each other and alone. We step out with
> them, people of the desert as we are all people of the desert,
> into silence. We find ourselves there, bearing the other within
> and the other without, the stranger without whom we cannot
> live, without whom we cannot be who we are called to be in

this holy emptiness, in this darkness which is sometimes filled with light, in the presence of God. And as we stay there, resting at peace in emptiness, and silence and darkness, we practice this presence and celebrate the other with whom we share, the other who makes us whole [p. 146].

Ben Zoma is quoted in *Pirke Avot* as saying, "Who is wise? He who learns from everyone" (4:1). This quotation supports the principles of studying with a friend, judging all people well, and recognizing how our own wholeness grows when we interact with and learn from the other.

Ben Bag-Bag said, "Study the Torah again and again, for everything is contained in it; constantly examine it, grow old and gray over it, and swerve not from it, for there is nothing more excellent than it" (*Pirke Avot* 5:26). This statement about Torah tells us that our community is shaped by our shared understanding of the world and of its meaning and value. Through the Torah, Judaism makes essential claims about who we are, why we are here, and what our life is supposed to be about. These claims, in turn, shape our actions, our history (what we choose to remember), and our way of being in the world. Ben Bag-Bag defines our community not in geographical or chronological terms but in terms of a chain of tradition: "At Sinai, Moses received the Torah and handed it over to Joshua, who handed it over to the elders, who handed it over to the prophets, who in turn handed it over to the men of the Great Assembly." David, whose bookshelf connected him to friends who had died and others with whom he had lost touch, lives out in his life the essence of community portrayed in *Pirke Avot*.

The Body and the Body Politic

To know who we are, we need to know the context in which we live. A lung unattached to its surrounding organs and blood vessels is a meaningless object. Its identity requires its function and context. Our own function and context in Egypt distorted our essential identity, and that is why the Exodus was so necessary. Our function was not to build the storehouses of Pitom and Ramses, nor to live in a polytheistic culture that was focused on the dead. Emigration is not only about fear, pogroms, and enslavement; it is also about finding a place that is consistent with the statement "Adonai, you have been our place for all generations" (Ps. 90:2). We must live in a place where this pronouncement can continue to be true.

Our theology develops consciously from our insights into our own experiences. The central Jewish experiences at the time of Lurianic Kabbalah were exile, wandering, and all of their vicissitudes. These states, then, became the primary symbols of cosmological reality, as God too was thought by the followers of Luria to be in exile and wandering.

The second half of the twentieth century brought two existential realities that led to new ways of understanding our place in this world. The first was the reestablishment of the state of Israel as a geopolitical reality, a dream that became real. Still, the realization of a dream is never the same as the dream, and the reality is not the Israel of our longings. The second reality is the sense of safety and security that Jews found in America and other Western countries. This, too, is a troubled picture: we've been there before, in Moslem Spain in the Middle Ages, in Germany for the first third of the twentieth century, and in dozens of places in between. Nevertheless, despite this long history, many people feel safety in their present homeland; the symbol of *galut,* or exile, does not resonate with them. They choose not to make *aliyah* (to emigrate to Israel), and they feel like members in their national communities, not like sojourners. So the question remains: What is our place, and how can this place be consonant with "Adonai, you have been our place in every generation"?

Jews and Telic Decentralization

Telic decentralization is heavy technical language for something that can be expressed more simply. The Greek term *telos* means the goal, purpose, end, or meaning of a thing. Biologically, *telos* refers to our instincts for self-preservation and maintenance of our species. In trying to reconcile the seeming "purposefulness" of *telos* with our susceptibility to disease and death, physiologist Hans Selye came up with the idea that the microbe that causes disease has its own *telos.* He writes that in cases of inflammation in response to microbes and cancer, "there are actually two *teleologic centers*; their interests are opposed but, within each of them, purposeful activity 'for its own good' is clearly recognizable. On the one hand is the interest of the patient, on the other that of the microbe or of the cancer. Indeed, the very essence of cancerous growth is the setting up of a center whose own interests are largely opposed to those of its host" (Selye, 1956, p. 245).

A verse from E. Y. Harburg's libretto for the 1947 musical *Finian's Rainbow* provides a lovely example of telic decentralization.

> My feet want to dance in the sun,
> My head wants to rest in the shade.
> The Lord says go out and have fun,
> But the landlord says, "Your rent ain't paid."

Psychologist David Bakan, building on Selye's work, adds that "the basic paradox is that organismic growth and development can take place only if there is a certain degree of telic decentralization, while at the same time, disease and death also result from such telic decentralization" (1968, p. 40).

In short, no telic decentralization means no growth, no movement, no life. Too much telic decentralization means disease and death. Prophets, gadflies, and Jews in their traditional role have awakened societies from their moral slumber but have been accused of weakening or causing moral disease in the society.

To what communities do we belong, and how do we set our loyalties in order? Some such ordering allows us to overrule the natural *telos* for self-preservation because of a deeper *telos* of loyalty to our people or our faith. Maimonides specifically addresses this issue in his letter of consolation to the Jews who were being forced to convert to Islam. He wrote that seven of the Ten Commandments are suspended when we are under the threat of death, and only three may never be superseded: the prohibitions against idolatry, adultery, and murder. Since conversion to Islam did not constitute breaking any of those three, he argued that the Jews must convert rather than accept martyrdom.

Jews have almost always stood on the edges of society, but this marginality has been important and even life-giving. Societies, like individuals, can falter and grow ill if they are torn apart by multiple conflicting *teloi*, just as they can grow moribund if nothing challenges their one goal. Socrates described his role as telic decentralizer in his famous defense, quoted in Plato's *Apology:*

> If you put me to death, you will not easily find anyone to take my place. It is literally true, even if it sounds rather comical, that God has specially appointed me to this city, as though it were a large thoroughbred horse which because of its great size is inclined to be lazy and needs the stimulation of some stinging fly. It seems to me that God has attached me to this city, to perform the office of such a fly, and all day long I never cease to settle here, there, and everywhere, pursuing, persuading, reproving every one of you. . . . I suspect, however, that before long you will awake from your drowsing, and in your annoyance you will take Antyus' advice and finish me off with a single slap, and then you will go on sleeping till the end of your days, unless God in his care for you sends someone to take my place [Plato, 1961, 30e].

Socrates served the role, in his society, that the Hebrew prophets served in theirs and that Jewish critics of Western culture serve in ours. The societies, like that of Socrates, awoke from their drowsing and finished off these stinging flies with a single slap. Because God has been our place in every generation, it is urgent that we retain our identity, value, and perspective even as they animate telic decentralization in other cultures.

Early Jews no more liked their prophets than the Athenians liked their gadfly. Now, from the safety of two thousand years, we can admire Jeremiah or Amos, but their contemporaries did not like having their ways of life denounced. People today who cry out for justice for oppressed peoples or question the ways of viewing reality in a complacent society are met with scorn, harassment, or disregard when they try to be heard or published. When they are finally heard, the price is frequently too high: Martin Luther King won the Nobel peace prize and yet was assassinated.

As mentioned in Chapter Four, the Suffering Servant Song in Isaiah 53 can be read as pertaining to an individual or to a community. Christians have understood this passage as a reference to Jesus, while for Jews it refers to all of Israel. Part of the difference in interpretation arises from the tension between the individual and the community. Is religion about personal salvation, or are we all part of something larger than our own lives and efforts, whether it is the body of Christ or the people of Israel?

But we are pursuing the wrong question. Rather than asking who the suffering servant is, we should try to determine in what context the righteous are chosen for suffering. Isaiah 53 describes one "servant of the Lord" who is disfigured, rejected, abhorred, and then saved. His suffering serves to atone for the sins of others. The crucial point this text clearly demonstrates is that the servant's suffering is not for his own transgressions but for those of others (Kraemer, 1995, p. 24).

What could have led the prophet Isaiah to this startling view? We have seen that theologies arise out of insight into experiences, and Isaiah confronted daily the undeniable suffering of the righteous, side by side with the comfort of the wicked. He concluded that personal guilt cannot be a factor in suffering, which he thought results from some greater *telos*. Our own historical perspective and our own experience have led us to recognize that the innocent suffer. We have witnessed more than enough wars, killings, and mass expulsions to rule out any belief that suffering is related to personal guilt.

In our organic model, each cell is a living being and indeed can be extracted from its normal habitat and preserved in a laboratory. We know that the medium in which the cell is placed affects its growth, its health, its longevity. Freud recounts a fascinating series of experiments with single-celled creatures—in Latin, *animalcula*—that bears on our consideration of individuality and community: "If two of the animalcula, at the moment before they show signs of senescence, are able to coalesce with each other, that is to 'conjugate' (soon after which they once more separate), they are saved from growing old and become rejuvenated" (Freud, 1920/1961, p. 48).

Freud goes on to suggest that it was the products of its *own* metabolism that had near-fatal results for the particular kind of *animalculum*. If we extend this concept to humans, we may fear drowning in our own juices. Looked at another way, we could say that for internal reasons, normal life processes bring on death, but union with a different living other introduces fresh vitality. This brings us back to the notion of telic decentralization and to the vitalizing and essential role that this marginality plays for the vigor of the body (be it an organic or a political body). In dealing with telic decentralization in the Book of Job, David Bakan describes sacrifice as "a manifestation of telic decentralization in that a part of the self is made into an 'it' for the seeming preservation of the remainder" (1968, p. 125). Much of what he says applies equally to the Suffering Servant in Isaiah.

We can conclude, then, that the Jew as marginal person is essential to the ongoing life of the community, but if the community is too far gone, it will destroy that which can vivify it. The famous call to Abram (Abraham), "Go from your native land, . . ." continues with

> I will make of you a great nation,
> And I will bless you;
> I will make your name great,
> And you shall be a blessing.
> I will bless those who bless you
> And curse him that curses you;
> And all the families of the earth
> Shall bless themselves by you.

> —Genesis 12:2–3

Jews, such as Bible scholar Gunther Plaut, have interpreted these verses to mean that the descendants of Abraham are the cause of both the blessings enjoyed by other peoples and the misfortunes that befall them: "The decline of a nation can often be clearly related to the way it has treated the Jew, and its prosperity stands in direct proportion to its sense of equity and human dignity" (Plaut, 1981, p. 94).

The Suffering Servant, then, represents those who keep their distinct vision, or critical edge, and offer it as a contribution to the community. The servant suffered not because suffering characterizes servitude but because the servant was trapped in a diseased environment that could not react to the life-giving stimulation of the other.

Just as commentators cannot finally agree whether the Suffering Servant is an individual or an entire community, we ourselves are confused about who we are—a part of community or an individual—and hold within ourselves all the tensions associated with this conflation. Nowhere is this tension played out more significantly than when we try to understand our relationship to death and to the continuity of life.

The greatest threat in biblical times was not death but exclusion from the community. Community is our guarantee of meaning, and Judaism argues that even death can occur within a meaningful system.

9

CONFRONTING DEATH

From Sheol itself I will save them,
Redeem them from very Death.
Where, O Death, are your plagues?
Your pestilence where, O Sheol?

—Hosea 13:14

WE ARE NOT ALONE, nor are we thrust out of community, even in dying.
Our ways of understanding death are shaped by the values and beliefs of
our community. Abraham's death was a gathering in to his ancestors;
Jacob's deathbed is the setting for the Testament of Jacob, in which he
foretells what will happen to each of his sons (the heads of the Twelve
Tribes). Joseph makes the men around his deathbed promise that when
they are liberated from Egypt (they are not yet even enslaved), they will
carry his bones out with them. Moses' death scene has been the subject
of multiple *midrashim*. His soul is supposedly extracted from his body
through a kiss by God.

Each of these deaths is entered into, understood, and accepted within
the value system of the people. "I look at our lives as a song we sing from
the moment we are born until God takes us. Death is not always the
timely, peaceful event that many of us would wish. Often, our melody is
broken off in the middle of our song. . . . It would be nice if we could sew
up our lives in six days, as God completed Creation, and rest on *Shabbat*,
secure in the knowledge that everything is complete. However, although
we may be made in God's image, we are not God" (E. Ochs, 1999).

We cannot avoid thinking about death. The existentialist philosopher Jean-Paul Sartre regarded death as proof that life has no meaning. But knowing that we are mortal colors much of life. Death—or more accurately, our awareness of death—allows us to be fully human, forces us to define ourselves, and makes meaning possible; indeed, like the artist painting on a finite surface, we create meaning and value out of finitude. We do not, for example, judge that one oil painting is greater than another because the artist used a larger canvas. The magnificence of the painting rests on its transcending the limitations of the canvas so that the finished work points to the limitless. It does so through the artist's use of design, color, and texture and through the interrelationship of the components of the painting. An infinite canvas, in fact, could not hold a meaningful painting at all, because meaning lies in the balance of part to whole, the motion of the eye caused by the interrelated shapes, and a thousand other factors that take the viewer *beyond* the work—a logical impossibility if the canvas itself has no limit.

What makes us human and allows for meaning are the decisions we make and the opportunities we forgo when we choose among alternatives. By selecting this and not that, we give value and meaning to life. Rather than trying vainly to fill an infinite canvas, we need to paint with all the creativity we can offer, so that our substance is too great to be contained in life's finite form, not too sparse to fill it. Only then can death be understood not as a negation of the temporal but as a different perspective on the same reality.

Judaism always opts for unity: mind is not other than body; head is not opposed to heart; the sacred can be found in and through the profane. Regarding death as totally other than life makes it alien and frightening. Death cannot, perhaps, be incorporated into our experience of life, yet knowing that we will die allows us to be truly human and to live meaningful lives.

How we regard death shapes our view of story, love, suffering, body, work, prayer, and community, but they in turn influence our view of death. There is no one-way causality at work here.

Story

If death means the end of the story, then the entire story is colored in one fashion. But if death is only one piece of the narrative with more to follow, then all the earlier pieces take on a different hue. A Japanese pilot assigned to a suicide squad in World War II displayed his own and his culture's view of death in a letter to his parents, which read in part:

"Please congratulate me. . . . I have been given a splendid opportunity to die. I shall fall like a blossom from a radiant cherry tree. . . . How I appreciate this chance to die like a real man! . . . Thank you, my parents, for the twenty-three years during which you have cared for me and inspired me. I hope that my present deed will in some small way repay what you have done for me" (quoted in Feifel, 1959).

Contrasting stories give us very different attitudes toward death. At the same time, we modify our narrative in light of our actual experiences.

JOAN

What I know about death I know from having lived through my father's passing. I read books about death; but they seemed to stop short of my own experience, which didn't abruptly end. It continued to occupy my thoughts even though I was sure I'd gone through all the accepted stages of the grieving process.

These early stages of loss have been amply described: numbness or disbelief, anger, bargaining, the full feelings of pain and despair, and finally, some acceptance and healing. The healing is not a mere deadening of pain, it is also the ability to remember with joy. The stage beyond healing is what I wish to describe, although it is difficult to do because I have no conceptual scheme that allows me to make sense of my experience. Nevertheless, I know that my own experiences are important, even if I can't as yet understand them, name them correctly, or place them within some consistent worldview.

Two statements give me some language to express what I am trying to say. The first is "Nothing good can be absolutely destroyed." Any contemporary physicist would agree that we live in a closed system, a universe that encloses everything that has positive being. Things can be transformed, but they cannot cease to be. The other statement, "Events don't happen; they are," I believed long before I could put it into words. It is the feeling that time is not "out there"; it is merely our way of structuring how we perceive reality. Time in our society is thought of as one-directional—it is the arrow that is shot at birth and lands at death. I had the experience first, and then I tried to find some way to express it. I'm not talking about paranormal happening but simply my own experience, which is as common (and as miraculous) as a new day. The experience is always present and yet, fully observed, I stand in wonder, awe, and profound gratitude. A world that was cold, unknown, dark, and frightening is suddenly warm, comforting, and bathed in the light of familiarity.

As we have seen earlier, our view of time is central to our understanding of death. Because Jews emphasize the sacredness of time, giving it priority over space, revelation takes place in and through time. Judaism has always formulated history as the unfolding of events leading toward some meaningful final goal. It not only recognizes change but makes the transformation of society a religious imperative.

Change has posed problems for all societies and for each of us individually. Some cultures deny the reality of change and declare it to be an illusion. Others recognize that change is genuine but find meaning and value only in the changeless. Jews tend to see a moral significance in change. Jewish history, which chronicles an enslaved people's move from bondage to liberation, demonstrates thereby that people's status can be modified and that Jews, in partnership with God, can bring about such change.

The value given to change also allows Jews to perceive the uniqueness of events, situations, and individuals. We are born into particular families at the time of specific events, and we are shaped in part by the choices our families have made.

Jewish history is both the story that begins with God's Creation and the context within which we live out our days and make our contribution to the world. Some cultures deny change because time and change lead irrevocably toward death. Jews, by comparison, see in time, change, and history the sense that there is a task to complete, a task that is larger than any individual life and effort: "You are not called upon to complete the work, yet you are not free to evade it" (*Pirke Avot* 2:21).

Love

Some things we can truly get to know only through love. Death is just a shadowy concept until it strikes someone we love. Then it stops being an abstract idea and impels us to search urgently for a way to maintain our relationship with the loved one. Through this quest, love alone can lead us to belief in afterlife, as we refuse to believe that love can die. Although love changes our view of death, death also affects our concept of love. A key Jewish argument for immortality is the belief that the mutual love between God and the Jewish people is too strong to end with death. On a personal note, you may have experienced that your love for someone continued even after the person's demise. The persistence of love raises the very real possibility that, in some way we cannot imagine, the person lives on as well, as the Song of Songs suggests in the words "love is stronger than death."

By opening up some of the boundaries between the self and another, death shows us a vulnerability we have that both frightens and exhilarates us. In Renaissance love poetry, the ecstasy of love (*ec stasis*, literally "standing outside oneself") is actually equated with the ecstasy of death

> Come again! sweete love doth now invite
> Thy graces that refraine,
> To do me due delight.
> To see, to heare, to touch, to kisse, to die
> With thee again in sweetest sympathy
>
> —John Dowland, *First Book of Ayres,* 1597

Suffering

We may regard death as the epitome of suffering as we voluntarily take on the acute pain of surgery and other radical treatments in order to postpone death. But how often have we heard it said when someone dies after a long, painful illness, "At least he is no longer suffering," an indication that death is believed to be the final cure for suffering? When we die, do we leave "this vale of tears" and go to a "happy land," or is, as Heschel believes, just to live a blessing?

Body

How can we talk about resurrection when we know how central the body is to our being and we see the flesh of the dead disintegrate? But we have been taught that matter cannot be created or destroyed, just transformed into energy.

Writing about matter, the modern British philosopher Bertrand Russell suggests we examine a table. To the eye it is oblong, brown, shiny, smooth, cool, and hard, and when it is tapped it gives off a "wooden" sound. But as soon as we try to get more precise about it, we run into difficulties. The color of the table depends on our viewpoint. It is not so much a property of the table as it is our interpretation of the light it reflects. The surface may appear smooth, but its roughness becomes apparent if it is viewed through a microscope.

But these problems with the table are insignificant compared to those raised by science. What we really know is not the table but different attributes that we assign to it: color, shape, hardness, texture. Scientists have explained that what we take to be a solid piece of wood is actually a countless horde of atoms and molecules unceasingly in motion. We agree that soul, or spirit, is a mysterious concept, but so, fundamentally, is the simplest physical object. To put it another way, we know as much, or as little, about matter as we do about soul.

If we don't really know what matter is, how can we say that resurrection of the body is any less possible than immortality of the soul? Yet the belief in resurrection held by many Jews does not simply affirm the mystery of matter; it declares the unique value of individuals; that is, we are who we are because of our bodies.

Work

In our work, we address a need to make a difference that persists beyond death. We read in Numbers that at the time of the Exodus, the Levites substituted themselves for the firstborn—of people and animals—that were to be sacrificed to God during the Ten Plagues. Their sacrifice did not entail being killed but belonging to God, a fascinating idea of sacrifice. Like the Levites, we are called to some work and we give ourselves over to it, use ourselves up, pour ourselves out. Even so, according to Ecclesiastes, "there is nothing better for man than to rejoice in his works, for that is his lot, and no one can permit him to see what shall be afterwards" (Eccles. 3:22). The connection between our work and what comes after we die is meant to show that through work we gain joy and meaning, not simply sustenance.

Prayer

Two prayers from the daily *siddur* give us ways to think about death. Upon returning to consciousness in the morning, we say: "I give thanks to you, Sovereign of the Universe, who has graciously restored my soul to me. Great is your faithfulness." The rabbis taught that sleep is one-ninetieth part of death. This prayer encourages us to imagine that God, who in faithfulness restores our soul to us every day, will at some point demonstrate even greater faithfulness by restoring our soul to us not from sleep but from death.

The other prayer that addresses death, part of the eighteen benedictions that form the *Amidah,* reads: "You sustain the living with kindness, and revive the dead with great mercy; you support all who fall, and heal the sick; set the captive free; and keep faith with those who sleep in the dust. Who is like you, Adonai of power? Who resembles you, O Sovereign? You bring death and restore life and cause salvation to flourish. You are faithful to revive the dead. Blessed are you, Adonai, who revives the dead." This prayer comes in the *Amidah* right after "You cause the wind to blow and the rain to fall." The proximity of the two prayers brings to mind the annual renewal of the earth in spring, a natural metaphor for our own renewal.

PATTY
When Patty was six years old, the owner of the corner candy store suffered a fatal heart attack. Because Patty knew him and saw him so regularly, her mother felt she had to tell Patty about his death. She asked Patty if she was upset, to which Patty responded, "No, he's going to rise again in the spring, isn't he?"

Patty's response to this prayer, which her mother recited aloud every day, displays the natural comfort that it could provide to a child her age. We may pass unthinkingly over the statement that God is faithful to revive the dead (although it appears frequently in the daily service) until someone's death causes the words to jump out and address us personally. This happened in different ways to three people who spoke about this prayer.

MARCIA
Having been diagnosed with cancer and undergone surgery and radiation, Marcia now finds herself in a long waiting period, unsure whether or not she will suffer a recurrence. One day, during prayers, she turned to her neighbor and reported that since she received her diagnosis, her husband had changed one of the prayers he recited every day. In the Reform Jewish *siddur*, the prayer reads:

With love You sustain the living,
with great compassion give life to all. . . .
Who is Your equal, Author of life and death,
Source of salvation?
We praise You, Eternal God, Source of life.

Her husband found the attribute "Source of life" too generic to help him deal with his specific needs in facing his wife's illness, so he adopted the traditional form, "You are faithful to revive the dead."

LOU

Lou made exactly the same change in the prayer, but for another reason entirely. He had endured an unhappy marriage for twenty-seven years when he reconnected with his college sweetheart. The painful dissolution of his marriage and his entry into the new relationship stimulated him to pray for revival of the dead and to bring up the concept of resurrection in his study group. When a close friend asked him privately why this topic was suddenly so important to him, he reported that for years he hadn't especially cared about his physical self. He had gone mostly numb to his own body about twenty years earlier and since then had merely been going through the motions of marriage. Now that he had someone who loved him completely, he found it hard to believe or accept that his body would be eternally obliterated.

JOSHUA

Joshua, an orthodox rabbi, had the reverse experience. Having prayed his whole life to "God, who revives the dead," he now admitted that after his wife left him, he could no longer believe in the resurrection of the body.

Clearly, our view of life is deeply intertwined with our view of death, and a full theology needs to address both.

Community

Camus wrote, as noted earlier, that there is only one genuine community: the human community united against disease and death. When we lose someone close, our first reaction is to imagine that no one has ever felt the way we feel, and we long to turn in on ourselves. But it is then, in our time of greatest emotional isolation, that we are required to recite the mourner's *Kaddish* for eleven months, a prayer that may be recited only in community, that is, when a *minyan* is present. We are forcibly reminded, then, that rather than cutting us off from everyone else, death unites us in mourning with all those who have ever mourned—a group that includes most adults, because there is no house in which someone hasn't died.

Death occurs in community—not just that of our family and fellow worshipers but also in the community over time of all the People of Israel. Our ways of conceptualizing, accepting, and mourning death have been formed by this selfsame community. Jewish law forces the mourner to connect with community in many ways and at different points in the process. Leaving the cemetery, we are obliged to walk between two columns of friends, relatives, and co-worshipers. At home sitting *shiva,* we are visited throughout the day and evening. When *shiva* ends after seven days, we are accompanied on a ritual walk around the block. For eleven months, we recite the mourner's *Kaddish* daily as part of a *minyan,* and on every *yahrzeit* (anniversary of the death), we again rise to say *Kaddish* in community.

Experiences That Lead to Belief in an Afterlife

The doctrine of an afterlife was formulated in part to resolve a seeming injustice—that the good would be rewarded only after they left this life—and in part because people could not imagine that their experience of relationship with God could end at death. Another reason given by people who believe in an afterlife is that they sense the continued presence of someone close who died. Such an experience has no value as evidence for anyone else, but it is utterly convincing for those who have had it.

OLLIE
Ollie reported that her fellow nurses working with the terminally ill found each other agreeing that Ms. Jones was dead, even though her monitor showed some slight brain activity, perhaps indicating that she was still alive, and that Mr. Allen was still present, even though clinically he had died several hours earlier. In another case, they reported that Mr. Thomas was still in his room, although the body had been removed the day before. They were unclear what exactly they were experiencing and why, but they were in remarkable agreement about these phenomena.

Unlike doctors, who spend scarcely ten minutes a day with hospital patients, the nurses, who spend eight-hour or even twelve-hour shifts on duty each day, become attuned to subtle signs. The nurses who had worked on the unit for more than two years all agreed that there is some form of afterlife.

LOUISE
Louise met Martin, whose young wife was killed in an auto accident six months earlier that left him with an eighteen-

month-old son. Even though the year of mourning was not yet over, Louise and Martin found themselves falling in love. Louise shocked him one evening when she announced in a whisper, "Your wife is here." Martin wondered if Louise had gone crazy, but she seemed perfectly rational, though deeply shaken. She finally said, "I have to speak with her." When he asked if she wanted to be alone, she nodded. Later, she reported her one-sided conversation:

"Stacy, I know that you're here. I'm not trying to take your place. You will always be Martin's first wife and Billy's mom, but I love your husband and son and want to be part of their lives. Billy needs a mom, and I can be that. And Martin, who will never forget you, needs a companion."

She said she was shaking by the time she got the last sentence out, and then she grew quiet, waiting to see if anything had changed. After a while, she felt that Stacy was no longer there, and she went to Martin to report what had happened.

Louise could find no Jewish context that explained her experience of Stacy's presence. She thinks of the ghost of Hamlet's father in Shakespeare and the old movie *Blithe Spirit,* but no biblical or rabbinic text tells a comparable story, except for the cautionary tale in which Saul meets the ghost of Samuel (1 Sam. 28:13–21). But where Saul asked a soothsayer to call up Samuel, who then predicts Saul's defeat, Louise did not consult a medium or call up anything. Did spirits wander the biblical world of their own accord? The spirit of Elijah came to rest on Elisha (2 Kings 2:15), but only to convey that the teachings and gifts of Elijah were finding new life through his disciple and survivor. Eliphaz reports in the Book of Job (4:15–17):

A spirit passed by me,
Making the hair of my flesh bristle.
It halted; its appearance was strange to me;
A form loomed before my eyes;
I heard a murmur, a voice,
"Can mortals be acquitted by God?"

But God reprimands the so-called comforters of Job, singling out Eliphaz: "After Adonai had spoken these words to Job, Adonai said to Eliphaz the Temanite, 'I am incensed at you and your two friends, for you have not spoken the truth about me as did my servant Job'" (Job 42:7).

A passage from Leviticus puts the experience of witnessing a ghost in an even worse light: "A man or woman who has a ghost or a familiar spirit shall be put to death; they shall be pelted with stones—their bloodguilt shall be upon them" (Lev. 20:27).

Not surprisingly, Louise found little comfort in these biblical texts. Her brother suggested that her experience resulted from a combination of guilt and an overactive imagination. He modified his analysis when he sensed that she was genuinely searching for an explanation and suggested that although life may persist after death, the Bible comes down hard on mediums because we are obliged to live in the present. That doesn't mean spirits don't exist, he said; it means that our concern is with the living, or as we are instructed in Deuteronomy, "Choose life" (30:19).

At Jeanne and Joe's wedding, the rabbi, following a folk tradition for marking a significant life-cycle event, invited Jeanne's dead father to be present at the service. Louise could easily make sense of the rabbi's invitation because she was convinced that life is much more mysterious than we know and that people's souls or spirits can survive death.

Death as the Great Change

The self resides in place—in the mind and the body. Dying is, in a sense, a radical form of moving on to another place. Perhaps one reason this move is so traumatic is that it disrupts our habits and connections, and it reveals the vulnerability we attempt to hide with permanent-looking possessions, outfits, and settings—even as we ourselves are transitory. Dying is moving on, but will our self be at home? Will it find a place in the next abode? And who or what is the self that moves on? Will we even recognize it? The fundamental answer to these questions is found in the psalms: "Adonai, you have been our place in every generation" (Ps. 90:1).

Death is not something external that comes to get us; it grows within ourselves and ripens, just as our adolescence and maturity do. The "problem" of death is really the problem of life: how to live so that we can die without regret for things not done, love not expressed, talents not used, contributions not made. How do we die without regret? How do we live so that dying will be the fitting end of having lived? "We must leave the earth not like scourged, tearful slaves," writes Nikos Kazantzakis, "but like kings who rise from table with no further wants, after having eaten and drunk to the full" (1965, p. 18).

AARON
Aaron told his spiritual adviser that his grandmother feels she
wasted much of her earlier life and therefore wants to continue living. The tragic paradox, Aaron notes, is that the
years she regrets and misses are the misspent years of her
twenties and thirties; the years she now clutches at merely
add to her time in a nursing home. For Aaron, the ongoing
lesson is to live now, in the present.

"If you haven't experienced Heaven before you die, you won't experience it afterward," a mystic once remarked. The rabbis regularly compared the afterlife to our experience of the Sabbath. Some mystics have
gone further, holding that different states of consciousness resemble and
even suggest death. These states engender our trust, so that just as we
awaken from sleep and are "resurrected" to life, we return from a mystical state of consciousness, a time of "no self," and are "resurrected" to
our ordinary consciousness.

Types of Symbolic Immortality

We can also think about life after death without the concept of an *olam
ha-ba* (world to come). I'll describe five forms of immortality: biological,
natural, theological, creative, and transcendent. Each of them is based on
some notion of memory, a central concept in Judaism.

We honor our departed loved ones with a prayer called *yizkor* (remem-
brance). We remember them by the tombstone we place on the grave,
which often includes a brief statement of the values held by the deceased.
We remember by sharing photographs of the dead, letters they wrote, and
stories that connect them to us. We also remember by treasuring objects
they once used: Dad's watch, Grandma's fountain pen, our great-grand-
mother's brooch. In some cases, the loved one may leave an ethical will,
a statement summarizing the faith and values that guided them and that
they hope will be carried on by their descendants.

Biological

We may live on genetically through natural-born sons and daughters and
their offspring. It was recently discovered that a large percentage of people whose last names are Cohen or Katz, or some other variation of the
Hebrew word *kohen* (a member of the priestly tribe of Israel), share
genetic markers, suggesting that they all have descended from the biblical

Levites. Beyond the tribe, a sense of immortality can be broadened to include other tribes, and indeed all the people of Israel. Further, we read in Lewis Thomas's *Lives of a Cell* of our kinship with various mitochondria and learn that our biological immortality can extend beyond family, tribe, and even species, to include all of being.

Natural

This form of immortality, which follows logically from the preceding, goes beyond genetics. It broadens our sense of self, allowing us to identify with all of Creation, as Job was invited to do in the Theophany. The increasing ecological awareness of recent generations makes this form of immortality a potent one for our times.

Theological

Judaism has no single view on theological immortality, placing its emphasis on life. Theological immortality includes various modes of personal afterlife that find some grounding within Judaism, such as immortality of the soul, resurrection of the body, and reincarnation. It follows from two statements in the Jewish tradition: "God keeps faith with those who sleep in the dust" and "I will be with you." Increasingly, Jews have demanded that we break the traditional silence about what happens after death. Chaplains and rabbis in the healing movement have remarked that terminal patients experience their last days more peacefully if they have a clear theological view of immortality.

Creative

Our works and creations may live on beyond us. Indeed, death may be the great motivator for our creativity. Michelangelo wrote that "no thought is born in me that has not 'Death' engraved on it." We hope to leave behind works of enduring value, but we're not always clear what that means. Pearl, whom we met in Chapter Five, was extremely creative, but because she built a nurturing environment, she could not easily point to enduring "works" as her legacy. In thinking about the house she kept clean, she was tempted to subscribe to the oft-expressed notion that we build our lives on sand. It took her daughter's love and appreciation to help her recognize that her contribution would live on.

But beyond biology, nature, doctrines, and works, we sense that memory itself is a place where those who once were still are.

Transcendent

Unlike the other modes of immortality, which are primarily symbolic, transcendence is based not on persuasion but on actual experiences cultivated by mystics of many faiths that eradicate time and death. The mystic anticipates the afterlife while still living in this world and feels that the mystic experience sheds light on the afterlife.

Our Story of Death

Our theology is the story that situates us in relationship to the rest of our world. It tells us which additional components must be considered as we construct our world: all of Creation, or only those entities above microscopic size; all of space, or only what we can actually encounter. Our story or theology reconciles us to some fundamental anomalies and guides us in our decision making. Thus our theology helps us understand the constituent elements of our lives: love, suffering, body, work, prayer, and community.

But can we tell a story about death? A story emphasizes human action (Do we do anything about death, or is death the end of our doing?), sequential order, and narrative perspective. We're not sure what agency is involved. Because death appears to break down our usual human interactions, we try to place it within a familiar framework, through such expressions as "being gathered to our ancestors."

A story has some character, but *who* is there after death? A story occurs in some place, but what is the place of death? A story implies some human agency, but if death indeed ends our ability to act, how can we continue to function as moral selves after death? Jewish views of what happens after death vary; they include immortality of the soul, resurrection of the flesh, reincarnation, and survival of a hidden self. Each, in turn, has been elaborated so that it fits in with a larger story.

Immortality of the Soul

Maimonides believed that the soul was immortal. An outspoken dualist in his view of human nature, he had no patience with the emphasis that folk religion places on celestial pleasures. He wrote that "to believe so is to act like a schoolboy who expects nuts and confections as compensation for his studies."

Resurrection of the Flesh

A belief in the resurrection of the flesh has been held by many mystics over the ages (we may note, for example, the view held by some members of the Hasidic Lubavicher sect that their departed leader will reappear as the Messiah). The view may be accompanied by elaborate material descriptions of the *olam ha-ba* that include, in one case, five chambers adorned with silver, gold, pearls, and fine drapery. The descriptions also display which issues are of central concern to believers. An overriding question they face is establishing which of God's creatures would be blessed in the world to come. One answer is all worthy beings, which would exclude only the serpent and certain individuals (such as all the enemies of ancient Israel). Believers in resurrection have also expressed great concern for justice, envisioning the world to come as a place where the blood of the slain would cry out. The deadness around the believers leads them to conclude that in Paradise plants would regain their powers, the stars they thought lost would be restored to the Pleiades, and we would at last perceive the real splendor of the sun and moon.

Further, the ongoing struggle we have with our humanity would be transformed: evil will disappear, as will desire, a major source of evil. All those who are defective will be healed. The pious man, such as the faithful laborer, will have his reward, and pious women too (although they are placed into a separate category). All holy days except the Day of Atonement will cease, and days will resemble an eternal Sabbath. All these beliefs held by many Jews about a world to come elaborate on this or that element of their own story.

Reincarnation

Reincarnation as a response to what happens when we die can operate as a story because a single consciousness passes through the vicissitudes of being to become its essential self. Although reincarnation has never been a major view in Judaism, mention of it is found throughout Jewish history. Flavius Josephus writes in his voluminous first-century work *The Antiquities of the Jews,* that the Pharisees "believe that souls have an immortal vigor and that virtuous souls shall have power to revive and live again on earth."

The Zohar sees reincarnation not as a reward for virtuous souls but as necessary learning for souls that have not achieved sufficient purity:

All souls must undergo transmigration; but men do not perceive the ways of the Holy One, how the revolving scale is set
up and men are judged every day at all times, and how they
are brought before the Tribunal, both before they enter this
world and after they leave it. They perceive not the many
transmigrations and the many mysterious works which the
Holy One accomplishes with many naked souls, and how
many naked spirits roam about in the other world without
being able to enter within the veil of the King's Palace [Zohar
III.99b; Sperling and Simon, 1934, vol. 3, p. 302].

Reincarnation became a universal belief among Hasidic Jews.

Survival of a Hidden Self

Once we have eliminated the possibility of total annihilation, which is
ruled out both by Newton's law of the conservation of matter and the
simple idea that we cannot fall out of this universe, we are left with only
two possibilities: that we survive either with our present consciousness
(the folk tradition, more or less) or else with a consciousness we cannot
imagine (an idea that forces us to accept that we contain a being superior
to the one we know). Such a belief in two selves, the one we already know
and the one we can fully claim only after death, is advanced in a *midrash*,
where the moon questions God:

"O Lord, why did you create the world with the letter Bet?"
[the second letter of the Hebrew alphabet, which also represents the number two] God replied: "That it might be made
known unto my creatures that there are two worlds."
     The moon: "O Lord, which of the two worlds is larger, this
world or the world to come?" God: "The world to come is
the larger."
     The moon: "O Lord, you created two worlds, a greater and
a lesser world; you created the heaven and the earth, the
heaven exceeding the earth; you created fire and water, the
water stronger than the fire because it can quench the fire . . ."
[Ginzberg, 1968, vol. 1, pp. 23–24].

Happily Ever After?

Despite Judaism's advocacy of four differing positions on what happens
after death, they boil down to two possible endings: "happily ever after"

versus "adventure that never ends." Happily ever after implies an end to the daily grind, to challenges, and to growth—or put another way, an end to time and causality. Adventure that never ends implies that human agency does not cease and that in life we go through all our learning and trials, all our years of shaping and self-discipline, for the sake of a self that endures. If we think of life as our school, do we take our final examination and then graduate (happily ever after), or are all our lessons preparation for advanced studies after death (adventure that never ends)?

If we consider our life as a deepening relationship with God, then our whole life is one long betrothal, and at death we finally enter into marriage. But those who have entered into human covenants of marriage know that "happily ever after" does not characterize the totality of this relationship. We know that nothing has ever challenged, stretched, nourished, comforted, bewildered, and assured us like a long-term marriage. We have had a lifetime to get to know God, our betrothed; are we ready to say "I do"? Just how much did we know about our beloved before we got married? Some people have long engagements; some people live together before marriage. Even so, it is amazing how much we don't, and cannot, know before we change perspective from "intended" to "actual." As we turn to our final challenge, what can we say about our relationship with God?

10

ENCOUNTERING GOD

"AND GOD, ANGERED by inaccurate reporting and editorial guesses about who he is and what he is about, hired the human person as scribe and began to dictate his story. For forty days and forty nights he dictated and for forty days and forty nights the scribe wrote. Finally the last word having been spoken, God stopped. The scribe finished the last word and stood up with the outrage of someone who has been plagiarized, 'But that is my story!'" (Shea, 1996, p. 53).

We develop a theology not by studying God, which we cannot do, but by deriving insights from our own experiences. Indeed, all we can know of God must be based on what we have experienced in our lives. At the same time, we believe that somehow our story is also God's story. Our story *is* God's story, shaped by God's presence in and through our experiences, and God's story is our story. So by examining the components of our lives as described in the preceding chapters—committing to love, enduring suffering, undertaking our work, claiming our body, engaging in prayer, living in community, and confronting death—we can find God, and find all we can hope to know or say about God.

Theologies, by definition, deal with God, but trying to describe God directly leaves us speechless. As the Torah repeatedly warns, we cannot look directly at God. But if we look at the world with an awareness of God, the awareness can transform our world. As children, most of us believed that God was one more being in a realm of beings that also includes plants, animals, and people. But as we grow older and bring more of our experience to bear on our attempt to think about God, we come to realize that God is not one among the various beings; God is that through which all that exists *has* its being.

Our thoughts about God, then, are not about God abstracted from all that is, but God as that which brings forth and holds together everything that is.

The Center Holds

Holding includes providing an environment in which Creation can flourish. Holding requires not only physical preservation but mental support as well. Our experiences are included in a larger whole.

Holding in Unintegration

We spend a large part of our lives trying to integrate our experiences in order to gain a sense of self and stave off integration's opposite, disintegration. But a third course, lying between those two, can be found if we release control and enter into what we don't know. Naming it *unintegration,* psychoanalyst D. W. Winnicott believed that it fosters our most creative times. In this sense, it also applies to the effort we make to understand our relationship with God. We spend innumerable moments holding on to and defending an unexamined self we have been developing since childhood. When we release our defenses, we can unleash energy for the new and the creative. We have countless hours of busyness going on inside, but though we convince ourselves of our own reality and existence, the self we are defending is limited. Our true self, which includes a component of mystery, takes us away from the ego-driven self so that we feel whole and real. These moments of "losing ourselves" can occur at death, during meditation, in the throes of love—really, any time we feel deeply moved.

We are much more than the story our ego-self can tell because, being in God's image, we do have the mystery component. If we allow ourselves to become unintegrated, we feel our selves expanding as we remain held by God.

Holding in Parenting

Just as God provides a nurturing environment for Creation, parents offer a holding environment for their children, a safe and supportive setting that fosters growth.

SHEILA
Sheila explained what she learned about God and God's presence through becoming a mother:
"My parents did not give me the 'good-enough parenting' that allowed me to be alone. I used to be terrified of being alone, but as an adult I've learned to find wholeness in solitude. What 'holds' me is God's noninterfering presence.

That's what presence is all about. For too long we've been
implicitly taught to associate presence with outcome—'Please,
God, defeat our enemies, heal the sick, make everything
good.' But as we all know, things don't work that way. Only
by not interfering in the world can God's presence guarantee
reality and existence. God's presence, as witness, helps us to
achieve wholeness in the real world. We come to realize this
as we stand in almost godlike relationship to our developing
toddlers. But what we do, we do imperfectly in flawed imita-
tion of God. So our attempt at providing our children with a
noninterfering presence is taken up by God's presence and
made whole."

Drawing out what Sheila was hinting at in her remarks, we can see why
the God of the psalmist is said to number all our tears and to see and
remember what befalls us—not so that God can eventually call the wicked
to account, but to sustain us in a shared reality. Every century has seen
victors who have tried to rewrite history. We would despair of ever knowing what really occurred if we didn't know that God remembers and that
God's seeing and knowing will support our own.

Holding in Commitment

We sometimes resist committing to love—of people, of this world, of intimacy—because we fear separation and death. The transitoriness of people and things keeps us from appreciating their present value. How can
we risk loving that which death will take from us? But a line in the *Amidah* ("You keep faith with those who sleep in the dust") is a good example of "holding." Even in the extreme "going to pieces" of death, we are
held by God's faithfulness.

Holding in Being

Can we "learn to be," that is, learn to fully accept being without doing?
We usually keep a constant stream of worries flowing through our minds
just to assure ourselves that we exist. Also, we concern ourselves with
monument building because we want to leave our mark and thereby
assure ourselves somehow that the world has been changed by our being
here. The monuments we leave—buildings, institutions, works of art,
laws, offspring—are external manifestations of our constant need to

assure ourselves of our own reality and existence (if we produce real effects, we must be real). As Sheila's adolescent daughter wrote:

I am!
I exist!
I am a nation newly recognized,
I received their ambassadors today,
    and spies (a diplomatic courtesy to send spies).
And they tempted me with
sweet pacts. I shook my head NO!
I like aloneness, it's all so new.
I bowed to the ambassadors and set up committees for the spies.
It was all a game, how jolly.
But I am recognized.
A new nation is born!
But a little nation and such big ambassadors
have recognized me.
I am!

But if we know that God knows and assures our reality and existence, we can simply let go and relax into quiet. The noise can stop, and we can experience the Sabbath. On the Sabbath we learn to emphasize being over doing, learn that we are more than what we do, and learn that we remain real even when we don't do anything at all. We find it hard to remain for long in a state of not doing because hours and minutes of nonaccomplishment both threaten and invite us to meet a different aspect of our self.

Weekday habits die hard. We find that we can go one day a week without phone, fax, and e-mail, but does knowing this change our relationship to time during the other six days? One hopes so, yet Josh's chain-smoking father, who used to stub out his last cigarette of the week every Friday when the candles were lit and didn't smoke again until after *havdalah* marking the close of the Sabbath, was never able to give up smoking. The Sabbath gives us an invitation, not a guarantee.

Where Is God?

One central question must be addressed in our theology: Where is God in and through our experiences? We may look for an answer by asking once again, Who am I? What can I know? Where do I fit into reality as a whole?

Who Am I?

It has become clear that in order to know God, we must know ourselves; conversely, true knowledge of the self requires knowing God. We should move beyond defining ourselves in terms of our various roles, relationships, place of origin, or other allegiances. We are God's creation, and our definition should be anchored in our conscious, deliberate relationship to God.

What Can I Know?

We can discern from the biblical account that knowledge has troubled humanity since the story of Eden. Eating from the Tree of Knowledge led to our separation from the Garden, but much more important, it led to the disastrous separation between head and heart. We come to know by opening ourselves to being known, recognizing this vulnerable state as a form of loving. Our understanding of what constitutes knowing has been transformed from a form of mastery to a trusting vulnerability.

Where Do I Fit into Reality as a Whole?

Understanding the self as a self in relationship to God also allows us to look at the rest of Creation's kinship to God. Understanding the self is our essential move beyond alienation. Once we start with a single Creator, we feel connected to Creation and to other creatures.

We rarely experience God directly, much as we rarely experience the sun in any direct way. But because the sun illuminates everything we see, we recognize it in and through the world around us. Looking at the sun directly risks blindness, so once we are consciously aware of the sun we can both see what the sun's illumination reveals about the world and begin to discern the sun as it is (perceived through its power to illuminate). In much the same way, we can view love, suffering, work, prayer, community, body, and death, telling the entire story from our own viewpoint and from the perspective of our focus on God.

The Contexts in Which We Encounter God

We encounter God through all aspects of our lives. God is the context of our story: of the love that illuminates those we love, of the meaning that lifts our suffering, of the force that binds our community together, of the energy that powers our work, of the creative force behind the body, of our partnership with God in prayer, and of our hope in the face of death. In this chapter, we look at each of these areas twice: first as if God were not part of the picture, and then with God illuminating each topic.

Story

If the punch line of our story read "and they lived until they died," the broken aspects of our lives would remain unresolved. This ending for our story would not allow us to address injustices we have suffered; nor would it heal the pain of the losses we have sustained. No ultimate design or purpose can be discerned from that final line. The curtain comes down; the farce is ended. Those who do not recognize God have little choice but to accept this ending and choose to focus on the process of life without regard to the end. All meaning and value must be found within this lifetime because there is no standing beyond this perspective.

The alternative ending transforms every moment of the life that preceded it. All becomes meaningful because "God has numbered all your tears." Nothing is lost, and our suffering now forms part of some larger harmony whose pattern we could not discern as we struggled in our lifetime. Now, at last, we can understand why things were as they were. The answer to all the questions comes down to God: the presence, the caring concern, the deliberate involvement, and the ultimate redemption of all the pain, injustice, loss, and confusion.

The poem "The Story We Know" in Chapter Two portrays the human story as it is seen by some people. In reminding us of the human condition and our shared vulnerability, the poem arouses tenderness and compassion. But it lacks direction or ultimate meaning because it finds no place for God.

We must be prepared to give an account of the hope that we carry and remember what we are called to be. Our story, as Jews, justifies what we've done by putting our lives into a different context. Our story depends on our sense of relationship with God, overcoming any alienation, and giving shape and meaning to our lives. We are part of God's story. We spend years as adults replaying, re-viewing, and reinterpreting the events of our childhood in trying to make sense of them. The effort is not wasted, because what we once knew but could not express is that our life is sacred text and thereby worth remembering, studying, and analyzing.

Love

The newest look at our story tells us that our life has taken on all its meaning and value through our loves. Love is so closely related to the essence of God that it is hard to examine it independently. Just as God allows us to release strict boundaries with trust, so love breaches all boundaries and allows us to expand. We begin with the wonder that we can love and the amazement that we can be loved. Along with love comes forgiveness, acceptance, renewal, meaning, and a transformation that makes of every place a home. Work, contribution, and sacrifice also accompany love. Think of the tale of the unemployed husband and father who seeks a job driving a truck carrying combustible materials. Several drivers have already met their end in explosions, but the protagonist is focused on being able to support his wife and child. He gets the job and is jubilant despite the risk.

This story is believable because we have all experienced love and sacrifice simultaneously. We want to contribute to those we love, spare them the pain and suffering we see before them. If we could, we would even take upon ourselves the pains they have to undergo. The offer feels so natural that we don't even think of it as sacrifice. It is the natural order of loving in general and parenting in particular.

The sacrifices made by others may leave us in awe, yet we often find it hard to recognize our own. But our consent to pain and difficulty also gives us a place to encounter God. It is frightening to love someone whose death can bereave us. But we find the strength and courage within to enter into deep commitments because we know about God's abidingness and believe that God "holds" those we have lost so that the loss is not final. Because love breaches all our boundaries, we dare to "fall apart" because we know that God will eventually bind up all that is broken.

Suffering

As Viktor Frankl (1973) pointed out, when given a *why*, people can bear almost any *how*. Is our suffering the random distribution of evil, or is there some greater meaning to what we do and endure in our lives? For those who view the world without God, suffering has no meaning. It is part of the human condition, and all meaning and value reside not in what suffering represents but in how we choose to deal with it. Do we bear it stoically? Do we join with others to try to forestall or alleviate it?

For the biblical figures, suffering is meaningful. We see their lives within the context of God, meaning that all they experience falls into their relationship to God: the good is a blessing, the evil is a test or tempering of their character. Everything is fodder for a journey to greater intimacy with God. The question is *how* to suffer and still find God in and through the suffering, as we might find a log we cling to while a sea of pain floods over us.

Body

Without God, the body becomes the gateway to death. We may respond by taking meticulous care of our body: exercising, watching our diet, avoiding unhealthy habits. Or, emphasizing denial, we may ignore or even disown the body and spend all our energy on the mind, as if it were disembodied. Positing the world without God, we would view time not as a creation of God but as an evil force bringing about feared changes.

In the context of God, we recognize the wondrousness of our bodies and see them as gifts and as splendid creations. We study them and use them, and we gratefully own them.

> LORI
>
> It is strange how going to the aquarium can bring us back to our bodies with a renewed sense of wonder and gratitude. As Lori stared at the tiny aquatic life, she tried to figure out what was a mouth, what was a sense organ. The strangeness led her to slow down and be drawn into a fascinating encounter with sea anemones, sea cucumbers, jellyfish, and many other forms of life. That night she looked at herself with the same frank curiosity she had brought to the aquarium and recognized that her sense organs were far more than her eyes, tongue, nose, ears, and fingers. Her entire skin covering sensed heat and cold, roughness and smoothness. "Adonai, our God, how wondrous is Your name throughout the earth" (Ps. 8:2).

Work

Without God, work becomes the desperate arena in which we strive for symbolic immortality. Yearning to make our mark in this transitory world, we focus on the monuments we leave behind. But if God is the context of our work, the product gives way to the process, and work becomes a setting where we may encounter God. Our sense of call, or destiny; our moments of inspiration; and our ability on occasion to exceed our presumed capabilities all present opportunities to find God. Our work is never done, but it need not be: "You are not called upon to complete the work, yet you are not free to evade it" (*Pirke Avot*: 2:21).

Prayer

It is hard to think about prayer in a system without God, yet certain types of praying can be done without any explicit theological commitment. Meditation and contemplation, for example, can be profound forms of prayer, or they can be "naturalized" as simple relaxation responses. One technique for entering these states has us focus on our own breathing, never once taking in the reality that we are witnessing the breath of life that God breathed into us.

Prayer as part of a belief in God is familiar enough that explanations seem superfluous; instead, a brief anecdote will express the concept well.

> RUTH
> In her daily prayer, Ruth collects the people in her personal world that she wants to lift up for God's concern. She names her spouse, of course, her children, her aged mother, and the friends in her life, whom she feels to be a holy gift. Sometimes she has specific concerns ("heal them") but often it is just a way of remembering them in the context of her relationship to God.

Community

Community can exist without reference to God; witness Camus's vision of the human community united against death and suffering. But as Ruth's prayer for the people in her world illustrates, there is also community in God, where we join in shared creaturehood and shared worship.

Death

Death is the ultimate challenge. Is God the death of death? In other words, does God finally triumph over death and free us from our mortality? Just as death shapes every one of our human activities—love, suffering, work, attitudes toward the body, community, prayer (and, by extension, what we can hope for)—so does God; there is a cosmic battle as to which shall gain the allegiance and loyalty of our consciousness.

As we saw in Chapter Nine, there are many ways of thinking about what happens after death, but essentially the two positions are death as the obliteration of self, or some form of preservation of self after death. If we believe that we can find God even in and through death, then we affirm that the shape of Creation that has change and death built into its design is a meaningful formation. We can affirm with God, as we read in

Genesis, that Creation is good. We affirm this at the same time that we know there is so much we don't know and can't know. We have spent this lifetime growing in love and trust. We have come to realize that our life story is our unique take on the story of God.

What God Does

Recognizing that we cannot say who God is, we can still examine what God does. We generate names for God from these actions: Creator, Judge, Healer, Liberator, Deliverer. A hymn of glory attributed to Judah of Regensburg (Birnbaum, 1949, p. 416) reads:

> I praise you, though I have not seen you;
> I describe you though I have not known you.
> [The prophets and sages] imaged you,
> not as you really are;
> They described you by your acts only.

In other words, whatever we say about God we are really saying about everything else illuminated by God. We don't contrast God and the world, which would be taking an essentially dualistic view. Rather, we recognize that "the heavens declare the glory of God, the sky proclaims God's handiwork" (Ps. 19:2). We Jews do not posit two worlds; we believe there is a single world that can be experienced in different ways. Everything, rightly considered, allows us to experience God.

Every story is also a story of God. This thought, which has been repeatedly rediscovered in the West, was so persuasive that the thirteenth-century mystic Meister Eckhart wrote, "We must learn to penetrate everything and find God within." German writer and dramatist Johann Wolfgang von Goethe made the same point: "So waiting, I have won from you the end / God's presence in each element." Nothing in the world is excluded from its goodness. Unclean animals are banished from the dinner table, but they may still be prized for other qualities, as the horse, mule, and camel are valued as beasts of burden. God is the light by which we see everything else: "By Your light we see light" (Ps. 36:10). We truly see and know people, plants, animals, and inorganic objects only in their relationship to God.

Encountering God in All the Ways We Think

We have been looking outside ourselves to learn about God, but we can look in our own minds as well. Our thoughts are organized by how we structure space, time, quality, relation, and quantity—the components of reality. Each of these fundamental categories displays traces of encounters with God.

Space, or Context

We organize our perceptions in terms of space; that is, we cannot think of an object without some notion of space. But even space itself colors our view. For example, 4′33″ a work by the composer John Cage in which the performer sits before a piano but plays nothing, has appeared on various concert programs. Because we attend the concert hall to hear music, we interpret what we hear there musically, and so when 4′33″ is "performed," we perceive any ambient noise in the house as belonging to the piece. Analogously, if our theology tells us that the holy appears in and through the profane, we expect to discover the sacred in our day-to-day activities. Being more receptive, we are more apt to perceive the holy than if we did not have this mind-set.

Time

Like space, time is essential for organizing our perceptions in the world. It also influences how we understand what we take in through our senses. Of course, our expectations are not always fulfilled. So although we may be told that the Sabbath is a holy day, we cannot always align our feelings with the date on the calendar. Yet when we can, as Joan did, we can reap our own rewards:

> JOAN
> Joan was a totally anxious graduate student on the Friday preceding the week of her doctoral examinations (one exam a day for five days). She was having recurring nightmares in which she wrote her examinations but failed to hand them in, or her adviser informed her that not only did she fail her examinations but she failed her courses as well.
>
> At 5:45 P.M. Friday, she lit Friday night candles and entered into a world of peace. For twenty-five hours, the acute panic of the preceding weeks abated. She could eat again without a nervous stomach. She could slow down and actually notice all the snow drops and the earliest crocuses pushing up through the ground. Her mind simply did not rush ahead to the ordeal awaiting her in the coming week.

She had no sense of losing time that could have been spent reviewing the material for her exams. Instead, she felt she had discovered an island of refuge in time. Even after the Sabbath ended, Joan did not open her books again until Sunday morning. On Monday, the tests began, continuing for a week without letup. At noon on Friday, she walked out of the exams dazed, feeling surprised that people couldn't see what an ordeal she had been through. She reached home, put away her papers, and at 5:55 P.M. lit the candles to welcome another Sabbath.

Quality

Quality, by which we judge and value what we perceive, can be beauty, goodness, truth, mercy, evil, vindictiveness, or any trait we may imagine. The tragic or the joyous can bring us into God's presence; we can recognize God by having a child or losing a child.

Relation

Our feelings of connectedness, expansiveness, and wholeness through love can open us to an encounter with God, but so does our sense of dissatisfaction—"our heart is restless till it rests in you," to quote Augustine of Hippo. We find God in our experiences of wholeness. We also find God in our fragmentation, which yearns for completeness. God lifts up the fragments of our experiences and makes them whole.

Quantity

Contemplating the expanse of the universe, with its preposterously large numbers, not only extends our imagination but inspires our awe and reverence: "If I ascend to heaven, You are there; If I descend to Sheol, You are there too" (Ps. 139:8).

But just as the very large can open us to encountering God, so can the infinitesimally small. As our measurements get ever smaller, they approach zero, a concept that has fascinated mathematicians and mystics alike. Zero can simply serve as a place marker: in the number 406, zero represents the empty tens place. Mystics suggest that God, analogously to the place-marking zero, holds the spot for whatever we cannot explain. But then we can ask whether we discovered or created zero, and similarly whether we discovered or created our God-images and God. Because zero is "nothing," we don't look *at* it but *through* it at everything else, just as mystics hold that in whatever we behold we are seeing God. We don't really know about zero, but we use it, as well as the concept it represents, as a way of viewing everything else. Analogously, knowing what we don't know and can't know, we can still use our relationship with God to help us see and understand everything else. God is the still point of the ever-changing world, the standard by which all is valued.

The categories just named—space, time, quality, relationship, and quantity—we have gratefully received from the Torah, and as shaped by the Torah, but the text to which we apply them is our own life. Like a holy person, the Torah is *not* self-referential; its truth, like that of the holy person, radiates out and makes us feel whole. Consequently, we do not study Torah for the sake of Torah but for the sake of life, as we read in Deuteronomy ("So therefore choose life!" not, "So therefore choose Torah"). Our immediate tasks are to live fulfilling lives, to love, to work, to contribute to community, and to accept whatever vicissitudes we may encounter. Because we can accomplish these tasks through loving God, our theology must help us grow in our relationship to God.

"Take Off Your Shoes, for You Are on Holy Ground"

We have just seen that can we locate God through the categories we find in our own minds. We have seen earlier that we can encounter God through what God does: create, judge, comfort, heal, and so forth. We may also discover God by studying what is said about God: that God is omnipotent and omniscient. But inevitably we want to experience personally the presence of God.

Personal experiences of the beloved permeate the Song of Songs, from its opening line: "O give me of the kisses of your mouth." The attributes of the beloved are discussed extensively throughout the text, the maidens of Jerusalem talk about him, and the protagonist thinks of him, but the main emphasis is on the *experiential*—what she feels about him and how she wants the experience of being kissed by him.

Our experiences are central to forming our theology. Here, naming becomes important: Do we dare recognize that what we experience is the presence of God? Sometimes we may hesitate to say so because we feel unworthy, but God's presence in our lives means that God is gracious, not necessarily that we are special.

In experiencing God's presence, we seek no ecstasy or "special effects"; we hope for a relationship that can deepen over time. We begin not by talking about God but by approaching this relationship obliquely. When are we struck with awe, with radical amazement, with a sense that we want to bend our knees or bow? When do we feel like using the word *holy*? Focusing on these experiences may take us further than formal study of such incomprehensible terms as *omnipotent* and *omniscient* that are traditionally applied to the Deity.

When, in fact, do we feel we have encountered God? Participants in a workshop on these questions gave a variety of answers, including being present at the birth of their first child, facing the death of a grandmother, and feeling a sense of wonder at the beauty of nature.

ILANA

Ilana, the social worker, reported that for her, "God had been a cognitive idea, a useful metaphor, but I had had no experiences of God. I complained to my rabbi, who asked me if I have any children. I told him that I have a daughter. He then asked me how it felt to be a parent. I suddenly became very moved and told him about how I felt rooted, connected, and opened up in remarkable ways. The rabbi interrupted me. 'So you do have an experience of God.'

"That absolutely floored me, because I'd had a similar exchange with one of my own clients. The client, in ill health, was facing prison on charges of welfare fraud and arrived distraught. I suggested that he pray psalms daily and give daily to charity. In time, his health improved and he remained out of prison, but he told me that although he continued to pray and give charity, God never spoke to him. I asked him to describe how he felt when he gave charity. He said he felt warmth, peace, and joy. 'That's God speaking.' I'm still amazed how I could help others but couldn't give myself the same advice.

"Belief has nothing to do with having an idea and seeing the world through the idea. That was what I'd originally thought, so believing in God meant believing in some idea of God. When I understood the belief to be where we stand in our whole being—heart and mind—I came to know God in and through all of myself. Now God is not just an idea but a deeply felt experience."

TINA

One of the most powerful answers came from Tina, whose teenage daughter had been killed in a car accident. She said she experienced God as peace amid the pain. A hushed silence

filled the room when she spoke; it seemed that only she could
follow up on her remarks, so she added, "Psalms of pain are
just as much psalms of praise as the joyous psalms because
God is found in and through all the moments of our lives, not
just the joyous ones."

In going through the exercise described in the Introduction, half the
members of the workshop were asked to tell their assigned partner a story
from their life, something they might tell their rabbi. The partners were
instructed to listen to the story as though they were hearing a sacred text,
and then help the storyteller name the story in a significant way. The partner's job was to help the other recognize God's presence in the chosen
story.

After that exercise, with the listener taking a turn at being the storyteller, the participants were asked to relate something that had happened
to them in the past twenty-four hours. Could they find God's presence in
something that occurred just yesterday? Could they be so close to God?

Once they had found traces of God in one another's stories (as they all
did), they were asked to look at the process itself. Central to Judaism is
the idea that each of us is formed in the image of God. Could they regard
the person they were working with as one who inspired an experience of
God?

GLORIA
Gloria described her difficult childhood and then remarked:
"I survived my childhood because God was with me. Early on
I felt God's presence. As panic rose, I turned to God—and
God was there. 'Though my father and mother abandon me,
Adonai will take me in' (Ps. 27:10). God always saw the pain
and the soul struggling to survive. I had such clarity as a
child, but can I find God today?" Gloria's partner responded,
"Haven't you found peace?" "Yes." "Then you've found
God."

MARGARET
Reflecting on the exercise with her partner, Margaret stated,
"I really do feel God's love. It is something like the dawn: it
rises almost imperceptibly and suddenly there is light all
around, all engulfing."

JULIE
When it was Julie's turn to describe her experience of storytelling, she said, "Criticism finds me open and vulnerable. My

reaction to criticism is directly related to my pride. I have to stop taking credit for my writing, my good looks, because all is gift. So when I doubt, I have stopped being a grateful receiver and I'm implicitly saying that I did it and therefore I can do it wrong."

TONI
Toni said, "I don't know who I am if I am not anxious and striving. Who am I?" Her partner responded: "Someone God has loved from the start, chosen from the start, called from the start."

SHEILA
Sheila gave the final reflection. She had already spoken of a poppy opening up as her image of the spiritual way. She described the sheath around the bloom, how it gradually fell away but the petals were still curled. Slowly, over the course of an afternoon, the petals uncurled. She thought about whether the uncurling came from the warmth of the sun, the force of the wind, or some other force.

"Often God's coming is as gentle as the rising of my own breath—and as intimate. I may know that I am in God, but I feel that God is in me—in the coursing of my blood, which I seem to be able to feel, in the tingling of all my organs. I cannot embrace God because God is too much a part of me. I feel excited and alive, and sense God's closeness and presence. My blood is ringing in my ears and I forget to breathe. Oh! The poppy! I understand. God warmed the poppy from within—not with probing fingers or a strong wind. By the force of God's inner embrace, the poppy opened up and blossomed."

We find God through God's actions, in the structure of our consciousness, and in our own most intimate experiences. We find God in silence and solitude in a level of mind that is deeper than consciousness.

The possibility of encountering God in silence and solitude is hinted at in two related passages in the *Tanakh*. In the first, Moses asks to see God's "face" but, as we read earlier, is told that only God's "back" can be seen, that is, only God's deeds and actions reveal God's existence and nature:

[Moses] said, "Oh let me behold Your Presence!" and [God] answered, "I will make all My goodness pass before you, and I will proclaim before you the name Adonai, and the grace that I grant and the compassion that I show. But," God said, "you cannot see My face, for man may not see Me and live." And Adonai said, "See, there is a place near Me. Station yourself on the rock and, as My Presence passes by, I will put you in a cleft of the rock and shield you with My hand until I have passed by. Then I will take My hand away and you will see My back; but My face must not be seen" [Exod. 33:18–23].

Taken by itself, this passage seems to say that we cannot have a direct personal experience of God. But the passage has traditionally been connected by commentators with Elijah's experience: "'Come out,' God called, 'and stand on the mountain before the Lord.' And lo, the Lord passed by. There was a great and mighty wind, splitting mountains and shattering rocks by the power of the Lord; but the Lord was not in the wind. After the wind—an earthquake; but the Lord was not in the earthquake. After the earthquake—fire; but the Lord was not in the fire. And after the fire—a still, small voice" (1 Kings 19:11).

The rabbis have identified Elijah's cave as the cleft in the rock where Moses stood, connecting these two experiences of God in the *Tanakh*, suggesting an experience that is more immediate than a discovery of God in retrospect.

Although thunder and lightning accompanied the revelation at Sinai, the essence of the revelation lay in the teaching of Torah. Wind, earthquake, and fire preceded Elijah's experience of God and were frequently identified with manifestations of God, but Elijah's story makes it clear that our capacity for stillness may be the most accessible gateway to God.

Our learning to be still may well need to be preceded by lots of wind, an emotional earthquake, or great burning desire, but in the end, we are told to "be still and know that I am God" (Ps. 46:11).

EPILOGUE

THEOLOGY PLAYS too significant a role in our lives for us to ignore it. For example, we encounter fervent theological debates about whether and how much we are determined by our DNA as opposed to the environment in which we were raised.

Now that we have looked at the basic components of our lives and discovered our own viewpoints and questions, we realize that these, not the predigested views of others, form the building blocks for our own theology. The story we come to tell about what we've experienced—how we choose to make sense of what has been given to us—is the greatest area of freedom we have. We don't need to falter before any expert's skill, because we each have a uniquely privileged perspective on our own life, and this life story is an important element in the story of God.

The Urgency of Creating a Personal Theology

Why is it important to recognize and create your own theology? For the same reason a psychotherapist would want you to make the unconscious content of your mind conscious: so that you can modify it, accept or reject it, and take responsibility for it. You can exercise your freedom in the domains of thought, naming, and evaluating. Our tradition tells us that God created by word alone ("And God said . . ."); since we are in God's image, we exercise our creativity most strongly through the products of these "word" creations—our conceptual images.

> FLORENCE
> How we can make sense of our suffering became an urgent question for Florence when she was hospitalized as a fifteen-year-old with pernicious anemia. "Why?" she kept asking. Her mother tried to answer, and the hospital chaplain spoke with her. But it was the long, empty hours on the ward, while she lay on her bed, that led her to begin working out her own story about the meaning of her illness.

At first, she did not share her story or theology with anyone. She just seemed more at peace and stopped asking
accusatory questions. But when her favorite aunt visited, Florence confided in her that she understood why she was ill:
"'The strength of the camel determines its burden.' I am
strong; I can bear this." When her aunt asked when she
thought the burden would be lifted, Florence smiled and said
she felt she would shortly be released from the task, and the
rest of the family would be fine.

Two friends of Florence's mother made essential points at
the time of Florence's hospitalization. The first simply told the
story of her own son's illness and how she realized she was to
blame for it. When Florence's mother protested, her friend
said, "Listen to what you are telling me." Then Florence's
mother recognized that secretly she too had blamed herself
for Florence's illness, and her friend had let her see the absur-
dity of that belief.

A second friend warned Florence's mother to stay out of
the way as Florence struggled to make sense of her illness:
"The issue is between Florence and God, and there can be
nothing more intimate. Just pray and trust God. You may
never know what Florence comes to believe, or she may
choose to share it with you, but it is her task."

The Ethical Implications of Story

When God made a covenant with Noah, it was really with Noah and his
sons. We could say that the word *sons* implies descendants or we could
say that it determines who is human. Are women human? How about
people of different races? Of different religions? We need to define which
beings are part of our moral universe. Such decisions are not made empirically. For example, before we undertake research involving the use of animals, we must ascertain the nature of our covenant with them, if any, and
then treat them accordingly—or decide not to use animals at all. We *name*
them as clean or unclean, as moral agents or as objects and possessions.

The same is true of people from different groups. We know enough to
recognize empirically that people are people, but our scientific information has not changed how we act or feel when tragedies occur to various
groups of people. Are children people? Are the unborn? If children are
deemed persons, then they are not the possession of their parents and the

law can limit certain forms of punishment, marriage agreements in the cradle, and the like, steps a parent might otherwise want to take.

It becomes clear that any worldview has practical implications. Camus argues that the death penalty only makes sense in a society that has a shared belief in an afterlife. If neither the sentencing judge (or jury) nor the guilty party believes in an afterlife, then the death penalty is not provisional and therefore cannot reform the culprit. Prisons, also called reformatories, were supposed to reform the inmates, not merely get them out of society's way. When belief in an afterlife is shared, torture has a certain logic to it: finite pain for infinite reward. Of course, coerced faith (or remorse) may not be good enough, but the point is that theology matters.

Whatever we may think, we *have* a theology that we need to dignify and empower; it is grounded in our own experiences, having shed the dead weight of the past. The strength of our theology is that its origin lies in our personal conscience, not in some unknowable higher authority. Our theology includes love and discovery. Love is a wayless way; we learn how to grow toward God by loving God and responding to God's love. We consciously create and adopt our own theology in order to become people who make free decisions of the heart. We can be religious—that is, take religion seriously—without necessarily taking the institutional forms of religion as binding.

What Criteria Do We Bring to Our Theologies?

We can evaluate our theology by noting whether it fosters engagement with life and the world, whether it offers a worldview that stretches us and calls us to grow. But whatever criteria we bring, we must finally ask, What about truth?

ELAINE
Elaine, a physicist, has gotten herself all tangled up in string theory, a recent buzzword in modern physics. She knows it will remain only a theory for a long, long time because there is no accelerator large enough to test it. But she wants to be able to test it, as all her training taught her to do. She finds herself frustrated because scientists have yet to draw out much of what happens if this theory holds, so even indirect verification is currently impossible. She is troubled that all those years and years of thinking and training have brought us only to a theory, albeit one that is elegant and beautiful.

Theories of Truth

Drawing out our theology does not mean theorizing about reality. We want to create a theology that helps us make sense of our basic beliefs and hopes about the real world. Unlike string theory, which offers elegance and beauty but cannot yet be tested, our theology is based on practical, lived experience. If our theology is never objectively true, then in what sense is it true? Can it be tested? What would count as truth? There are various theories of truth, so how do we choose one over the other?

CORRESPONDENCE THEORY. The *correspondence theory of truth* holds that a true statement is one that corresponds to a state of the world. In other words, the statement "it is very hot today" is true if it really is hot today. But a theological statement, such as "prayers are answered," neither corresponds to the real world nor fails to correspond, because we don't know all the possible meanings of *answered*. (Think of praying to catch a flight, missing it, and then learning that the aircraft crashed.)

COHERENCE THEORY. The *coherence theory of truth* requires a statement that agrees with all the basic axioms of a system and sticks (coheres with) the rest of the system. The most familiar example takes us back to plane geometry, where we learn that a triangle cannot have two right angles (much less three). That's true within the Euclidean system, but not necessarily true about the external world, as a practical test shows. Imagine yourself standing on the North Pole. Now walk one hundred paces due south, make a 90-degree left turn, and walk one hundred paces due east; then make another 90-degree left turn, and walk one hundred paces due north. You are back where you started, and the triangle you paced out has two right angles and coheres with the real world—because the surface of the earth is a sphere, not a plane.

We often employ the coherence theory of truth without knowing the system to which the truth must cohere. For example, we accept a scientific system that rules out the existence of gnomes and leprechauns, on the ground that we have no credible evidence of their existence. So if someone now makes a statement about gnomes, we automatically rule it out. Indeed, there are whole statements we never investigate because they simply do not cohere—fit in—with our fundamental worldview (Kuhn, 1962). As a test for a theology, we have already ruled out the correspondence theory of truth for theological statements, but the coherence theory is hardly better. We can easily build a coherent theological system—complete with gods, angels, devils, and even gnomes—where a statement about leprechauns fits right in.

PRAGMATIC THEORY. The *pragmatic theory of truth* defines truth as whatever takes us where we aim to go and not astray, or, as Nikos Kazantzakis (1965) colorfully defines it, "Truth is whatever gives us wings." But we ourselves must determine the destination, and any goal we set can satisfy no more than our present state of awareness and knowledge. Since we are not yet who we can be, the pragmatic theory doesn't hold for theological statements. Theological truth must be larger than we are so it can enlarge us.

When we read a story, we want it to teach us something about reality and to adhere to certain conventions. In a story about cavemen, we don't want the characters to use helicopters. Good fiction writers spend a great deal of time and research to make their stories consistent with all that we already know about the story's time and setting. We also demand that the story be internally consistent; that is, if a character suddenly acts in a surprising way, we want to know that we will be able to find the seeds for this transformation earlier in the story. But we demand more: we believe that great literature is one way to get at the meaning of life. We finish reading Tolstoy's *War and Peace* and feel that somehow the experience Tolstoy has put into Andre's character has allowed us to perceive reality in a new way that takes us into what is most real.

Three Levels of Truth

In addition to developing three theories of truth, philosophers have identified three levels of truth: *noetic, ontic,* and *absolute.*

NOETIC LEVEL. *Noetic truth* refers to the truth of a statement, which is the usual sense in which we understand truth nowadays. A statement is noetically true if it correctly describes a state of the world. Still, fictional truth has nothing to do with noetic truth, so we need to talk about the sense in which a story is true. The truth we seek in theology may also be separate from noetic truth. Indeed, silence may be more to the point than any statement, so we need to know what we don't know—allowing us to recognize those times when the most appropriate response is to shut up!

ONTIC LEVEL. *Ontic truth* is the truth of being. Something is true if it is rather than fails to be, and if it is what it is rather than being other. This notion of truth affirms the positive achievement of being and comes close to what we mean by integrity or authenticity. There is an implied value in the notion of ontic truth, captured by Heschel's statement, "Just to be is a blessing." Noetic truth, the truth of a statement, depends on ontic truth. If there were nothing, then there could not be any true statements. So we find a deeper sense of truth in ontic truth. Our theology should foster our authenticity—but theology is not psychology. Although the true story of our childhood may foster healing and growth, thereby becoming the psychologically true story, theology demands more because in the end we are not the measure of all things.

ABSOLUTE LEVEL. Our theology may be ontically true, but it must not stop there. *Absolute truth* is the sense of truth we mean when we say that Truth is one of God's names. Just as noetic truth depends on ontic truth, ontic truth—our being and our essence—depends on absolute truth. This dependence explains how a story can be an invitation to absolute truth, and how our theology serves our relationship to God. We discover, create, and formulate our theology to help us become conscious and aware of God's reality, presence, and guidance. Our theology helps us treat all of Creation with greater reverence.

Historically, much of theology has operated on the noetic level. We find wonderful statements that are brilliant, even elegant and beautiful. Some operate on the ontic level, variations on the psychoanalytic story that help us feel good about ourselves and our world. The real task is the absolute level, which allows us to know and be known, to love and be loved, and to be fully caught up in the covenant.

We return to the questions we have been asking all along: Who am I? What can I know? How do I fit into reality as a whole? After we have tried to answer all these questions, we find we know nothing else as well as we know ourselves. Who are we? We are meaning-seeking creatures looking for our story, forming our commitments, enduring suffering, working, praying, being in community, all with an awareness of our mortality.

Our basic tool for forming our theology, standing at both the beginning and the end of our journey, is story. We begin with the story of our people, which gives us the fundamental ideas that help us make sense and put into some order all that happens to us. En route, as we encounter a variety of experiences and gain insights into our experiences, we modify the story. At the end of our journey, our story is a report of our discoveries along the way.

We are always making associations with earlier parts of our lives. As a people and as individuals, we often use the past to help others on their journey and to help ourselves as we face the future. Those who have come through a certain experience can serve to guide others en route; as René Daumal writes in *Mount Analog*, "If you come to an impasse or a dangerous spot, remember that the trail you have left could lead people coming after you into trouble. So go back along your trail and obliterate any traces you have left. This applies to anyone who wishes to leave some mark of his passage in the world. Even without wanting to, you always leave a few traces. Be ready to answer to your fellow men for the trail you leave behind you" (1959, p. 106).

Our ancestors have left us a story that offers guidance by reporting the false moves they made along the way:

> Give ear, my people, to my teaching,
>   turn your ear to what I say.
> I will expound a theme,
>   hold forth on the lessons of the past,
>   things we have heard and known,
>   that our fathers have told us.
> We will not withhold them from their children,
>   telling the coming generation
>   the praises of Adonai and God's might,
>   and the wonders God performed.
>
> —Psalms 78:1–4

How does our story—our theology—fit into the larger story of our people, that is, Judaism as a whole? We do not create our theology any more than we create the world: we cocreate both. Abraham didn't dream up monotheism; he entered into a relationship with God. He *responded* to a call. In our lives, we each play out the formative stories of our people: we respond with curiosity and enter into relationship. We wander in many strange places, entering into new experiences, even forms of servitude. We feel ourselves drawn to new values and a new way of being. We face trials and gain insight.

Each of our stories is part of the larger story and is understandable in terms of it. It also influences the larger story, which we are thus constantly renewing and modifying in light of our experience. The enterprise of making sense of our lives therefore not only rewards us personally but also contributes to the larger story we are all building together.

The story of God is being written. We too have contributed our narrative line—the text of our lives—to flesh out God's story. God's story has given solidity and meaning to our own story. Together we are creating a life-enhancing theology.

The opening words of Genesis are *Bereshit bara elohim et.* The *alef* (first letter of the alphabet) and the *tof* (last letter of the alphabet) that constitute the word *et* are said by mystics to mean "In the beginning *(bereshit)* God created the alphabet." As proof that Creation is accomplished through words, *Shemot,* the Hebrew title for the second book of the Torah, means "names." Letters and naming are both functions of Torah. *Vayikra,* the title of third book, means "and he called," thus letters, names, and calling. The fourth title, *Bamidbar,* translates as "in the wilderness" but can also be read as "in speaking." The final book of Torah is *Devarim,* whose title means "words."

What the mystics are saying about the Torah parallels what we have learned about theology: we create worlds of meaning by our use of language, our ways of naming and calling, our speaking, and our words. In short, it is through our theology that we shape a world in which we can live fully human lives.

REFERENCES

Ausubel, Nathan (ed.). *A Treasury of Jewish Folklore*. New York: Crown, 1948.

Bakan, David. *Disease, Pain, and Sacrifice*. Boston: Beacon Press, 1968.

Becker, Ernest. *The Denial of Death*. New York: Free Press, 1973.

Belford, Fontaine Maury. *The Uses of the Heart*. Pembroke, Mass.: Campbell & Lockwood, 1996.

Birnbaum, Philip (ed. and trans.). *Daily Prayer Book*. New York: Hebrew Publishing Co., 1949.

Birnbaum, Philip (ed. and trans.). *High Holyday Prayer Book*. New York: Hebrew Publishing Co., 1951.

Blake, William. *Songs of Innocence and of Experience*. London, 1789–1794.

Bloom, Anthony. *The Courage to Pray*. Mahwah, N.J.: Paulist Press, 1973.

Cioran, E. M. *Tears and Saints*. (Ilinca Zarifopal-Johnston, trans.). Chicago: University of Chicago Press, 1955.

Cohen, Morris Raphael. *A Dreamer's Journey*. Boston: Beacon Press, 1949.

Collins, Martha. "The Story We Know." In *The Catastrophe of Rainbows*. Cleveland, Ohio: Cleveland State University Poetry Center, 1985.

Daumal, René. *Mount Analog*. San Francisco: City Lights Books, 1959.

Dunne, John. *A Search for God in Time and Memory*. Old Tappan, N.J.: Macmillan, 1969.

Feifel, Herman (ed.). *The Meaning of Death*. New York: McGraw-Hill, 1959.

Folberg, Neil. *In a Desert Land*. New York: Abbeyville Press, 1987.

Frankl, Viktor. *Man's Search for Meaning*. Boston: Beacon Press, 1973.

Freud, Sigmund. *Beyond the Pleasure Principle*. In J. Strachey (ed.), *The Complete Psychological Works of Sigmund Freud*. Vol. 18. London: Hogarth Press, 1961.

Fromm, Erich. *The Art of Loving*. New York: Bantam Books, 1963.

Gilbert, William Schwenck. *Iolanthe*. Libretto. New York: Stoddart, 1882.

Gillman, Neil. *The Death of Death*. Woodstock, N.Y.: Jewish Lights Press, 1997.

Ginzberg, Louis. *Legends of the Jews*. 7 vols. Philadelphia: Jewish Publication Society, 1968.

Green, Arthur, and Holtz, Barry W. (eds.). *Your Word Is Fire: The Hasidic Masters on Contemplative Prayer.* New York: Schocken Books, 1977.

Grudin, Robert. *Time and the Art of Living.* New York: Ticknor & Fields, 1982.

Harburg, E. Y. *Finian's Rainbow.* New York: Random House, 1947.

Heschel, Abraham Joshua. *The Sabbath.* New York: Farrar, Straus & Giroux, 1951.

Heschel, Abraham Joshua. *God in Search of Man: A Philosophy of Judaism.* New York: Farrar, Straus & Giroux, 1955.

Hillesum, Etty. *An Interrupted Life.* New York: Pantheon Books, 1983.

Kaufmann, Walter. *Religion from Tolstoy to Camus.* New York: HarperCollins, 1961.

Kazantzakis, Nikos. *Report to Greco.* New York: Simon & Schuster, 1965.

Kraemer, David. *Responses to Suffering in Classical Rabbinic Literature.* New York: Oxford University Press, 1995.

Kravitz, Leonard, and Olitzky, Kerry M. (eds. and trans.). *Pirke Avot: A Modern Commentary on Jewish Ethics.* New York: UAHC Press, 1993.

Kuhn, Thomas. *The Structure of Scientific Revolutions.* Chicago: University of Chicago Press, 1962.

Lane, Belden. *Landscapes of the Sacred.* Mahwah, N.J.: Paulist Press, 1988.

Leech, Kenneth. *Experiencing God.* San Francisco: Harper San Francisco, 1985.

Levine, Robert. *A Geography of Time.* New York: Basic Books, 1997.

Maeterlinck, Maurice. *The Children's Blue Bird.* (Georgette Leblanc, ed.; Herbert Paus, ill.). New York: Dodd, Mead, 1916.

Maimonides, Moses. *The Guide of the Perplexed.* (Shlomo Pines, trans.). Chicago: University of Chicago Press, 1964.

Milne, A. A. *Now We Are Six.* New York: Dutton, 1955.

Milner, Marion. *Eternity's Sunrise.* London: Virago Press, 1987.

Mitchell, Basil. "Theology and Falsification." In Walter Kaufmann, *Religion from Tolstoy to Camus.* New York: HarperCollins, 1961.

Morris, David B. *The Culture of Pain.* Berkeley: University of California Press, 1991.

Newman, John Henry. "The Pillar of the Cloud." In *The Poems of John Henry Newman.* London: Lane, 1905.

Ochs, Elisabeth. "Sermon for Rosh ha-Shanah 5760." Unpublished sermon, Congregation Sha'ar Zahav, San Francisco, 1999.

Oliver, Mary. *Winter Hours.* Boston: Houghton Mifflin, 1999.

Plato. *The Collected Dialogues.* (Edith Hamilton and Huntington Cairns, eds.). New York: Putnam, 1961.

Plaut, Gunther. *The Torah: A Modern Commentary.* New York: UAHC Press, 1981.

Scholem, Gershom G. (ed.). *The Book of Splendor: Basic Readings from the Kabbalah*. New York: Schocken Books, 1949.

Selye, Hans. *The Stress of Life*. New York: McGraw-Hill, 1956.

Shea, John. *Stories of God*. Allen, Tex.: Thomas More Publishing, 1996.

Sher, Gail. *One Continuous Mistake*. New York: Penguin Putnam, 1999.

Sperling, Harry, and Simon, Maurice (trans.). *The Zohar*. 5 vols. London: Soncino Press, 1934.

Spinoza, Baruch. *Ethics*. (W. H. White, trans.; rev. A. H. Stirling). In James Gutmann (ed.), *Ethics, Preceded by On the Improvement of the Understanding*. New York: Hafner, 1949. (Originally published 1883.)

Spinoza, Baruch. *On the Improvement of the Understanding*. (R.H.M. Elwes, trans.). In James Gutmann (ed.), *Ethics, Preceded by On the Improvement of the Understanding*. New York: Hafner, 1949. (Originally published 1884.)

Stilgoe, John R. "The Puritan Townscape: Ideal and Reality." *Landscape*, 1976, 20(3), 4.

Thomas, Lewis. *Lives of a Cell*. New York: Viking, 1974.

Tolstoy, Leo. *The Death of Ivan Ilyitch*. (L. Maude and A. Maude, trans.). In Walter Kaufmann, *Religion from Tolstoy to Camus*. New York: HarperCollins, 1961. (Originally published 1886.)

Urbach, Ephraim. *The Sages*. Cambridge, Mass.: Harvard University Press, 1973.

Weil, Simone. *Gateway to God*. New York: Crossroad, 1982.

Wiesel, Elie. *Souls on Fire*. New York: Random House, 1972.

Wisdom, John. "Gods." In Walter Kaufmann, *Religion from Tolstoy to Camus*. New York: HarperCollins, 1961.

THE AUTHOR

CAROL OCHS has been lecturing and writing on theological topics since the early 1970s. Following a twenty-five-year career as professor of philosophy at Simmons College in Boston, she joined the faculty of Hebrew Union College–Jewish Institute of Religion (HUC-JIR), New York, where she now teaches, directs the Graduate Studies Program, and serves as spiritual guide to rabbinic and Doctor of Ministry students. A graduate of The City College and The City University of New York, she holds a Ph.D. degree in philosophy from Brandeis University. She is the author of *Behind the Sex of God* (1977), *Women and Spirituality* (1983; revised and expanded 1997), *An Ascent to Joy: Transforming Deadness of Spirit* (1986), *The Noah Paradox* (1991), and *Song of the Self: Biblical Spirituality and Human Holiness* (1994), and coauthor of *Jewish Spiritual Guidance: Finding Our Way to God* (1997, Jossey-Bass). She has also written numerous essays and journal articles. Ochs and her work are recognized in *Who's Who in America*.

INDEX